This is Communist Hungary

This is
Communist
Hungary

Edited by

ROBERT FINLEY DELANEY

HENRY REGNERY COMPANY   CHICAGO
1958

To St. Stephen,
the First King of Hungary,
whom the Communists neither know
nor understand
and to the late
John MacCormac
whom the Communists knew
and feared

To St. Stephen,
the First King of Hungary,
whom the Communists do ... not
understand
and to the late
Jozsef Mindszenty
from the Communist prisons
until freed

Contents

Hungarian Prayer

Mothers have always detested tyranny in all its forms
And, believe me, when we could, helped.
Now we must see our children suffer, waiting and praying:
O Men! When are you to make peace as you made War?
It is more than enough from words and lies and propaganda,
No one shall tell us how to raise our children,
How to be happy and what to think and believe.
When will everyone go home where he belongs?
When will heaving tides, evil waters return to their beds?
When, O when will there again be light?

And on a day our young children, our heroes stand up
And with their lives win the salvation of their country.
But, see, there come the frightful tanks again,
To crush our new freedom, to crush our suffering souls.

Help, O help most powerful of Men! Give us peace at last,
Peace for our long suffering country, for our bleeding children!
But, if you have not time or mood to trouble with us,
Being a nation little and poor,
Or if some business or policy should let us be slaves again,
I beseech you to have mercy upon us, a single mercy,
Throw down one of your atomic bombs
And kill us quickly, because that will be far better for us all.

We will have a free and human life, or die, please comprehend!
Our fate is there, before You!

O Men! My voice is low, only the echo of millions
But hear me! Hear me there in the councils
And before you write down a decision,
Remember your mother, or a child, who was once the center of
  your eye.
Think: "What if they should share this fate?"—O think!
O Men. Give Hungary a human life, hope and peace.
Give us justice.

A HUNGARIAN MOTHER
November 4, 1956
Budapest

Acknowledgments

I am indebted to many people in many ways for the arrival of this book in published form. High on the list are the contributors themselves who shared with me a need for such an explanation of past and current Hungary as is here attempted. My patient and loyal secretary, Dr. Konstantina Dina, did the very difficult job of urging, co-ordinating, and typing contributions from two continents. Faithful friends, Canadian, Austrian and Hungarian, saw to translations without a murmur, especially Mrs. Ilona Paul. Irene Howard and Norma Palma were indispensable in the last few days of the manuscript's preparation.

To the others who know and understand, but who cannot be here mentioned, my thanks and gratitude.

Foreword

The starkness and horror of Soviet Communism's brutal and continuing repression of the Hungarian people is today very much before us. Only recently have we witnessed once again the Soviet Union's complete disregard for world opinion on Hungary, when it flagrantly refused to heed United Nations' efforts to provide some measure of relief for this suffering country.

Today Hungary lies on the rack of communist revenge. But her cause is not lost, because it far transcends purely political and diplomatic problems. The people of Hungary in their insurrection accomplished for history what the Free World had been unable to achieve. They proved the futility of communism as an acceptable way of life. The Hungarian people destroyed the myth of paradise on earth, Soviet style. For here was the final proof—common cause in revolt against a tyranny cloaked in deceit and inhumanity. It was the overwhelming unity of the entire population which frightened the communists and destroyed their philosophy—sending Communist Party functionaries scurrying for safety into neighboring countries, the bravado all gone, as it always is with defeated dictators.

They returned to exact a terrible price for having been exposed. Yet, despite the horror of an entire country in chains, Hungary and Hungarians resist. For there is no other course. The reality of Hungary is after all but a reflection of the age-old struggle of the indestructibility of the soul of man versus the power of evil as currently expressed by Soviet colonialism.

It is comforting to know that the spirit of man will ultimately triumph. We saw ample evidence of this possibility during the tragic days in Hungary during the fall of 1956. But if we saw, did we really understand? Did we absorb the lessons? Do we somehow know a little more intimately the insidiousness of communist control? Do we face this problem with a greater determination to stand fast by freedom?

The story you are about to begin is a mirror of communism in action. It is told by the people who have earned the right by fire to explain to the world what communism does to individuals and all aspects of life in its insatiable search for control. The Hungarians who made this book possible came from all parts of Hungary, from all major walks of life. There are among them ex-communists and anti-communists; they have really only one thing in common: they are revolutionaries for freedom.

This book concerns itself with a view into Hungarian society under communism. While it contains occasional insights into the experiences of our authors, it does not rate as autobiography. Yet here we have collected a group of quite remarkable human beings. Many of them I met in Vienna as they stepped into freedom. There are the Martons, who suffered imprisonment simply for knowing Americans and Britishers and who left Hungary only because the very real alternative was arrest and quite possibly death. There is Mayor Koevago, a man of heroic nature, who twice has chosen the cause of freedom to communist compromise. One day in Vienna I heard a soft spoken Hungarian voice speaking in English of Bela Bartok in such beautifully constructed phrases I presumed an introduction. Today, Peter Budai, a brilliant young musicologist and idealist, is rebuilding his life as a member of the internationally known *Philharmonia Hungarica*. Paul Landy looks back on the exciting days of the revolutionary free press and his role which led to his ultimate flight to the West. Now his interpretative pieces on post-revolutionary Hungary are beginning to attract world attention. To wish to become a priest and to be denied the vocation by communist *diktat* is the role assigned to Jozsef Magyar, who persisted in his theological studies as a layman. He provides us with a picture of a church divine, yet human, in the full throes of persecution.

These, then, are some of our contributors. They speak for a nation under suppression.

August 20, 1958   ROBERT FINLEY DELANEY
Feast of St. Stephen the King   Washington, D.C.

Introduction

BY JOHN MAC CORMAC

It is a truism that revolutions, though heralded by intellectual dissent, are planned and made by small but determined minorities. History may one day label the Hungarian revolution with the seldom deserved word "unique." For although it ran true to form in originating in the minds of the Hungarian intelligentsia, it was not made but broke out like an epidemic or a forest fire. It was not organized but had to find its organization after it had begun. It assembled around no mesmeric leader—for Imre Nagy's chief desire was to brake, not to encourage insurrection. It was not made by an army—for only part of the Hungarian army joined it. It was not engineered by a class—for every class supported it. Least of all could it be called an ideological revolution since it was a revolt led by communists against communism. It was mostly, but not wholly, a national uprising. No one, least of all those who had most to do with it, foresaw the lengths to which it would go.

The world first heard of unrest in December 10, 1955, when the Hungarian Communist Party indignantly noted that certain members of the Hungarian Writers' Association had denied the necessity and right of the Party to direct literature. They had prepared a memorandum protesting against Party control and this had been signed by many writers who were also Party

* John MacCormac was the Vienna Correspondent for the *New York Times*. He died unexpectedly, July 6, 1958.

xv

members. Some of them were Stalin prize winners. Under the "June road" program of Imre Nagy, with its relaxation of thought control, they had enjoyed an intellectual freedom which they were loth to surrender, when Matyas Rakosi deposed Nagy and restored Stalinism. But they were careful to confine their protest to literary dictation. They did not champion Nagy's economic program with its emphasis on fewer guns and more butter.

Their protest, though mild, was not mild enough to appease Rakosi. Several writers were expelled from the Communist Party and control of literature was tightened. But the authors did not take this lying down and the journalists joined in. By the summer of 1956 they and other malcontents began to find a more public platform for the expression of their dissents in the Petoefi Circle, an offshoot of the communist youth organization DISZ. Scientists, professors, former members of the Spanish Brigade and finally Julia Rajk, widow of the foreign affairs minister executed by Rakosi in 1949 for Titoism, joined them there.

The Petoefi Circle speakers protested not only against thought control but restrictions generally. Well-known writers demanded the resignation of Matyas Rakosi, Ernoe Geroe and other leaders of the Party or the regime. Professor Lajos Janossy, the cosmic ray expert who had resigned his position in Dublin University to return to Hungary, told the Petoefi Circle that although he was vice-president of the Hungarian Atomic Energy Commission he had not been informed officially that uranium had been discovered in Hungary. Geza Losonczy, a communist recently rehabilitated after a long term of imprisonment, demanded that Imre Nagy be allowed to reenter public life.

This happened in June. In July, Communist Party boss Matyas Rakosi was dropped and succeeded by Ernoe Geroe. Geroe had been Stalinist number two. Nagy was readmitted to the Party but not to its central committee. The Hungarian workers, who had been slow to echo the discontent of the intellectuals, began to press for the creation of workers' councils as a step toward the system of economic decentralization pioneered by Tito after 1948. In Gyoer, in what was described as "the first entirely free public and outspoken debate" since 1948, the withdrawal of Soviet troops from Hungary and the release of Cardinal Jozsef Mindszenty were demanded.

This was the situation as October drew towards its end. Neither the army nor the workers had moved. Nothing had yet happened in Hungary which had not happened before in other "people's democracies," and there had been no Poznan. So deceptive was the surface calm that a young American reporter who heard during a visit to Budapest mysterious hints about "the underground" concluded in all innocence that these must be references to the Budapest subway—one of the oldest in the world.

Then discontent began to spread from youth as represented in the Petoefi Circle to university youth. This also had happened before in the satellite world—for instance, in Czechoslovakia—and nothing much had come of it. But in Hungary it was to be the beginning of the end.

A student who a month later was to escape to Vienna has recorded: "On October 22, a placard bordered with the Hungarian national colors summoned me and other pupils of the Technical Academy to a meeting in the Auditorium Maximum. Young workers from the Budapest working class suburbs of Csepel, Ujpest, and Kispest were also invited.

"We knew what had been happening in Warsaw. We had observed how the communists, who wanted to save their positions, had heaped all the sins of the last eleven years on Stalin. Hungary also had its scapegoat—Rakosi. The whole country longed for democracy. But there was no open opposition.

"The meeting began at 6:30 P.M. One speaker after another addressed us—and said nothing. Finally one asked the question which was in all our mouths: 'I ask this meeting, with what right are the Russians in our country?'

"As one the meeting rose from its seats and cried out: 'Away with them; away with them.' We put it in the form of a resolution, one of sixteen. Other resolutions demanded equality with Russia, publication of our economic agreements with her including that for the exploitation of our uranium, a reshuffling of the Government with Imre Nagy as leader and secret general elections with more than one party participating.

"A Csepel worker rose to say: 'Friends, I have no fine words. I belong at the bench not on the platform. I just want to thank you. I want to say the workers need leaders like you. Csepel accepts the sixteen points. We are ready to follow you into hell for them!'

"At midnight we agreed that next day, the 23rd, we would hold a demonstration around the statue of the Polish General Bem, who fought for us against the Russians in 1848. The meeting closed at midnight with the national hymn, 'God bless the Hungarians.' "

The demonstrations started next day. The students began to march. Then the unplanned happened. White-collar workers from nearby offices, artisans from the factories, communist youth organizations and even soldiers joined their ranks. The demonstration in Bem Square, beside the Foreign Office, swelled to 10,000 and then to 20,000. It was noted that the marchers carried Polish and Hungarian national flags, but no red ones. From Bem Square the demonstrators marched to the Parliament. There they heard Geroe in a broadcasted speech condemn their demands as contrary to "international proletarianism" and inspired by persons who wanted to establish not socialist but bourgeois democracy. Angered, the crowd cried: "Put out that red star." An hour later it no longer glittered from the peak of Parliament. Meanwhile, in front of the Budapest radio station, another crowd sent in a delegation to demand the broadcasting of the sixteen points. The AVO—the Hungarian security police—tried to disperse the crowd with tear-gas bombs and then fired on them, killing one and wounding others. That was when the peaceful demonstration turned into a bloody revolution.

Up to this point the crowd was unarmed. But an "ambulance" hurrying to the radio station under a Red Cross flag was stopped and found to contain ammunition for its AVO defenders. Hungarian soldiers and city police handed over some arms. Workers from Csepel Island brought others. The crews of Hungarian army tanks ordered to the scene fraternized with the crowd. Other demonstrators who had been hauling Stalin's giant statue off its pedestal in Stalin Square arrived. The radio building was stormed. The crowd moved off to the offices of *Szabad Nep,* the Communist Party organ, and there had another clash with the AVO. Fights began to break out all over the city. Barricades were set up at street corners.

At 4:30 on the morning of October 24, Soviet armored columns entered the capital. Mikoyan and Suslov came by plane that same evening. At 8 A.M. the Budapest radio announced that the Government had requested the Soviet garrison, stationed in Hungary under the Warsaw Pact, to restore order. It added that Imre Nagy was now head of the Government. The general impression was that Nagy had ordered in the tanks. Nagy and his lieutenants have since denied this. His version was that he was called by the students at 8:30 Tuesday evening at his home, that at 11 o'clock he had told them in front of the Parliament that he agreed to their demands but had no power and had then gone to the Communist Party headquarters. There, he said, he had been kept incommunicado until informed by Geroe at 9 o'clock the next morning that he was prime minister. At 8:45 A.M., however, the Budapest radio had announced without his knowledge that he had decreed martial law.

Perhaps the situation could still have been saved without further bloodshed had it not been for the sanguinary and mysterious massacre on Parliament Square at noon on October 25. Into an unarmed and utterly peaceful crowd, which had been fraternizing with the equally friendly crews of three Soviet tanks, AVO machinegunners opened fire from one flank. Evidently the Soviets, thinking they had fallen into a trap, fired back. The crowd, like the Soviets, thought they had been led into an ambush. From that moment nothing was the same. The AVO, always the evil spirits of Hungarian politics, had acted their part as provocateurs with fatal success.

But the spirit of the revolutionaries, which meant that of the man in the street, was undaunted. Less than ten minutes after the massacre on Parliament Square, new demonstrations began to form only a few blocks away. The Hungarian army refused to fire on their own people, and more and more officers and soldiers slipped away from their barracks to join them. The revolutionaries found two able military leaders in Colonel Pal Maleter and General Bela Kiraly. Under their command some 1,500 students, workers, soldiers and youngsters barricaded themselves in the Killian Barracks, a 200-year old building with meter-thick walls. The Csepel workers entrenched themselves in their Danubian island. Over in Buda two focal points, the Moscow and Moricz Zsigmond Squares, became rallying points.

The Soviets had made the mistake, inexplicable from the viewpoint of military tactics, of sending in tanks. The tanks were usually preceded and followed by armored trucks, but the soldiers who crouched down in them were merely more vulnerable to attack from the housetops, not more mobile in the fashion required for street fighting. Not until the very end of the fighting, when they had brought in reinforcements of more than 200,000 men, did the Soviets send in infantry to accompany the tanks. Perhaps their leaders felt that the green troops under their command could not be trusted except behind armor. It often looked that way to the crowds which—lined up in food queues around the corner from some hot spot—openly laughed at the cowering troops in their trucks.

The tactics of the Soviets were partly dictated by the unfitness of unaccompanied tanks for city fighting against an embattled populace, partly perhaps by their desire to make a horrible example of Budapest. Their reply to even a single shot from some window or housetop was to blast the whole street. The revolutionaries were handicapped by a lack of bazookas. They made Molotov cocktails, but out of every hundred only three proved effective. Sometimes they greased a street so that the tank treads slipped. They would cover the visibility-slit of a tank with paste and paper so that its crew could not see where they were going. They would stuff rags soaked in gasoline in the exhaust so that it would catch fire. The aim in all three cases was to have the tank crews get out so that they could be shot down.

It must have been uncomfortable fighting for the Soviet crews. They never knew when they were safe. Soviets like children; but children hardly too old to play with marbles were playing with grenades and sometimes throwing them into open tank turrets.

During the lull between the first and second Soviet attacks on Budapest two freedom fighters came into my bedroom to tell their story. They had been in the Killian Barracks. One was 17 and the other 14. Finally the 14-year-old said: "I must go now. Mother says, now that the fighting is over, I must get home on time."

A mother sighed: "It's terrible about the children. I can't keep them home. They want to be out fighting. Such babies, really, and yet some of their friends have destroyed Soviet tanks."

The youth of Budapest had another weapon against the Soviets. Not only had they been forced in their schools to acquire some military training but some knowledge of Russian.

They would ask the Soviet tank crews: "Why are you fighting against us?"

When told "You are all fascists," they would answer: "How can we be fascists? I am a university student. Fascists aren't allowed to go to our universities. I belong to the DISZ [communist youth organization]. This man here is a worker and Communist Party member. Why are you in our country, shooting us down?"

Only the Soviet army command knows what effects such conversations produced on the morale of its men. But it was noteworthy that for the second and final attack on Budapest it removed the original Hungarian garrison and brought in new troops, most of them Mongolian or Kirghiz.

While this was happening in Budapest the workers were striking throughout the country. Revolutionary councils were formed in provincial towns, in big factories, in the army and the universities. More and more army units joined the revolutionaries. Finally, on October 30, the Hungarian air force threatened to bomb Soviet troops if they were not withdrawn.

Because the revolutionaries had no organization and no recognized leader (although Nagy was becoming their symbol) their demands were at first uncoordinated. But they were rapidly hardening. In addition to free elections and the departure of the Soviets they came to include abrogation of the Warsaw Pact and the transformation of Hungary into a neutral country like Austria.

As the fighting went on, the Government changed its composition and its character. "National communists" were added to the Politbureau on October 24. But it also included such Rakosi-Stalinists as Geroe, the former prime minister Hegedues, Antal Apro and Arpad Kiss. Geroe resigned on Suslov's orders and was replaced as Party secretary by Janos Kadar, who claimed to be a national communist since he had been imprisoned in 1951 as a Titoist. From Nagy's new Government were eliminated such anti-revolutionary communists as Istvan Bata, minister of defense, and Laszlo Piros, minister of the interior; added were non-communists Bela Kovacs, former general secretary of the Smallholder Party, and Zoltan Tildy, former president of Hungary. But it also included a majority of communist holdovers from the Rakosi era such as Antal Apro, Istvan Kossa, Karoly Janza, Sandor Czottner and Zoltan Vas.

This Government reluctantly yielded ground before the growing demands of the revolutionaries. On October 28 Nagy admitted that the revolution was not a counterrevolution but "an elemental force . . . an all-embracing, unifying, national and democratic movement." He promised to negotiate for the immediate withdrawal of Soviet troops from Budapest and eventual departure from Hungary and to disband the AVO as soon as order was restored. But this did not satisfy the partisans. They continued to fight and the Soviets continued to attack them until November 30. On that day Janos Kadar, on behalf of the Communist Party, Tildy for the Smallholder Party and Ferenc Erdei for the former National Peasant Party, broadcast a promise to hold free elections, to proclaim Hungary a neutral country and to insist on immediate departure of the Soviet troops.

This eleventh hour grant of the demands of the revolutionaries was made after they had stormed the headquarters of the AVO, hanged or shot many of its members, burned down Communist Party headquarters in Buda and set fire to every Soviet bookshop in the capital. On the same day the Soviet Government announced it would discuss with the Warsaw Treaty powers the withdrawal of its troops from Hungary, Poland and Rumania. The Soviet forces in Budapest actually did leave.

So ended the first phase of the revolution. Optimists believed that it had been won. After a week of fighting the defenders of the Killian Barracks emerged from their fastness. There were hollow-cheeked men with week-old beards, white-faced girls in a state of shock, children carrying rifles as tall as themselves. The Soviets having gone, the partisans proceeded to hunt down the AVO. A terrible vengeance was exacted from those they found. But of the approximately 60,000 members of this force of public enemies, the great majority either escaped or went to jail to be freed less than a fortnight later.

Political prisoners were set free. The Government stopped the compulsory collection of produce from Hungarian farmers. In the countryside the collectives began to dissolve. A meeting of "revolutionary councils" was called, this being the first official word that such bodies existed. Colonel Maleter became Major General Maleter, minister of defense, and Major General Kiraly was appointed commandant of Budapest. Nagy declared that: "The Revolutionary Armed Forces Committee shall operate until the new Government to be formed through general and secret elections takes office."

Nagy began negotiating with the revolutionary councils on a number of demands which had been broadcast by them. They included independent political parties, free elections, freedom of religion, freedom for small manufacturers and traders to set up in business, abrogation of all agreements with the Soviet Union, and economic aid from the West. None of these proposals, which represented the most extreme demands ever made by the revolutionaries, warranted the claim later fabricated by the Soviets and their sycophants that "reactionary fascist forces" turned the revolution into a counterrevolution. Freedom for small manufacturers was part of the last Polish Five Year Plan. It has been claimed that Cardinal Mindszenty, who was freed by a Hungarian tank unit on October 30, broadcast an appeal to restore its lands to the Church. The writer was never able to find any proof of this. But he heard it publicly and privately stated not only by the Nagy Government but by various revolutionary councils that agricultural land would never be restored to the big landowners nor industry to its former proprietors.

On October 31 Nagy cabled the United Nations that Hungary wished to withdraw from the Warsaw Treaty and become neutral. Next day word was received that new Soviet forces had begun to enter Hungary and to surround Hungarian airfields and army units. Nagy remonstrated with the Soviet ambassador in Budapest, protested to the secretary general of the United Nations and asked him to invoke the aid of the great powers to protect neutral Hungary and to bring her case before the United Nations assembly.

The reply of the Soviets was to agree to the appointment of a joint committee to discuss a timetable for the withdrawal of the Soviet forces from Hungary. Major General Maleter and his chief of staff Istvan Kovacs were invited to come to Soviet headquarters on the evening of Saturday November third to negotiate. They never returned.

Instead of withdrawing, the Russians attacked Budapest for the second time in this revolution and the fourth time in Hungary's history. They attacked at 1 o'clock Sunday morning, November 4, and this time in overwhelming force. The third phase of the revolution had begun.

By arresting Hungary's military leaders under promise to negotiate with them and surrounding every Hungarian unit and airfield while still discussing their departure from Hungary, the Soviet leaders had struck a shrewd blow. The new Government had had only four days to consolidate and was still discussing its enlargement by the addition of three Social Democrats, two National Peasants and a leader of the revolutionaries when the blow fell. The Hungarian army, as an army, had little chance and no orders to resist. The five or six armored Soviet divisions assigned to the task entered the capital after little more than an hour's bombardment.

The Nagy Government was ordered by the Soviets to capitulate by noon, and a new puppet Government was set up. Four of its members, Janos Kadar, Antal Apro, Gyoergy Marosan and Sandor Ronai, had been members of the Politburo named by Geroe four months earlier. A fifth member, Imre Horvath, had been Geroe's foreign minister. Its minister of interior was Dr. Ferenc Muennich, present premier and a former chief of Budapest police. As head of the Hungarian Trade Union Congress, Apro had already been repudiated by several of his own unions. Kadar had been considered a Stalinist when, in his then capacity as minister of interior, he had had his friend, Laszlo Rajk, arrested in 1949. Two years later, he, himself, had been jailed by Rakosi for alleged Titoism and, according to his own account, tortured in prison by his former comrades.

Nagy left the Parliament before the Soviets entered it and escaped to the Yugoslav Embassy, where he took refuge. Cardinal Mindszenty, after a brief interview in the Parliament with Nagy and his ministers, also sought sanctuary, but in the United States Legation.

The Soviet Government had pledged itself in the Warsaw Treaty which it signed with Hungary and its other satellites, to abide by "the principles of mutual respect for their independence and sovereignty and non-interference in domestic affairs." Its armed emissaries, after being instructed by the Hungarian Government to get out, had now broken into the Hungarian capital, deposed the Government and set up a shadow regime of its own.

Making it stick was another matter. The strange silence which followed the entry of the Soviet tanks into the city did not last long. Maleter was in the hands of the Soviets, but he had drawn up a plan of defense should the Soviets attack. Some 1,200 officers and cadets barricaded themselves in the Killian Barracks and prepared to fight to the last. Others manned the Citadel, the Gellert Hill, the ruined Var or castle-fortress, Obuda post office and Moscow Square in Buda, the West Station and the Varosliget or city forest. The workers made themselves ready for the fight in Csepel and the Ujpest factories. The defenders tried to connect up these points and thus to establish two crescent-shaped defense lines, one on either side of the Danube.

But the students, workers and soldiers who fought for the Nagy Government had only a few medium tanks and a small number of light and medium guns against four complete Soviet

armored divisions with some 1400 T-34 and Stalin tanks. The
odds were hopeless. The defenders could only choose the manner of their death, and they chose to die fighting. The Soviet
tanks soon cut the connection between the different bastions.
All that was left then was for their defenders to hold them as
long as they could, while small mobile groups tried to take a
toll of the tanks as they raced up and down the broad boule-
vards. Few or none of these Soviet monsters seemed to be
equipped with stabilizers which would have permitted them to
fire their cannon in motion. A few thousand bazookas or recoil-
less rifles in the hands of the besieged—in their *kamikaze* willing-
ness to die—would have made an incalculable difference in the
result. But, as it was, the tanks roared past, spraying both sides
of every street with their machineguns, or stationed themselves
at a safe distance from individual bastions and battered them
with indirect fire from their tank cannon, medium field guns
and mortars.

The Killian Barracks were breached and entered after two
days' bombardment, but the defenders continued to fight from
its ruins until early Thursday morning, November 7. On that
day, the West Station also fell and the Soviets stormed the ruins
of the Var. The Students' Revolutionary Committee broadcast
at this stage instructions to the Freedom Fighters to fight their
way out of Budapest when their positions became impossible,
and to build partisan groups in the countryside. Not until Sunday, November 11, did the workers in the Ujpest factories give
in while the Csepel workers in their island fastness held out two
days longer. The workers and Freedom Fighters in the iron and
steel center of Dunapentele were also overrun on the 11th. But
partisans assembled in the Buekk mountains near Miskolc, in
the Matra mountains northeast of Budapest, in the Bakony
hills and forests north of Lake Balaton, around the coal and
uranium mines of Pecs and in the marshes of the Danube and
the Tisza. There they prepared to hold out indefinitely.

In the process of mopping up, the Soviets picked up not only
disarmed Freedom Fighters but every wounded man, everyone
accused or suspected of having participated in the fighting and

finally, in sudden street raids, every man of military age they could lay hands on. The news soon leaked out that these were being loaded into boxcars and deported to the Soviet Union. Meanwhile the Soviets arrested Imre Nagy when he left the Yugoslav Embassy for his home, after Kadar had promised President Tito that he would not be molested.

The end of the fighting in Budapest was not the end of the revolution there. The workers had taken advantage of the revolutionary situation to form workers' councils, of which that in the capital functioned as the central body. These now took over the representation of revolutionary interests. They demanded the replacement of Kadar by Imre Nagy, cessation of the deportations and withdrawal of the Soviet troops. They said that when these basic demands had been granted negotiations must begin for the establishment of Hungary's independence and neutrality, free elections and the complete dissolution of the hated AVO.

Kadar at first affected to negotiate with the councils. But he made promises only to break them and finally began to arrest their leaders. When the councils responded by calling a general strike he ordered them dissolved, thereby destroying his best means of access to the revolutionaries—which meant, for all practical purposes, the Hungarian people. His purpose was obviously to atomize Hungary and, when he had reduced it to a state of near anarchy, to reintroduce a regime of pure compulsion enforced by a reconstituted AVO backed by a permanent Soviet garrison. But few believed that this was really Kadar's doing. Revolutionaries who had known him described him as no Machiavelli but a man broken by the tortures he had suffered at the hands of the Stalinists. Most of all, they say, he is a fanatical communist to whom the Party is life and law.

When word of the deportations began to spread, the youth of Hungary began to flee their country. Some 18,000 sought refuge in Yugoslavia. But the great bulk of the fugitives poured into Austria and from there into the United States, Canada, Australia, Great Britain, and every corner of Europe. Hungary became a stricken warrior bleeding from two wounds, one in each side. Now the flow has stopped, but only because Kadar has rebuilt the Iron Curtin, with its minefields, its barb wire and watch towers.

Why did the revolution get out of hand, instead of taking a more ordered course like that in Poland?

Some of Nagy's followers were inclined to blame themselves. "We had no plan," they said. "Our program should have been merely to get Nagy elected, representing him to the people as the symbol and guarantee of the revolution. But the Stalinists had compromised the situation before he ever had a chance. After that, because he had come in without a program, the people pushed him too fast and gave the Soviets an excuse to attack."

But the writer has also met others once close to Nagy who hinted that their leader had been pushed only in the direction he himself wanted to go. According to their account he had become in his thinking another Djilas, convinced that communism must face free elections and thus prove its worth in competition. That may explain why the Soviets arrested him and caused his death.

THE SOUL

The concept that nations, as well as individuals, have souls, was so forcefully expounded by the German philosophers during the 19th century that it has remained a dominant idea up to our own day. It is not surprising, therefore, that imperial communism would seek to destroy this idea of national soul in their search for absolute control. But what is a nation's soul reduced to flesh-and-blood terms? If we did not know before, the communists have defined it for us. Recognizing that the family and religion form the core and spirit of a national soul, they have attempted the pitiless extermination of these twin foundation stones of a healthy society. Why? The answer is not difficult to find. It is in the intimate nature of family life associated with and in the eternal verities of religion that communism faces its most basic challenge. Domination and control of a population are impossible without capturing the influence of parent and church. This, unfortunately, the communists understand far better than the average citizen of freedom. But if the communists know where to strike, the lesson of Hungary questions their knowledge of how to strike. For here is a real problem. Soviet power and communist terror may frustrate the normal functions of family upbringing and religious faith, but they have yet to devise an appeal or force which can bring about the total disintegration of these basic social units.

In this first section of the book, Mrs. Ilona Marton, a former uncooperative prisoner of the dreaded AVO (security police) for many months, tells how she was able to rear her two daughters to believe in God, right and wrong, and the political facts of life, without endangering her own safety and that of her famous husband, Endre Marton, former Associated Press correspondent for Hungary. Not an easy task, as you shall see.

Jozsef Magyar is the pseudonym of a prominent Hungarian lay theologian, whose real identity must be withheld to protect family members still held captive in Hungary. While his story deals with the brutal Red assault on the tradition-laden Hungarian Catholic Church, his analysis of tactics and principles can be generally applied to the communist suppression of all religious groups in the country. We, who live in security and freedom, can only pray for our suffering and persecuted brethren in their moment of decision.

Family Life in Hungary

BY ILONA NYILAS MARTON

Hundreds and hundreds of times during the revolution, we reported from Budapest that those who fought Soviet tanks, self-propelled guns and all the modern armor of a great power, were mainly teenaged boys and girls. Almost every reporter added that this was the greatest slap in the face international communism had ever received, but only a few drew the final conclusion: that it was also the victory of the family, the victory of parents and—last but not least—of the mother over communism.

Communism, the antiquated nineteenth century Marxist theory in practice, has failed in every human respect, and the unforgettable weeks of the Hungarian revolution have unmistakably proved it. Here, on the following pages, I shall explain how and why it failed in the family.

Family life in Hungary before World War II was not different from family life in any other conservative European country, like France or Austria. "The family is the basis of society" is a hackneyed phrase, but as so many platitudes, it is true. Children in prewar Hungary—whether they were rich or poor—

* Dr. Marton is a former United Press correspondent for Budapest, and a co-winner of the 1957 George Polk award for journalism.

were brought up as law-abiding citizens, respecting elders in general and their parents in particular. There were moderate religious and educational requirements, and though the system was outmoded and too much on the German line, standards were high and teachers severe. All in all, it was neither better nor worse than in any other country in the Old World.

World War II and its consequences marked a drastic change in this respect; communism could not afford to tolerate another power, the cohesive force of the family.

The typical postwar phenomena and pattern of life, the war on Hungarion soil and especially the siege of Budapest, with all its major and minor family tragedies I do not wish to describe here, but the total effect of these events helped the communists in their efforts to disrupt traditional family life in Hungary.

It goes without saying that the communists were aware that they had only one chance to win. They had to win over the youth, the young people who had no memories of prewar life. But to win over the children, born immediately before, during or after the war, they had to break the influence of the family, the respect of parents. They tried and they failed. The communists overplayed the game in this respect, as they so often did.

Schoolboys and girls in Hungary became young rowdies in the late forties, respecting nothing and no one. Teachers, afraid of the powerful communist youth organization that practically ruled in the schools, obeyed the pupils; the various youth organizations sponsored by the Communist Party disposed of their free time and overworked, tired parents were generally helpless.

When I say "parents" what I really mean is the mother. Relatively few women worked in Hungary before the war, at least not in the sense that they had to work after the war. When I say "work" I mean work outside the home, and "women," in the sense of family life, are married women, most of them with children.

Of the women who worked before the war in factories, offices, shops and in the fields, most of them were girls living with their parents and only an insignificant minority were married women with children.

All this has drastically changed since the war. The mad over-ambitious program of industrialization, and the mushrooming bureaucracy needed more and more manpower. Communists openly proclaimed as dogma that it is a shame for a woman to be the "slave" of the family and of the household, instead of helping to build "glorious" socialism.

The other factor, naturally, was want. Few families could have a decent life with only the man's salary and that fact alone compelled tens of thousands of women to go to work. There was constant propaganda popularizing female "heroes" of work, women tractor drivers and weavers, bus conductors and even female soldiers. There were even "Stakhanovites" among them who received decorations of various orders, including the Kossuth Prize, the highest award postwar Hungary gave to her greats.

On the other hand, the communists did very little to make life more comfortable for the mother, who had to look after her husband and child, if not children, in addition to working in a factory or an office. Life undeniably improved in one respect after the war. Most of the factories had nurseries for the babies of woman workers, state owned factories and offices supplied their workers with lunch at reduced prices, but Hungary still remained an extremely backward country with almost no facil-ities of the type that make life so much easier for the housewife in the West, especially in the United States.

It remained the mother's task to make the fire, prepare break-fast and dinner for the family, to mend the clothes, clean the house, usually also to help the children prepare their homework; in short, all the chores around the home, in much the same way she had to do before the war, but without the added task of going to work for at least eight hours a day. There are no washing machines in private homes in Hungary, shops do not deliver foodstuffs and most of the women have never heard of the dozens of small household devices that are taken for granted by the housewife in the West.

Moreover, women are more conservative than the men. The Government made efforts to persuade housewives to use deep-frozen or prepared food. There was also heavy advertising recommending canned foods, but to little avail. Some years must elapse before the Hungarian housewife discovers that dinner need not be prepared in the same way her mother and grandmother did. It is still the standard of a good housewife in Hungary to see that her larder is filled with home-made preserves, fruit, vegetables, tomato-juice, etc., and no housewife would dare to face the critical women in the neighborhood if her pantry was not sufficiently stocked with all these foodstuffs each autumn, however hard she had to work otherwise.

But the regime not only compelled thousands of mothers to join the country's labor force, it also aimed at indoctrinating them. This meant additional hours far from the family. It was part of the hair-raising nonsense of the Stalinist era that three, four, sometimes five times every week, both manual and white collar workers, men or women, had to stay in the office or factory after working hours and attend hours long Party or trade union seminars, discussions on the eternal problem of how to raise production, meetings discussing foreign policy, which meant, naturally, worship of the Soviet Union and Stalin and censure of the "imperialists." In the mornings workers had to arrive early so that someone could read to them the official communist organ *Szabad Nep*, a paper to which everyone had to subscribe in any event. And all these extra hours were, of course, without extra pay. Imagine a woman returning from her work, exhausted, nervous, worn out, only to work at home again, striving desperately to maintain some faint semblance of a warm home.

At that time, there was a popular joke circulating in Budapest. It told the story of a family of four, two parents and two grown-up children, with all four working. The father returned home first, but had to leave and so he left a note fixed to the door: "Have gone to the Party, will be back at nine." The mother added: "Went to the women's federation, will be back at nine." Then came the girl: "I've got to go to a seminar tonight...." And finally the boy: "There's a meeting in the DISZ, will be back at nine." When, at last, the family returned later that evening, a fresh note was tacked to the door: "I've been here—will not return at nine—hooray for the Party!" The house had been robbed by a witty burglar.

Even the Communist Party's humor magazine *Ludas Matyi* carried at this time a little story ridiculing "family life" in Hungary. It described how a man and his wife, both working in different places, tried in vain by telephone to make an arrangement to see each other, but it turned out that either one or the other had some important discussion, seminar or Party school to attend every night—so finally they agreed to spend the weekend together.

Imagine family life under such circumstances. And there was still another factor: housing.

The housing situation in Hungary, especially in Budapest and in the other major cities, has been appalling ever since World War II. The reasons were manifold.

Firstly, the 1944-45 seige of Budapest destroyed many homes, but the greatest concern of the communist regime was to build new factories, concrete and glass fortresses for the secret police, for the Party and, last but not least, plush villas for the Party bosses, but no apartment houses for the population. Secondly, the state forced about 600,000 peasants to give up their land and come to the cities to become industrial workers, without caring how these people lived.

The consequences were disastrous. A decree was issued shortly after the war permitting only one room for a married couple plus an additional one if they had up to two children. There were exceptions: intellectuals, physicians, writers or engineers could have a second room, a kind of study, but no more. Matyas Rakosi and the other communist bosses were also exceptions. They lived in their luxury villas, shared only with their body-guards. That decree, thirteen years after the war, is still valid. If you go into a big apartment house built during the first decade of the century in downtown Budapest, you will sometimes find four or five calling cards fixed to a single door indicating that this comfortable flat of five or more rooms which housed one family before the war is a co-tenancy now, one of the most hated institutions of the communist regime. According to the law, the original owner could keep only one or two rooms according to the number of his children. The rest was occupied by co-tenants on orders of the district council. But the flat built for one family only, which usually meant only one bathroom and one kitchen, now had to be shared with four or five families. How many bitter jokes there were over the constant bickering among co-tenants, on the many petty tragedies and, sometimes, real dramas. Imagine three or more housewives returning approximately at the same time from work all wishing to give warm meals to their families, yet with only one outmoded stove in the kitchen. To say nothing of the mornings, when everyone needed the bathroom at the same time.

But apart from that, the intimacy of family life was destroyed. A co-tenant was next door on the left, another perhaps next door on the right, with only a single thin door dividing all. This condition, not unnaturally, facilitated a slackening of morals, especially among the young. There are sometimes a dozen people if not more belonging to several families, in one Budapest flat, people of all ages and both sexes, and it is only too easy for the teenagers to observe various phenomena of life which he (or she) would not have the opportunity to notice under normal circumstances. The boys and girls know all the "secrets" of life in Hungary well before the age they should and this does not help to maintain necessary discipline and right order in a family.

There were other factors that helped youngsters to become enlightened before their due age.

Co-education and the early co-mingling of the sexes are controversial matters. They have their merits and demerits. The practice was introduced in Hungarian general schools (ages 6 to 14) after the war and it was a failure. The situation was especially bad in the late forties, when the regime's policy was to flatter the youth in every respect in order to win their active support against the "unreliable" older generation. As with the grownups the same technique was employed. A totalitarian regime can control its citizens easiest by keeping them busy, preferably in one flock, by allowing them as little free time as possible. The grownups had their seminars and Party schools, the young ones had their organizations, the pioneer movement for the small fry, the DISZ, the monolithic and powerful youth organization for youth above 14. The regime did its utmost to reduce the time the young ones could spend within the family. The DISZ kept them busy, there were clubs for the young people where they met without a chaperon and camps for them in summer.

All this would be all right normally. There are clubs for young people in the West, the boy scouts go to camp, too. But during those postwar years, hearing and reading nothing other than that they were the backbone of the regime, the basis of the future, these young people really thought that everything was drawn only to please them, that they could snub every authority, teacher or parent.

Only when the most unpleasant things occurred, did the Government realize that it had gone too far. The common camping of teenaged boys and girls resulted in illegitimate children of 14-15 year old mothers. This, alone, was not a crime in communist controlled countries. In those mad years of production records, when the regime pretended that there was no such thing as unemployment in a communist country and the nation needed more and more manpower, the slogan "To bear a legitimate child is a duty, to bear it out of wedlock is glory" appeared on the walls of maternity wards.

Things in school were more complicated. The overwhelming majority of teachers were brought up before the war and they were terrified. They got a limited time to re-educate themselves, to learn the sacrosanct theories of Marxism-Leninism-Stalinism that formed for so many years the basis of the Hungarian educational system in elementary and secondary schools and in the universities. But besides the feeling that disaster always hung over their heads because they were part of the pre-war intelligentia, suspected of disloyalty toward the regime, there was a new menace for teachers: the pupil.

The youth organization DISZ controlled life itself. Their representatives were sitting on the boards which controlled the instruction and marking. The Government constantly accused teachers of demanding too much from the reliable cadres, those offsprings of workers and peasants whose number was artificially increased year after year. It was not enough for the child of a middle class family to have good marks when he finished general school at 14. The good cadres had preference going to secondary school and, later to the university, and even if a worker's son was only a mediocre student, he had a much better chance to be admitted to the secondary school than the unhappy son of a middle class family, however good the latter's certificate had been.

There were unheard of scenes in schools in the late forties, even communist newspapers had to admit them—later. Students terrorized the teachers, there was neither discipline nor order and not much learning either. Conscientious teachers who wanted to flunk a student who happened to be a good cadre member were threatened by the DISZ, or even the Party, which was the same, since the DISZ was the preparatory school of future Party members. This was later partially stopped when renowned scientists, old university professors warned the regime that universities were in an impossible situation, as they were obliged to admit students without a minimal basis of knowledge. It was a seriously bitter question in Budapest in the early fifties whether it was too risky to call a young physician or to go over a bridge built by a young engineer.

Family Versus Communism

Though some kind of order was restored in schools and teachers regained at least part of their authority, the fight between the communist rulers and the family continued. It was a blind alley. The children were taught materialism in school and then returned to their parents who feared, detested and abhorred this doctrine. Furthermore, many a smart child detected rather soon that the teacher also, pattering indifferently about Marxism, did it only half-heartedly like someone who had to do it, but does it against his will. The parent was helpless. He felt not only "ideologically" outmoded, but it was rather difficult for him to help his offspring in doing his homework. Every subject was interwoven with Marxism, small children of six

learned about Lenin and Stalin, long before they were told
about Hungary's national heroes. The school, whether the
teacher liked it or not, ridiculed traditions that remained the
basis of the family. The Church no longer had any say, it was
a permanent feature of education to belittle religion, to discourage the youth from going to church; priests were depicted
as unnecessary evils and likely as not the same boy or girl heard
just the contrary at home.

Take Christmas for instance. Hungarians used to celebrate
Christendom's greatest holy day in the German way. Christmas
Eve was a family feast, there were no theatres open, restaurants
were closed, even streetcars and buses stopped early in the evening. Christmas for centuries was the feast of the family and of
the child. Non-Christians also celebrated it. Jewish families had
Christmas trees, its candles were lit in practically every house,
rich or poor. It was one of the many stupidities of the communists that they wanted to abolish this beautiful tradition. They
were bound to fail. They ordered theaters to be open on Christmas Eve and state-owned restaurants advertised extra menus
for customers. It was a ridiculous attempt. Unfortunate actors
had to play to empty houses and restaurants catered only to
their staffs. The communists also aped Moscow in this respect.
"Father Winter" was advertised as bringing presents for the
small ones and the holiday was called "the feast of the Pine
Tree."

We had a neighbor, the man was a high ranking Party functionary. They had a daughter, only a few years older than my
Juli, now 12. The girl was brought up in good communist "traditions" and although otherwise a good girl, she tried to ridicule
my two daughters' belief in little Jesus bringing Christmas
presents.

"Don't be fools," she would say, "your parents buy them, I
know."

Still I always had the feeling that Zsuzsi, the neighbor's
daughter, envied my Juli and Kati for their illusions. The
Christmas after the revolution, Zsuzsi had great news to tell my
daughters. For the first time in her life they were to have a
Christmas tree and she asked whether she could come and see

how we decorated ours. The communists had failed with their own Party members.

We also had another communist family in our neighborhood. Contrary to Zsuzsi's father, who had been some kind of intellectual, they were simple peasants, both father and mother working in the Party headquarters. These people, of course, ignored Christmas, too. The old mother of the woman, a typical Hungarian peasant woman wearing a kerchief on her head, lived with them and looked after their children. It was one of the most characteristic and also most moving things I experienced when one morning before Christmas some years ago, I caught sight of the old woman bringing a small Christmas tree from the market trying to hide it behind her back.

Such double-dealing could not lead to anything but lies. The child heard one thing in school, and even there he sometimes sensed that the teacher did not speak according to his belief, and another at home. They were abusing the West in school and the parents were listening to the Hungarian broadcasts of western radio stations at home. According to the school, everything was wonderful in communism, and yet everything was just miserable when the child listened to his parents. Where could this lead?

I myself (and my husband, of course) had many unhappy hours because of this double standard. For years we did not talk about politics in the presence of our children, but this was easier for us than for the average Hungarian. We worked together, politics was our profession and so we did not have to talk about it in those hours we spent with our daughters. But the average Hungarian spent his day in the office or in the factory and met his wife only when he also met his children. How could he restrain himself?

Still I was worried. I am by education a teacher and I was afraid of a psychological disaster when my daughters found out that there are two worlds, the world worshipped in school and the other their parents live and work for. I was amused to find out how easily the children overcame what I thought to be an insurmountable difficulty. And this was true not only with my children. I talked with many parents who had the same worries and they experienced the same solution. I did not know what to do and chose the easiest way. When they went to school the first time I did not tell them anything. Of course, here again, it was easier for us because of our profession. We were acknowledged to be the "enemies" of the regime; it was no secret that we had friends among western diplomats—a mortal sin otherwise—and that we listened to foreign broadcasts. So informed, an inquisitive teacher might have asked my daughters about such things, but it never happened, to my knowledge, and it would not have harmed us if they had told the truth. We were beyond the pale.

An amazing thing happened when my Juli went to school the first time in 1952. She was six and, of course, taught never to tell a lie. The school mistress, an amiable elderly woman, told the children one day to bring in the next day the toy they liked best. Juli had many nice things and I let her select the one she wished to take to school. She chose a little monkey that played the drum and danced in a circle when wound up. I was not too happy with her choice. The monkey was obviously a western product, something no Hungarian child could have had in those years of complete isolation. But I did not interfere, though Juli naturally also knew that she got the little monkey from Ruth Tryon, an American diplomat, who had been declared *persona non grata* by the communists just one year earlier.

Next day when Juli came home I asked her how it was.

"Mine was the nicest," she boasted. "Aunt Margit (the school mistress) liked her very much, I had to wind her up twice and make her drum and dance. She also asked where I got her."

"What did you say?" I asked. Juli looked at me, I will never forget the premature wisdom in her eyes.

"I did not tell her I got it from Aunt Ruth, I said I got it for Christmas," she replied. A six year old child, taught never to tell a lie, but she instinctively knew that it was more clever not to reveal that her favorite toy was the present of an American diplomat.

How often I have witnessed this premature wisdom of little children during all those bleak years. How often I felt my throat tighten because of the children, my children and others, who had to learn so prematurely the cruel realities of life. I do not know, of course, how much children in the West today know about life, about politics, but I have met too many uninformed adults from the West to assume that their children have reason to be precocious.

I should like to relate an example of what I mean by political sense taken from my own family. It happened during the revolution, when my two little ones were nine and ten and when we no longer saw any point in trying to conceal anything from them. We had after all been in prison, the two had been left alone, and they knew the reason why. We talked one evening about a teenaged boy who left his family and fled to Austria.

"Oh, he will come back, he's stupid," Kati, the younger one, remarked with unmistakable authority.

I asked her whether she would go, leaving us behind.

"Yes, I would," the answer was. "At least one member of the family must have brains, and I would send you food parcels from abroad."

Those parcels coming from the West were for years the dream of every family in Hungary. Partly because thousands of impoverished middle class families made their living by selling the contents of such parcels, and partly because their contents for years represented the richness of the West with unheard of luxuries like nylons, pure wool and good razor blades.

This same Kati asked me perhaps the most dramatic question I heard during the revolution. It was November 4, the date of the Soviet onslaught on Budapest and Hungary's short-lived freedom. "Tell me, Mamy, have you ever been free in your life except during these past few days?" she asked.

What could I tell her?

And how exactly they knew, girls of nine and ten I must repeat, that the patriots hid "three carloads" of weapons and ammunition somewhere in the hills around our house. And they told me exactly what the cache contained: tommy guns, pistols, handgrenades, all things I myself learned to know only during the revolution. I still do not know whether it was true or just street gossip, but they spoke so seriously about it as girls their age customarily talk about their dolls.

Recently, when we were finally on this side of the Curtain, we were sitting in the lobby of a Viennese hotel with some western diplomats waiting for lunch and talking, of course, politics.

We spoke about Turkey. My daughter Kati, who so far had listened attentively, turned to me: "Mother, where's Turkey?"

I explained to her.

"No," she said, "I mean politically, West or East?" My diplomat friends were flabbergasted.

But it was another lie that finally turned thousands of teen-aged boys and girls against the regime, shaking the very foundations of international communism. It was the lie they, the communists, told them for years, and then had to repudiate.

One of the greatest blunders communism made was the obsequious aping of everything in the Soviet Union, including the personal cult, which led to the worship of Stalin, and in Hungary, of Stalin's "most loyal pupil," Matyas Rakosi.

It was an accepted fact in Hungary that Rakosi was a clever man, furthermore, most of the western diplomats thought he was. I question this for various reasons. One of them is that had he been a clever man he would never have made the mistake of this special Soviet feature. He should have known that the Hungarians, a proud people, would never stomach it.

Still, while the personality cult nauseated the adults, it could be feared that the new generation, which did not know anything else, would accept it as a matter of course. They did, many of them, for some time. But then Stalin was denounced and later so too was Rakosi, "father" of Hungarian youth. Try to imagine the state of mind of a teenager who never heard anything else, who was taught in school, on posters, through loudspeakers, in the youth organizations, that Stalin is the benevolent god and Rakosi his resident in Hungary. That they are the best, that only superlatives can be used in describing them. Then, suddenly, all this was revoked in a most brutal and abrupt way. It was small wonder that the youth went wild. To rob them of their illusions, to trample their artificial idols into the mud and still expect them to remain loyal to the system was such naivete that one has to question the cleverness of such leaders.

It was a tragic comical farce that just those youngsters, the teenaged boys and girls whom the regime trusted most, who were brought up by them, who should have been the Janissaries of the movement, the Party's weapon against the "reactionary" elder generation, spearheaded the revolution.

I interviewed dozens of such youngsters during the fighting in Budapest and one of my stereotyped questions was "how did you learn to fight tanks?"

The answers were unanimous: in official courses sponsored by the Government, from Soviet text-books and films describing in detail the activities of young partisans in World War II.

Another thing that caused constant friction between the regime and family was religion. Hungarians in general and particularly Roman Catholic Hungarians, nominally representing some 65% of all Magyars, are religious people.

The teaching of religion was compulsory in Hungarian schools till the communists abolished it. The western reader may lift his eyebrows and ask "So what?" I agree with him and I agree wholeheartedly with the separation of church and state, as it is in the United States.

But in Hungary, the communists wanted to break the religious sentiments of the people. The consequence was that churches were more crowded than ever before. The communists abolished compulsory teaching of religion. The consequence was that even mothers who did not especially care, like myself, saw to it that their children should get religious instruction. This, I think, is understandable. It is the primitive reaction of man toward a hated system that tries to impose its will on the people. The regime might have been right in some respects, still the sole fact that they were hated was enough for the people to resist.

The communist state abolished nearly all the religious orders in 1950. But many of the disbanded monks, and especially nuns, continued their Godly work without the habit of their vocation. It was a powerful illegal organization. Parents learned through the grapevine that a certain nun was willing to come to the house and teach religion. In our house I learned of it from my little daughters. They came one day saying that Sister M. is teaching the children of neighbors and would I please let them learn, too. I did not object.

In prison I had a nun as a cellmate for some weeks. She confirmed what I already felt: the Catholic Church never gave up the fight for the souls of the younger generation and it was amazing how well organized they were.

The state, of course, was smart enough not to forbid the teaching of religion in schools, it only abolished the compulsory teaching of religion. This meant that those pupils whose parents insisted on religious instruction, and there were very few, had to return to school outside the normal school hours.

But this was not the major obstacle. Every parent had the "right" to declare when the school year commenced whether he wanted religious instruction for his child or not. Few dared to ask for it and those who did were discouraged by teachers, usually in the friendliest way. It was so easy. In a communist country, where everything is state owned, almost everyone depends on and gets his pay from the state. It was enough to hint that higher authorities would not be happy and even fathers determined to let their children enroll changed their minds.

It was characteristic indeed that in 1953, when the new look of the post-Stalin era was introduced in Hungary, it was a Jewish woman who went around in our neighborhood, a district inhabited mostly by a rather conservative, Christian middle-class, persuading parents that the time had come to enroll children *en bloc* for religious instruction in the schools.

The revolution also changed things in this respect. Whatever the final verdict on the revolution will be, there stands one fact. Hungarians are no longer frightened, they have changed completely, the former cringing, toadyish attitude has disappeared. The communist system of teaching religion has not changed, the Kadar Government has maintained in force the former regulations. But it is interesting to note that the communist press has already published anxious reports of children and their parents being "pressed" to request religious instruction. Who would "press" them in a country where the terror of the worst period of Stalinism has already returned? There is, of course, no question of such pressure. The simple answer is that the fathers and the mothers are no longer afraid. They ask now for a right under communist law—religious instruction for their children, something they did not dare to do for so many years.

One of the first things that startled my daughters in the West was how empty the churches were. We arrived in Vienna on a Thursday and the following Sunday, as they have done since they first were able to walk, my daughters went to Mass at the beautiful Karlskirche close by the place we lived. The huge cathedral was almost empty, an unbelievable thing for anyone coming from the other side of the Iron Curtain. Churches in Hungary were always rather full on Sundays even before the war, but have been practically packed with Hungarians since the end of the war.

This is partially a natural phenomenon. Religious feelings are always stronger after a national tragedy and the war certainly was very much a tragedy for Magyars. But, again, the main reason was resistance to communism. The communists wanted to break the church, let's show our sympathy by attending Mass or religious service.

The communists were smart enough not to interfere directly. Their aim was to break the political and economic power of the churches and to eliminate their direct influence on the children by closing their excellent schools. They also saw to it that priests, ministers and rabbis should not say "inciting" things in their sermons. Those who did were jailed.

But otherwise the regime was exceptionally clever in this respect. They knew two things. First, that the main thing for the really religious man is that he can go to church whenever it pleases him and there to pray to God. Everything else, including Cardinal Mindszenty or even the parish priest whom he used to see every Sunday, is of minor importance. Second, the regime was aware that either it closes all or almost all the churches, as was done in Russia after World War I, or that it accepts the reality that nothing could stop the average Hungarian from going to church on Sunday.

This does not mean that the communists did nothing to discourage people from attending church. There were over-ambitious Party functionaries, Party secretaries in offices and factories, who watched the churches on Sundays.

The Communist Party strongly objected, of course, that Party members and especially functionaries went to church. Still everyone, including myself, knew personally Party members and also functionaries, mainly opportunists, who managed to go to church on Sundays.

It was amazing indeed how the regime also failed concerning the younger generation in this respect. The Party and the communist youth organizations did everything to lure the children away from church, there was always something for them on Sunday mornings, some entertainment, excursion, sport event. Still the number of young people in churches was steady throughout the years.

Some years ago I took my elder daughter Juli to one of the Budapest churches to receive Holy Communion. It was a weekday, everything was arranged with the priest who was waiting for us. The church was open and I expected to find there only the usual number of elderly women, who have more time than others and like to sit in church. The ceremony lasted for about thirty minutes and during this time three young men, all wearing the overalls of workers, came in for a few minutes, just long enough to kneel down before the altar and pray.

The Plight of the Children

But alongside this example Hungarian youth appeared depraved, immoral and equipped with appallingly superficial knowledge. This is a sad fact but let's make it clear had they been decent, well-behaved children, as their fathers and mothers had been a generation earlier, they would never have ventured to fight the Soviets in Budapest streets. Had they been children like children in any decent western country are, they would probably have stayed "behind the skirts of their mothers," as Hungarians used to say, and not go out in the streets to blow up monster tanks with their amateurish weapons.

Among the hundreds of incredibly bad Russian novels (in Hungarian translation) I was given to read in prison, I found one really good book. It was written in the late twenties by a Soviet educator named Makarenko. I hope it has been translated into English. It is a great book written by a great man. Makarenko was the headmaster of a "college" in Soviet Russia after

World War I, a school to which were admitted only underage petty criminals, little scoundrels of both sexes who were roaming all over the Soviet Union after the terrible years of civil war, without parents, cheating, sometimes robbing. Makarenko described in his book how these little monsters became decent humans in a relatively short time and he stressed that there was no miracle in the process, because they were basically decent, only circumstances compelled them to turn into tramps.

Every comparison is, of course, artificial, but I could not resist thinking of that book during the revolution. I saw the same "Teddy boy" in his ridiculous trousers and long hair whom I noticed with disgust in a dance hall only a few days earlier doing his rock n' roll, on the barricades with a rifle in his hands. It was the same young brat from the neighborhood who had been the menace of the whole district, whom I met early in the morning November 4, on the street in front of our house, cuddling his tommy gun in his arms. "Where are you going?" I asked in a rather silly way.

"The Russians came back," he said seriously and hurried off, obviously to die.

I hope nobody will misunderstand my narrative. The sharply dressed "Teddy boy" whom I watched fight and die, the brat from the neighborhood became heroes when the right time had come. I leave it to the psychologist to explain the change in their souls. They fought on the side of the hundreds of young workers, factory apprentices, university students and the offspring of middle class families. There must have been an unbridgeable cleft between them in many respects, but they were firmly united in one respect: "The Soviets have to go."

But let's come back to that "depraved, immoral" youth who became the heroes of the revolution.

I have already explained the whys. Parents, in general, had little time to care for the children, moreover, the parents realized that they belonged to another world, ridiculed by both the regime and the younger generation. Youth was idolized by the state and it is small wonder that this went to their heads. The result was disastrous. Young people were impolite, they pushed aside their elders, packed the cheap dance halls and squandered money recklessly. How could they do it? Western observers in Budapest, including many diplomats, frequently asked the question how was it possible that in spite of the low standard of living and low average incomes, restaurants and dance spots were usually jammed, mainly with young people. To answer partly is that there was nothing else for the young ones to do but to spend their money that way.

Several years ago I talked at length with a young technician in an effort to find out how he could afford to go to a cabaret three or four times a month.

The boy, he was around twenty, worked in a Budapest factory. Though not a Stakhanovite, he was considered a good worker and had an above average income of about 2,000 forints monthly.

I could convert this amount into dollars (actually it would be 166 dollars at the official but artificial Hungarian rate of exchange) but it would make little sense since it represents only 65 dollars in purchasing power. The average income is between 1,200 and 1,500 forints per month. Those in the lowest income brackets (like charwomen, for instance) get about 6-700 forints, while famous opera stars might get a monthly pay of 10-12,000 forints, plus royalties from records, concerts, etc.

Now, of course, if my young man had a family, he naturally could not afford to go to such places, he likely could not afford to go to the movies more than once a month. But my friend lived with his parents. His father was a foreman in another factory (2,600 forints per month) and the mother, though close to fifty, was a renowned weaver in a textile plant making almost 3,000 forints a month. The parents made more than 5,000 forints, a respectable amount in Hungary, still they remained a simple, honest couple, content with their modest two-room flat in one of the cheap tenement houses in a suburb with low prewar rents.

"I do not contribute to the household, because they do not need it," the boy told me. "This doesn't mean that the old people are happy with the way I'm spending my money. Sometimes, when the old man is in an ugly mood, he calls me names, says I'm a spendthrift and reproaches me for not saving money, as he did when he was young. But tell me, why should I? What is the point? Can I buy a car? Obviously I can't. Can I go abroad? Nonsense. To save money for the time I'm old? Hell, I'm still young and meanwhile there will be war and the money will lose its value as has happened twice already with my old man. So what?"

The explanation can be accepted as the general way of thinking of Hungarian youth, and one has to admit that they are more or less right, however cynical their reasoning sounds.

Hungarians were always renowned for their devil-may-care attitude toward life, that included the tendency to live above their means.

Still, people saved money for their later years, mothers collected the dowry of their daughters for years, and it was the ambition even of the poor classes to have a comfortable home and a bike for junior.

This changed, too, after World War II. Life as a whole seemed to have some kind of temporary character, nobody believed that it would last, the third world war was in the minds of the people, even if few talked about it. The soaring inflation of 1945-46 that was created largely by communist pressure, a fact of which most people were aware, also discouraged Hungarians from saving. Furthermore, there were reports published in the Hungarian press about the appalling monetary reforms in Rumania, Czechoslovakia and other communist countries, robbing practically everyone who had a small amount saved. For years, people were frightened that something similar would happen in Hungary.

All this is by the way of explanation why, for instance, Vienna restaurants appear to be empty compared with similar spots in Budapest. Or why the younger worker or clerk who could be seen with his sweetheart in a fashionable place in Budapest having his cheap drink and pretending to be a man of means had no real pretensions. He wore a relatively cheap ready made suit of bad Hungarian cloth, his Sunday best, and he had another one for the office or factory.

Take a characteristic example, something for which many young people in the West are putting money aside: a car.

One of the many things that struck my daughters in Vienna were the shiny automobile display rooms with the cars in the show windows. Nothing like that has existed in Budapest since the war. A car is not only luxury in Hungary, it is like crying for the moon. Hungary does not manufacture automobiles— only trucks—and there are, theoretically, only two ways of getting a car—either to import one or to buy a ramshackle jalopy of prewar vintage. I know of only a single case where a private citizen brought in a car from abroad. He was Mihaly Szekely who returned from his tour in the United States in 1950 with a Metropolitan Opera contract in his pocket. He did not receive a passport again until 1955, but as a kind of compensation he was permitted to buy and bring in an American car with the money he had made in America.

Perhaps five or six others in Budapest had modern postwar cars. We did because of our profession, as did certain opera stars and famous physicians who made sufficient money. But these were secondhand cars bought with the special permission of the Government from diplomats who departed. Such permission was rarely given. Finally, there were about two to three thousand cars in private hands, all small prewar European cars, old Opels and Skodas mostly.

But even these cars could not be bought by just anyone. Special permission of the Government was required to buy a car, apart from the driver's license, and according to the law only those belonging to the privileged classes, doctors, engineers, Stakhanovites, writers, actors, and of course, soccer stars got such permission. As a consequence, to buy a car remained a dream, apart from the fact that the price was prohibitive. Only a state-owned undertaking could buy and sell cars and the Government made enormous profits in 1950 when it took away the licenses of thousands of people and ordered them to sell their cars to Government offices at ridiculous prices of 1,500 to 2,500 forints (125-200 dollars, at the official rate of exchange). Then, weeks later, after the cars had stood rusting in open courtyards, the regime demanded 20-25,000 forints (1,660-2,000 dollars) from the lucky ones who received permission to buy. This was one of the many official rackets.

There was really only one thing that interested Hungarian children: sports.

Much has been written about the sports madness of Magyars,

on the exceptional abilities of this small nation in athletics. One of the explanations for Hungarian successes in the Olympics was certainly the enthusiasm of the youth. The soccer star and the Olympic champion were national heroes and idols of the young people. This sports mania doubtless had its bad effects on the youth. Certainly it was not sports itself. No modern man can object to the young generation engaging in athletics, unless it hinders them in the business of learning.

But the communists overplayed the game here, too. Hungary held a large role in international sports before communism, for example, she (unofficially) placed third at the 1936 Berlin Games when she was represented by real amateur sportsmen.

Postwar Hungary introduced what Avery Brundage, president of the International Olympic Committee, has called "state amateurism," exactly on the Soviet model. Mr. Brundage, who is a champion of true sportsmanship, probably invented the term "state amateurism" to save the Olympic Games, but I really cannot see why athletes of communist countries should be called amateurs at all. They are not. They are professionals. No one can object against professionalism in sports, but every honest man should object against hypocrisy, calling professionals "amateurs." Every Hungarian "amateur" sportsman gets some kind of pay, even unknown second rate fencers, skiers, and the like receive at least 300 forints "pocket-money" a month. Those who make real money are, of course, the soccer players. Stars like Ferenc Puskas, made easily one hundred thousand forints a year, which is enormous, considering the average annual income of, let's say, 18,000 forints.

The demoralizing effect on the youth was that this payment was no secret. It was never admitted, of course, papers never wrote about it, still everyone seemed to know the amount Puskas and company got for a single match, the youngsters knew that they had large villas, cars, and, what was perhaps more important, the wonderful things brought home from their tours in the West, radios, cameras, long-playing records, tape recorders, all unheard of luxuries, not to speak about their shoes, shirts and suits.

What was the result? Many a teenaged boy when asked the

usual frivolous question of what he wanted to be when he grew up, answered most seriously, "a soccer player." In school students could clearly see that to excel in some sport usually paid better than to excel as a student. The age limit in competitive sports dropped remarkably during the last decade and many of our best swimmers and tennis players are today around or under twenty.

The regime in Hungary did not conceal the fact that it exploited the world's sports mindedness for its own propaganda purposes. They conveniently forgot, and tried to make the people forget, that Hungary was a power in sports long before World War II and boasted that only a communist country can achieve success in sports.

It is no wonder that the secondary school swimming starlet believed her training far more important than preparing boring homework. It is no wonder either that the others envied her and tried to swim or run as fast as she did, because that meant fame, travel, forbearance in school and, last but not least, pocket money.

What could the parents do? Obviously not much. The teenaged boy was clever enough to realize that to kick the football better than his friends would bring much more wealth and fame than other pursuits, moreover it would bring things that nothing else would through touring the West and the possibility of buying western consumer goods.

The following joke characterized the situation. A sexagenarian scientist was noticed playing table tennis in the university club. "What is the idea? We never realized you were an athlete," he was chaffed by his colleagues.

"Nonsense," the old man snorted, "I just want to go to Paris again and they intend to have the next world ping-pong championships there."

Family and Marriage

Love, of course, is something that has been, is, and will be whatever the political system may be. But romance and chivalry are gone, they are obviously against the doctrines of materialism.

Furthermore, communism created some kind of strange hypocrisy in this respect. Novels, films, plays carefully avoid all realism dealing with the eternal connection between boy and girl. The "boy loves tractor" concept of modern love dominates these literary products and it is apparently a shame to write a novel or play with a central problem of love or marriage. This nonsense went so far that even an inveterate Hungarian communist intellectual, the chief ideologist of Hungarian communism, found it opportune to ridicule such sterile literature. Jozsef Revai, a veteran Moscovite, himself a brilliant writer and orator, raised the question at a congress of Hungarian playrights and film scenario writers some years ago: "How is it that for years I haven't seen a kiss on the stage or the screen?" he asked. At first the audience reacted with giggling uneasiness, then with an outburst of applause. But that was all. The kiss did not return to the stage or to the screen.

The same holds with painting and sculpture. A few years ago, at a press conference preceding the annual December exhibition of Hungarian artists, my husband, pretending to be uninformed, raised the question why Hungarian painters and sculptors never depict the naked human body, a subject of art since time immemorial. Again it was a veteran communist, painter Gyula Poor, a septuagenarian, who sided wholeheartedly with my husband, "Yes, why don't we?" he asked. The official answer, given by a young Party spokesman, was rather incoherent and never again were we invited to the annual art press conference.

This hypocritical and false shame is unexplainable all the more since Hungarians, and especially Budapesters, probably spend more time in the city's numerous swimming pools than any other people in the world. And swimming suits, I assure you, do not begin to cover everything. The reason is hardly lack of textiles.

Still, the two phenomena combined probably give the real answer to the lack of romanticism in the life of Hungarian youth nowadays. Life itself, with its labor competitions and also with its nakedness in swimming pools, does not inspire romance, and there is no romance in our literature and art either—the excitement of romance is largely missing from the life of the young people in my country. But it is missing from the life of adults, too. Hungary's marital morals fell into the general European milieu. To speak frankly, there always have been minor scandals, gossip about flirtations and affairs, the triangle problems of French comedies. This also has more or less ceased in the "society" of Budapest under the communist rule. The reason, again, is the utter drabness of life. People are too worried, too much engrossed in physical survival. There is little free time for frivolity and flirtation.

The communist leaders themselves were against all levity in life, at least outwardly. Almost nothing was known about their private lives. They lived in a secluded villa district, guarded and completely isolated from the rest of the city. Except for very few minor figures, one would never see them in restaurants or theaters with the exception of official gala performances. They had no friends and lived only among themselves. But despite all secrecy and vigilance, or perhaps just because of that, some details leaked out and outraged the man in the street.

The consequence of such nonsensical secrecy always is that people are inclined to exaggerate things. When President Eisenhower leaves Washington to spend the weekend playing golf, a flock of newspapermen accompany him and anyone who is interested may find his latest estimate of his game in the papers.

But when Rakosi left town, nothing was disclosed. However, within a few days people observed the disappearance of the policemen who guarded the route he drove twice daily in his convoy of three limousines going to his office and coming home. Then the gossip started. He was called to Moscow, he is seriously ill, even wounded, fallen into disgrace, dead. A simple vacation? Nonsense, who would believe that?

When, during the revolution, newspapermen were conducted through the "forbidden zone" of villas of Communist Party bosses, some of us were disappointed. They were fine villas indeed, certainly they outraged those young revolutionaries, who guided us and who had to share their shabby homes with others. But they were nothing special by western standards. Of course, there were telephones in every room, facilities to play films at home, a bomb-proof air-raid shelter in the center of a park containing three villas, each connected by underground passages. But where was the helicopter airfield in Rakosi's garden, where was his covered swimming pool with heated water and artificial waves, both said to be there by "well-informed" Budapesters? They were created by the phantasy of people who were never told the truth.

And naturally it leaked out that there were luxuriously built and secluded places for the Party bosses on Lake Balaton and in the mountains. Old castles, the best hotels, newly built villas were reserved for these men and their families, for the new aristocracy of the Party and the secret police. There they spent their weekends and their vacations, and in this seclusion it was relatively easy to maintain the appearance of an ascetic life. In one spot along Lake Balaton there are three or four fine modern villas in a park for the children of second-rank Party officials, surrounded by a fence and guarded by AVO troops. No one could enter, but occasionally a minister's wife would need a hairdresser, or a doctor had to be called, and then the next day everyone would know in what luxury the children of the Party bigwigs live.

I often had the feeling that the communist leaders had no idea of what money was, that they probably do not even see money. The fact is that they are supplied with everything by the Party: homes, cars, consumer goods and foodstuffs from special stores. It is understood that their salaries go directly to the Party treasury, and everything they need they receive from the Party.

I remember how indignant I once became when accidentally I observed how well they lived.

It happened in the summer of 1950, a particularly trying period with the stupid economic policy and the scorching heat and drought, all of which resulted in an unprecedented scarcity of foodstuffs. There was no meat, only few vegetables and people had to queue up for ice, as only very few had refrigerators.

The parents of my husband lived in a house on the Hill of Roses. The next house was a villa, reserved for VIP guests of the Party, fully equipped down to the AVO guard. One morning we drove up to my parents-in-law, bringing them carefully hoarded butter and other scarce foodstuffs. Going in the garden door we became bewildered. Somewhere someone was listening to the Hungarian broadcast of the BBC with the radio blaring the news so loudly that the well-known voice of the commentator could be heard throughout the neighborhood.

Knowing my father-in-law, an elderly man who never could conceal his hatred toward the communists, we first thought that this was one of his reckless deeds, but the AVO guard lingering in the adjacent garden obviously realized our thoughts and pointed to the open window of the VIP house. "It's the old man, he listens to it every day," he said with a grin.

"Who is he?" my husband asked.

"Jeno Varga," the answer was.

Professor Varga is known to be the Soviet Union's leading economist. He was born a Hungarian, but became, as I recall, a Soviet citizen immediately after World War I. After World War II he used to come to Hungary regularly every year and spend some months there.

While we were chattering through the fence, a small truck stopped in front of Varga's house and we watched while two men started to unload the most precious things one could imagine in those times of semi-starvation. The men carried in a huge chunk of veal, a kind of meat only sick people could get in good clinics. There was naturally plenty of butter, milk, and canned goods with western labels. Encouraged by the friendly and unusually communicative guard, I asked him, when the truck left, "Where do they get all these things?"

"From the Party shop of course," came the reply.

Why do I tell all this? Because in spite of every secrecy everyone knew about the careless luxurious "family" life the "upper thousand" of the Party was living and this, like the privileged life of soccer stars, undeniably had its effect on the average Hungarian family. But, strangely enough, while soccer ace Puskas and the others, though envied, were also idolized by the masses for years, nobody envied the communist leaders their life, and nobody loved them either. They were hated for their "eccentric life," and while a child did not conceal that his dream

was to become another Puskas, I never heard anyone dreaming
of becoming another Rakosi.

Outwardly, however, the communist bosses lived a rather
"ascetic" family life. They were always neatly dressed, usually
in dark business suits, their wives, most of whom held some
post in the regime, too, popularized the simple black suit, jacket
and skirt, without makeup. I had the opportunity, and being
a woman journalist, it was my duty, I thought, to investigate
the cloth of which the impeccable and inconspicuous suits of
Rakosi and the others were made. It was not difficult. One had
the chance twice a year to stand close to them in the corridors
of Parliament, the only time and place a western reporter got
near to them. May I declare with some measure of authority
that all the clothes I saw Mr. Rakosi and his lieutenants wearing were made of finest English cloth, something nobody else,
except the sport stars, could afford to have simply because such
cloth was not imported into Hungary.

This false and sham hypocrisy often led to disastrous results.

Some years ago Hungary had a woman minister of health,
Mrs. Anna Ratko, a former textile worker. This woman had
the task of increasing the birthrate as quickly as possible, partly
because this belonged to the communist mania of "surplus production," and partly because, as it was thought, Hungary
needed a greater labor force.

The question of abortions is a delicate one in every country,
I assume. Hungary had adequate legal regulations in this respect, mainly intended to protect the family and to prevent
criminal abortions being carried out under unsanitary conditions by midwives, quacks, and other charlatans. But Mrs. Ratko wanted to carry out her assignment by any means and she
called on the assistance of the police. Draconic sentences for
abortions were made public, physicians and would-be mothers
were sent to prison for 8-10 years. That was not enough. The
police, using a typical communist tactic, employed informers
and agent provocateurs to discover more criminal doctors. The
private consultation rooms of gynecologists, for example, were
watched by plainclothesmen. Only a special board of specialists
could give permission to carry out abortions in some state con-

trolled clinics, and as is customary in totalitarian countries, members of this board were thoroughly frightened and refused to give permission even in cases when normal human concern might consider it necessary.

The result obviously was an increased birth rate. But there was still another result. What honest physicians were unable or unwilling to carry out was done by unscrupulous charlatans for enormous sums of money under unhygienic circumstances often resulting in the death of the woman. When this stupid measure was quietly abolished in 1953, Mrs. Ratko turned over her post to a physician, who, one has to assume, knew more about such things than the former textile worker. The jailed doctors were released.

The communist regime, on the other hand, had more luck with another anti-family activity. It almost wiped out prostitution. Here again Hungary, and Budapest, were neither better nor worse than other countries. There were brothels and street-walkers, their medical control was said to be rather effective. The Government clamped down on them swiftly in the late nineteen forties. The houses were closed, the streetwalkers disappeared, many of them were retrained and some, for instance, became rather good taxi drivers. Prostitution, of course, could not be abolished altogether. Some of the girls remained, working "free lance," but Budapest on the eve of the revolt could still be regarded as a city without the problem of unrestricted prostitution.

A strange category of such women remained, however. They could be found in hotels reserved for foreigners, in some international night clubs and bars. Rumor has it that all of them worked for the secret police being entrusted with trying to find out from visitors from abroad whatever they could. The fact that they were tolerated indicates that the rumor was true.

I have written at some length about the young, the chief concern of every mother, but I have barely touched upon the subject of marriage. The relatively high wages young people got during the period of forced industrialization encouraged many young people under twenty to marry, which was an unusual thing in my country before the war. There might be pros and cons, but my experience was that marriages between the youngsters around or under twenty were mostly failures. On the other hand, there was little possibility to redeem such a faulty step. Divorce had been made more than difficult by our cynical regime.

A law introduced several years ago continues to regulate divorce proceedings in Hungary. It gave all the authority to the judge to determine whether a marriage should be dissolved or not. There is no such thing as the common consent of the two parties, even admitted adultery does not compel the judge to dissolve a marriage. Characteristically there is one good reason for divorce: divergence in ideology. Imagine a judge in the United States declaring a marriage contract to be dissolved on the grounds that the man is a Democrat and the woman a Republican! Still in Hungary, where the judge, according to the law, has primarily to consider "the interest of the society" this is the chief concern. If either of the two partners stated that the maintenance of marriage became impossible because he (or she) is a faithful communist, while the other is hostile to this doctrine, the judge will dissolve the marriage without further deliberation.

But let's return to marriage without thinking about divorce. Marriage, everyone will agree, is not just romance and love. It is the day to day, year by year partnership of two people, who freely chose to share all the joys and worries of life. I have already related that the average man in the street in Hungary needs his wife's income to have a more or less decent life. I also wrote of the nuisances that make life dull, sometimes grim in my country. There are others. Take, for instance, the daily worry of every housewife all over the world: what shall we cook today? This was never a problem in prewar Hungary, a God-blessed agricultural country, the bread basket of central Europe. But it is a problem in Hungary today. I do not mean the prices. Every reasonable housewife knows how much she can spend on food. What I mean is the exciting problem in Hungary, what shall I find on the market? It is no good to decide that today I will have beef and carrots for dinner, it is most likely that I will find neither beef nor carrots on the market, but pork and cabbages. Why? Nobody knows.

Housewives got accustomed long ago to take what is offered to them. With vegetables and fruit it is relatively easy. These items can be brought to the market by the peasant and to the greater glory of a state-run food supply system, there is in a normal year plenty and a fair variety of both. But with meat, butter, lard, cooking oil, sugar, flour, and other such things controlled by state monopolies it is different. Here the housewife is at the mercy of the state and of its inadequate, inefficient, bureaucratic distribution system that would break the nerves of any woman who stubbornly insisted on having this or that for a certain day.

I cannot remember a single period since World War II when there was not a lack of something, and I think not only with foodstuffs, but also with other primary consumer goods. Would the western reader believe that ten years after the war one could rarely get needles, ordinary sewing needles in Hungary, in a country that bragged of its communist industrialization? Or, to mention just one other example, that there were weeks on end when there was no toilet paper in the shops. In the summer of 1954 the aged parents of my husband were permitted to emigrate from Hungary. On their way to Australia they stopped in Vienna for a few days and from there my mother-in-law wrote us, "I had to think of you in our hotel, because we have such fine toilet paper here!"

I could list, of course, other examples. There were mysterious temporary scarcities, once soap, then perhaps buttons another time. And what was available was of inferior quality. Fashion, I readily admit, is of secondary importance, still it was a pity to watch how Budapest, once the city of well-dressed elegant men and women, became a drab place of badly dressed people. This fact of communist life became a source of desire after nice things, of longing after something unattainable, of impatience and discontent.

For many years we belonged to the very few Hungarian families who regularly obtained western magazines. It was a matter of course that we distributed them among our family friends who hungrily devoured all their contents including the beautiful advertisements. But it was also my habit to bring a copy of *Vogue* or a similar fashion magazine to my hairdresser on my infrequent trips, to show it to the manicurist, a simple young girl who knew nothing else but what communism could offer her. It is hard to describe the effect such a fashion magazine had on the manicurist, on my dressmaker, and on others.

I know, for I heard it often enough, what a good razor blade means to a man. The communists, in their doggedly stubborn drive for autarky, ordered some factories to manufacture razor blades. They proved so bad that even the Government-controlled press found it necessary to criticize them. After all, these newspapers were written by men who shaved. The result was that people paid exorbitant prices on the black market for western razor blades, five forints (42 cents) or even more per blade. It was a most treasured Christmas present when my husband gave a pack of blades or a tube of shaving cream to one of his friends, however ridiculous it sounds.

This stupidity about autarky was something no reasonable man could understand. It was, of course, understandable that Hungary could hardly afford to buy consumer goods for hard currency in the West, but what no one could explain was why Hungary did not import such things from industrially more developed communist countries, like Czechoslovakia or East Germany. Only the 1953 new look brought some progress in this respect, when consumer goods from these countries became available in limited quantities.

Another custom which disappeared from postwar family life in communist Hungary was entertaining. It is a platitude that Hungarians are hospitable people. It belonged to the everyday life of all social classes to invite friends for dinner. Traditionally, the middle and upper classes had given parties and balls.

All this has almost entirely ceased during the communist era. The main reason obviously was that very few could afford it, most families were happy if they could maintain a certain standard for themselves. Another reason was the lack of family space.

The comfortable homes disappeared, people were jammed into one or two rooms. Entertaining was reduced to after dinner invitations, when a guest got a small cup of black coffee and, at most, a glass of Hungarian brandy.

Captive Families

A chapter on family life would be incomplete without a special section, not uncommon in Hungary: family life in prison. Part of it I know from personal experience.

The communists take emancipation very seriously. Women are frequently among the political prisoners and their lot is not an easy one. I know of many cases where the woman of the family was imprisoned and the man remained free. In 1953, when Imre Nagy became prime minister, "legality" was restored at least to the degree that political prisoners could receive visitors twice yearly and also get parcels containing simple food, toilet articles, and underwear, usually twice a year.

A husband's love, fidelity, and attentiveness were judged by the wife and her fellow inmates by the care with which these parcels, mindful of the limitations on the quantity and the contents, were made up. And women prisoners are sharp-eyed judges.

Everything is drab and grey in prison, one never sees the green of grass, the color of a flower, and only for fleeting minutes the blue of the sky, when one is taken for a walk in the narrow court yard. Even then one is not supposed to see the sky. The regulation is to go round, hands clasped behind the back, eyes cast down on the filthy cement floor.

It is natural then that every husband who has the ingenuity to send things in color to his wife in prison is regarded as a dear thoughtful man. I have seen a woman weeping for joy because her husband found and sent her green colored hand soap instead of the usual white. And if he is especially gifted, he has scented the parcel. Of course, no perfume or even *eau de cologne* much less a mirror is permitted, but no one could prevent the man from scenting the underwear or the towel he sent, and that is a special feast in prison, the cell mates coming and asking to be permitted to smell. This sounds funny but it is not. These are the small things in prison that can make a woman happy for weeks, make her dream, and dreams help time to pass quicker.

With us it was different. We both were in prison at the same time. But we also had our "family life," a rather strange one.

In a prison of the AVO no prisoner is supposed to know about any other. The cells are for one or two persons and the convict or the arrested man awaiting trial never sees anyone else but his cell mate, if he has one.

You never leave your cell, except when taken to be interrogated, in the morning to fetch water to wash yourself, or the four to five times a week when you are taken for a walk. But even then you cannot see anyone else but the jailers and your cell mate. Cell doors are opened only one at a time and the vast courtyard is divided into several roofless cells. There you take the air alone or together with your cell mate.

In November 1955 we were tried for the first time. The court room was in the same building. I was in a cell on the fifth floor. After the trial the jailers brought us back to our cells together. First we stopped on the third floor, the jailer, a goodwilled man, told us to say goodbye to each other and turned his back. We were in front of cell number nine on the corridor, I knew it was my husband's.

Next month, in the course of one of the periodic reshuffles, I was brought down to the third floor and given cell fourteen, almost opposite to my husband's. I was happy, this was something, we were on the same floor.

But how shall I let him know it? One morning, when I was let out to fetch water in a tin wash basin, I coughed on my way to the washroom at the end of the corridor. I repeated it later, when taken to walk, and then next morning again. Back in my cell I listened. Did he hear it? Did he recognize my cough?

Two days later the answer came. He coughed back when he was let out. Can I describe how happy I was? No one would understand it except perhaps one who has been in the same situation.

This went on for months, until I was released. "Family life

in Hungary, 1955. They cough to each other," my husband's cell mate remarked, as he told me later.

When I was released my husband was not told about it and the letter I wrote to him was never received. I do not know the reason, it was again one of the senseless cruelties.

My husband went on coughing for weeks and got no answer. He was desperate and believed that I was transferred to another prison. One morning, when he coughed louder than usual, one of the friendlier jailers guarding the corridor told him, "Don't cough, she isn't here anymore." That was all. He learned that I was free only two months later, when I received permission to visit him.

I think I have come to the end of my narrative. However, there is one more thing, perhaps the most tragic part, family life during and after the revolution.

Boys and girls fought in the revolution, young workers, secondary school pupils and university students. They had parents, many of them in deadly fear of the life of a son or daughter. But I did not hear of a single case where a mother tried to keep them from going to fight. I have seen many mothers trembling, praying with slowly moving lips to God, in agonizing fear when the son had not come home for two days, but they did not stop them.

They became mothers again, as we understand it, only when the armed revolution was crushed and the manhunt began. Many of those fearless little heroes became kids again, with chattering teeth, afraid of being taken away. Then the mothers became tigers. They hid their sons and daughters and whenever a Soviet armored car came or was thought to have come with the purpose of taking away the young, the women from all over the neighborhood came out screaming and more than once they succeeded in frightening the Russians away.

I had good reason to be proud to be a Hungarian, and I had good reason to be proud of being a woman, too. I watched the women's demonstrations on December 4 and 5, 1956, one month after the treacherous second Soviet onslaught on Budapest. I saw how those two thousand women whose only weapons were flowers they wanted to place on the tomb of the Unknown Soldier, terrified hard bitten Soviet troopers and caused the mobilization of dozens of tanks and armored cars. I saw them advising their men to stay away. "It's now our turn, go away from here," they told the men on the streets.

And I knew mothers who sent away their young sons and daughters without a tear in their eyes. I especially knew one of them very well. First her son left, perhaps 24, he had just graduated from the university, some days later the daughter, less than 20. The mother was not the heroic type, but she behaved like the Roman mother of the Gracchi. "They should go and see a better world. I'm too old to go myself," was all she said.

There were hundreds if not thousands of tragedies. Let me tell you yet another one.

The Communist Party secretary of one of the Budapest university clinics had been a former charwoman, a typical embittered comrade, who poked her nose into the scientific work of doctors and became a general nuisance in the clinic. She was a widow, had a son, whom she brought up strictly in accordance with communist principles. Having been a loyal Party member, she managed to enroll her son in the university.

Then the revolution came, and one day the son did not come home. The next day he was brought home dead, his body covered with a red, green, and white flag. He died in the Killian Barracks area fighting the Soviets.

Doctors and other personnel of the clinic watched what happened. The mother dug a grave in the hard-frozen garden of the clinic, alone, with bullets whistling around her head. She refused help. She stood over the grave for a long time, tears rolling down her wrinkled cheeks. Then she took the weather-beaten flag of free Hungary to her shabby room in the clinic and covered her son's bed with it.

She is now a common charwoman again, she did not rejoin the new Communist Party.

The revolution is over though resistance will continue.

Whatever else the result has been, it was a victory for the family, for the mother over communism. The child had been indoctrinated for years, flattered, cherished by a regime that had no other hope but one: to win over the young generation to form a firm foundation for its cause. They knew that they had to stand or fall on this and they failed. The child chose the family and resorted to arms to fight his masters.

The revolution for freedom was crushed with the help of a foreign power. The result remained the same. Communism in Hungary can count neither on the older nor on the younger generation.

The Cross of Religion

I should observe by way of introduction that we shall discuss
religion and communism from the viewpoint of the experience
of the Catholic Church in Hungary with which I as a Catholic
am particularly familiar.

Catholics are generally aware that Pope Pius XII in his en-
cyclical *Mystici Corporis* stressed Saint Paul's teaching that "the
Church is Christ's Mystical Body" and this fact should be the
central thought for the entire world of the faithful. Thus, the
Church is not a rigid human institution, but an organism living
a supernatural life, which is Christ Himself, its visible head the
Pope, its members the faithful, its soul the Holy Spirit, Who,
in addition, lives separately in each individual. This is the
mystery, hence the name Christ's Mystical Body; the supernatural internal life of this organism is the world of dogma and
grace, the world of the liturgy, and the propagation of faith.
The bearer of this mysterious internal life, however, is an external visible institution, seemingly a human organization. But for
the faithful to see only that aspect of it would be just as absurd
as seeing in Christ only a man, let us say the son of the carpenter
of Nazareth. Finally, one of the eternal marks of the Church is

* Jozsef Magyar is a Hungarian lay theologian.

that the ruling and teaching power is of divine origin. Christ ordained Peter, and his temporal successor appoints bishops and each bishop leads and directs his clergy.

As with any institution the Church created its own legal code, regulating the outward activities of that organization. It is vital to our story to remember that the Church's apostolic character is divine and eternal; its outward regulations change with human ways of life and are not eternal, as for example, the size of the Sacred Colleges or the number of hours required for Eucharistic fast, which may change from one day to the next. The garment of the Mystical Body is the social-economic-political constellation in which the Church is living and which has no organic relation to its essence. The Church may live in an empire or a republic, in a capitalist or a non-capitalist society, in any color garment, provided it is not so restrictive as to hinder the proper functioning of the basic human freedoms. In other words, the society must not deprive man of his elementary God-given rights.

To complete our framework I should add the following quotation from St. Paul, "If one member suffers, all other members suffer with him." The reality of communist persecution of religion must be seen from a supernatural view. It may happen that the loss of merely human institutions, humiliation and torment may be more advantageous for the Church from a supernatural point of view, considering the very essence of things, than state protectionism maintained for external political reasons.

There were close ties between church and state in Hungary before the communist transformation; theoretically, or rather institutionally, the church enjoyed state protection. There were Catholic Church estates, Catholic schools, bishops could be and were members of the Upper House. But the church was unable to influence the political trend. The Christian Party which was of predominantly Catholic character ceased to be a decisive factor in the years following the 1919 Bela Kun communist regime.

There was a rather drab daily paper, *Nemzeti Ujsag* supported by the episcopate; and while the paper was anti-Nazi it failed dismally to represent Catholicism adequately especially with respect to social problems, since it feared the loss of large capital's support. In the thirties ultra-conservative circles declared that the forceful representatives of *Quadragesimo Anno* were "pacemakers of communism." Hence, early in the forties the Hungarian Catholic Church was not a decisive factor in political life, nor did it exercise the cultural influence in the country it should have due to its size and intellectual achievements.

Why? Had we not been told that the Hungarian Catholic Church had undergone a regeneration during the first third of our century? The answer is simple. The inheritance of the secularist era was so strong, the anticlerical factor was so important, that this internal development, the revival of religious life, was not yet able to change the features of external life. Further, due to state support, Hungarian Catholics did not immediately recognize the importance of self-sustained Catholic Action, that movement created by Pius XI which called the lay apostolate into action. The first steps toward the building of a genuine Catholic Action movement in the western sense of the word were taken only when Hitlerism was at the very gates, and the specter of a complete totalitarian, anticlerical state emerged on the horizon. After 1945 events developed even more rapidly, and more happened between 1946 and 1948 in Catholic Action than in any previous comparable period.

Catholicism did experience an enormous revival during the first third of this century. There was, for example, a radiant, revolutionary, and apostolic personality of the times, Bishop Ottokar Prohaszka who possessed considerable literary and oratorical talent. He educated an entirely new generation of serious-minded priests, produced excellent youth institutions, societies, newspapers and a religious-educational literature. Within three decades the spiritual face of Hungarian Catholicism was transformed. The children of religiously indifferent fathers became fervent Catholics going to Communion every month. Monastic schools educated hundreds of youngsters in a religious and patriotic spirit. But, unfortunately, not enough emphasis was placed on the education of youth so as to install in them lives of cross-bearing Christians with a courage of their own, with a sense of social responsibility. The Catholics of Hungary saw no need for the support of organizations urging a program of Christianity in practice. Of all the alumni and fraternal groups, perhaps only the boy scout movement and the Marian Congregation contributed to serious and fruitful work.

Despite the evidence of revival, a diagnosis of Catholicism during this period is not encouraging. Bela Bangha, a well-known Jesuit, has described statistically the spiritual situation of the Hungarian Catholic Church in the thirties: 20% of the membership were, in fact, non-religious, freethinkers, Marxists, etc.; 35% were traditional Christians who went to Church only on principal holydays, who married in the Church and arranged beautiful family baptisms; 35% went to Mass every Sunday, "good Catholics," at least on the surface but whose non-weather-proof creed forsook them in critical situations if called to sacrifice a career for the sake of faith, for example; finally, there were about 10% who really lived according to the law of Christ and were willing to make sacrifices for Him and His Church. But, as Father Bangha indicated, half of them lived in the country which resulted in an approximate urban figure of 5% who would be heard in public life. Yet one was always struck by the close traditional attachment of the great percentage, some 80%, of Hungarian Catholics to their faith and to their Church. And as any action entails reaction, in 1945, when attacks against the Church commenced, the faithful's attachment to the Church intensified and culminated in the 1948 Marian year, as shall be seen shortly.

Something one must keep in mind when observing the fate of Hungarian Catholicism is the close connection between religious and national feeling. Hungary's first king Saint Stephen commended the country to the protection of the Virgin Mary. Our favorite hymn is "Blessed Virgin, Our Mother, our ancient Great Patroness, being in great distress, our country implores: do not forget Hungary, our ancient country, do not forget poor Hungarians." Few ruling dynasties furnished as many saints to the Church as the house of Arpad. During the Catholic restoration in the Baroque age, crowds of hundreds of thousands paid homage to Our Lady of Hungary and thus satisfied both their religious and national feelings. It was then that the concept of the *Regnum Marianum* (the Kingdom of Mary) developed among serious Catholic statesmen. The idea of a *Regnum Marianum* also played a very important role during the Hungarian Catholic renaissance at the beginning of the twentieth century. The cult of Our Lady assumed a dominant position in the youth movements and in the pages of the Catholic press. Male youth also paid its devotion to Saint Emeric, our first duke. The celebration of Saint Emeric's day in 1931 was the first great mass action of a renewed Hungarian Catholicism. This led to the convocation of the 1938 Eucharistic Congress in Budapest. This close entwinement of religious and national feeling finally found a symbol in one man: Prince Primate Jozsef Mindszenty.

There were great anticlerical but not necessarily militantly hostile political trends in Hungary resulting from the revolutionary spirit of 1848, as everywhere else in Europe.

During the "Christian trend" of the twenties following the Bela Kun defeat social democrats, assisted by the communists (from the underground) represented the militant anticlerical position. But 1945 revealed that strong anticlerical forces had not died but were only asleep. Violent attacks broke out against religion following the war, ending in the destruction of the monument to Bishop Prohaszka. It became quite clear at this time that anti-religious feeling was being carefully nurtured by Hungary's tough atheistic communists.

Tracing the course of religion under the communists several distinct phases are distinguishable:

1. The relatively free phase from 1945 to June 1948;

2. The initiation of forcible measures against religion (secularization of schools, arrest of the Prince Primate, etc.) from June 1948 to June 1950;

3. The anti-religious campaign from June 1950 to July 1953 (when Imre Nagy became prime minister) followed by a new phase of terror from March 1955 to June 1956;

4. Moderately quiet periods from July 1953 to February 1955, and from June 1956 to the revolution.

During the first period of the transformation into a people's democracy the motto of the anti-religious forces was "the Church is the ally of feudalism." All those who cherish democracy must stand up against the Church. They reproached the Church for the existence of "three million beggars" (the agrarian proletariat) whom certain writers had frequently mentioned even during the Horthy era calling them "the beneficiaries of the Horthy era." This assault took place on the political level. In the social sphere the extreme leftist MADISZ (Hungarian Democratic Youth League) carried on intensive propaganda against the Church. And finally on the administrative side with the Ministry of Interior and police in communist hands, oppositional elements were arrested. From the start the police summoned priests and laymen working in clerical institutions for short periods of interrogation. The Church replied with reference to the declarations of Pope Pius XII concerning democracy as the ideal but reminding the faithful of the distinction between the divine entity of Christ's Mystical Body and its changing human garment.

Another important area of attack involved the offensive mounted against youth, whom the communists wished to isolate from any and all religious influence. A rather vile, but unfortunately, not ineffective method was adopted, demoralization which made a technique of licentiousness and promiscuity in "people's colleges" and coeducational schools. As a result, a part of our youth was a willing tool against religious influence which symbolized moral restrictions and discipline. Moral licentiousness assumed such an extent that, years afterwards, when the communists had consolidated control, purges and discipline among Party cadres were launched against moral depravity.

The seizure of the large ecclesiastical estates meant financial loss for the Church. There was lost some 994,000 acres of agricultural property. This cannot in truth be called an anti-religious action, since the estates of the aristocracy and wealthy bourgeoisie were also confiscated. The unjust distribution of land and property had long been a seething problem in Hungary. To indemnify the Church for this expropriation the clergy was given state salaries, bishops were even to be accorded salaries comparable to ministers of state—it is interesting to note that Cardinal Mindszenty rejected this payment for himself—and the clergy in general was to receive stipends on a graduated basis. The Church, however, did not suffer any basic financial loss, for all the parishes down to the smallest village community assumed the task of furnishing the necessary provisions to the clergy. The laity brought food to the seminaries and to the bishops' residences and gifts were made so generously that cathedrals which had been neglected for centuries at a time when the Church owned large estates were now refurbished, as in Eger and Vac.

In 1947 after the stabilization of the currency and when the ruins of war had gradually receded, the Church began to undertake more and more work in the social sphere. Catholic Action under the direction of Msgr. Zsigmond Mihalovics became very active, its weekly magazine, the *Uj Ember* (New Man), was well received and regular distribution exceeded 100,000. As a result of the elections early in the fall of 1947 an unexpectedly large number of the Catholic-oriented People's Party entered Parliament. I mention this only in order to characterize the upswing, since months later the communists forced the dissolution of this and other small parties by administrative decree. The representatives were faced with a choice of flight or imprisonment.

The climax of the post-war religious life in Hungary was the 1948 Magyar Marian Year. During the Marian days outdoor Masses, pageants, and meetings were arranged everywhere. The Prince Primate and the bishops of the land participated and the country witnessed a religious and national demonstration and sentiment missing for centuries. The communist clique watched with helpless rage. "Non-official elements" frequently disturbed processions, police molested pilgrims, and hoodlums took the occasion of the Marian Day at Celldoemoelk to attack pilgrims with refuse and garbage. Hungary had entered the second period in the war against religion.

The press campaign against the Church started in precisely the same spirit. The major objective was to prevent clerical influence upon youth. A campaign for the secularization of schools was started and in June of 1948, Gyula Ortutay, a crypto Communist of the Smallholder Party, who had himself studied at a monastic school, ordered secularization of all 3,163 religious primary and secondary schools. Mindszenty forbade religious cooperation with the state authorities who had so confiscated the schools. Initially, to be sure, the regime would have preferred to keep the religious orders teaching in civilian clothes under the leadership of governmental supervisors. The religious orders obeyed the Prince Primate's instructions with impressive discipline. With the refusal to cooperate the Government suffered a shock when it had to fill this teaching gap and the level of education dropped immediately. This anti-religious trend increased, the ranking officers of Catholic Action were arrested and their activities prohibited.

But the greatest shock was the arrest of Cardinal Jozsef Mindszenty at Christmas 1948. It struck western public opinion like lightning. In no other period before the revolution was world public opinion so mobilized and interested in Hungary. The trial caused another sensation. It made the world's flesh creep to realize what satanic powers must have been unleashed to damage the very being of such a personality as Mindszenty and to turn him into his own denouncer. But the communists failed to reach their goal of destroying the country's most popular man and symbol. Hundreds of thousands prayed every day for their primate, for this martyr of religion and national feeling.

People were so intimidated that no open demonstrations took place. But the episcopate exercised a form of passive resistance at least in the political sector. The bishops refused to take the oath of allegiance to the Government, which was mandatory for the parish clergy, and they refused to negotiate with Minister Ortutay, who had confiscated the schools. "Father" Istvan Balogh stressed the necessity of an agreement between church and state both in his political activities and in the columns of the crypto Communist *Magyar Nemzet,* and Archbishop Gyula Czapik also inclined to this viewpoint. But Archbishop Jozsef Groesz was not willing to budge for the time being. The regime was forced to employ stronger measures.

The measures came in the summer of 1950, when the greater number of priests from religious orders were rounded up and deported to various "concentration" houses, while their own houses with all equipment were seized. Shortly thereafter all the religious orders were summarily disbanded by direction of the communist regime.

Under the threat of still additional terroristic measures, Archbishop Groesz started to negotiate with the regime. The episcopate acknowledged the Government and encouraged the clergy to take the oath of support. The Government in turn restored eight high schools (six boys' and two girls' schools) defining precisely how many members the religious orders maintaining the schools might retain (a total of seventy religious with two novices per year admitted for replacement). This was the first agreement, which the Vatican itself disapproved in a letter written to Archbishop Groesz.

In the summer of 1950, and in accordance with Rakosi's famous "salami" tactics, the Government created the "peace priest movement" whose head was "Father" Istvan Balogh who collaborated with the communists. So long as no serious terror measures were enforced the episcopate steadfastly refused to legalize the movement and only a small proportion of the Hungarian Catholic clergy, less than 5%, joined the movement. The bishops did not hide their disapproval of that movement. Hence, the communists took the road of sheer force.

I shall only mention here the most important measures and phases of the regime's frontal assault on religion. One step was the declaration that state and church were separate. The Ministry for Religion and Public Education was replaced by a Ministry for Public Education, while a Government Office for Ecclesiastical Affairs (AEH) designed to last a decade was entrusted with religious affairs. Another important step was direct interference in the duties of the hierarchy. When Jozsef Mindszenty's vicar for Esztergom, Janos Drahoss, died, another vicar capitular was elected by the Canons of Esztergom in the person of Auxiliary Bishop Zoltan Meszlenyi. A few days following his appointment he was arrested by the AVO. The cathedral chapter of Esztergom convened again and elected Canon Charles Gigler. But the AVO arrested him also. At the same time the secret police sent a message suggesting if the chapter would elect Canon Miklos Beresztoczy, he would not be arrested. The situation was clear. Beresztoczy was unanimously elected. Rome nullified this illegal step and appointed the Bishop of Csanad, Endre Hamvas as apostolic administrator for the archdiocese of Esztergom, by which act the office of a vicar capitular ceased to exist. This victory, however, was pyrrhic. Bishop Endre Hamvas was confined to house arrest and, under constant pressure, was compelled to appoint two deputies, Miklos Beresztoczy to preside over the archdiocese of Esztergom, and the Budapest parish priest Laszlo Szecsy over that of Csanad. Both were prominent members of the "peace priest movement," and Beresztoczy later became successor to Istvan Balogh as president of the movement, while Balogh, his usefulness over, was interned in some small provincial parish.

While these events were taking place, the crushing of the Catholic Church's external organization proceeded with dramatic speed. The establishment of the Government Office for Ecclesiastical Affairs (AEH) was the beginning, then followed the Groesz trial, which was intended to frighten both clergy and laity into total submission. Agents provocateur circulated widely among the clergy throughout the nation accusing, trapping, and deceiving with the result that many hundreds of men were imprisoned as defendants in the "Groesz trial." The trial was broadcast nation-wide by radio, and it was characteristic of the regime that the three most intransigent members of the episcopate then under house arrest, Jozsef Petery, Bishop of Vac, Endre Hamvas, Bishop of Csanad, and Lajos Shvoy, Bishop of Szekesfehervar, were required to listen to the transmissions. The world was once again dumbfounded. The defendants did not use their own natural languages but indicted themselves in a Marxian jargon heavy with examples of "anti-people's" deeds.

By the end of the Groesz trial certain of the "peace priests" had successfully infiltrated the hierarchy. Then, on July 3, 1951, a black day in the history of religion in Hungary, the decimated episcopate held a meeting under the chairmanship of Gyula Czapik, Archbishop of Eger. Two archbishops were in prison, three bishops were confined to their residences and represented by their vicars. And for the first time two emissaries of the communist enemy sat among the vicars. I intentionally do not call

them representatives, since it was generally agreed that Beresztoczy, the senior visitor, was a broken man after his long internment and only assumed his role under physical compulsion. In
the presence of these two intruders, the bishops dared not speak
openly to each other.

There was only one subject to discuss at that dismal meeting.
Archbishop Czapik made the announcement. He requested the
members of the episcopate to sign "without comment" a declaration which he would read aloud "in order to prevent unfore-
seen consequences." He then read a three-point statement. Point
one renewed the state-church pact concluded a year before but
"violated" by the Church. Point two condemned the persons
involved in the Groesz trial. Point three involved the most tragic
consequences of legalizing the "peace priest movement," which
so far had enjoyed the unconcealed disapproval of the bishops
and thus had made practically no headway.

This was the moment when the inner bastion's key fell into
enemy hands. The next step was obvious. If the bishops had
already been persuaded to accept the "peace priest movement,"
it was not at all difficult to pick the "least disagreeable" of two
or three suggested "peace" candidates and appoint him to a post
of vicar or "deputy" bishop. Within a few days, AEH officials,
in fact, secret AVO representatives, whose purpose was to assist
the vicars (the people soon called them "moustached bishops"),
were sent to each diocesan seat. To make the entire action more
impressive, the regime even delegated an AVO official to each
bishop with authority to seize both the keys to diocesan safes
and the bishop's seal. From that moment on bishops' mail was
opened in presence of the "peace" vicars and AVO representatives. The Church's physical authority grew weaker and gradually fell to the enemy. For if a bishop refused to sign any document desired by the regime, he was immediately confined to
house arrest and the document was signed by his vicar. Later the
communists felt strong enough to convene the vicars for a conference.

This fateful conference was held in camera and, therefore, did
not cause noticeable public reaction. More painful, however,
was the next step. Following the conference, a high AVO func-

tionary stepped out of a car to see each bishop requesting him to enter the car and travel to the capital, attired in episcopal robes with all his decorations, as is customary when one is received by the head of the state. The bishops were assembled in the central seminary of Budapest, even those who had been confined to house arrest. Imre Kisberk, assistant Bishop of Szekesfehervar, was the only exception, that ramrod of a man, whose attitude was so staunch that they dared not take him knowing that his resistance might influence the other bishops. The bishops then were driven by car to the Parliament where Archbishop Czapik read the loyalty oath in the presence of the Presidential Council, President Istvan Dobi, Prime Minister Rakosi, and President of Parliament Ronai. The members of the episcopate took the oath as a sign of the agreement between state and church. Actually this oath did not matter too much, since the lower clergy had already taken it a year before. But what happened after the ceremony deeply shocked the country. The members of the Bench of Bishops all walked into the adjoining hall where refreshments were served, and a friendly clinking of glasses took place between the leading regime people and the leading prelates. Flash bulbs popped, photo reporters appeared, and the following week a newsreel showed this solemn act of "reconciliation" between church and state. To make their humiliation complete, priests were ordered to commend the picture from the pulpit. It is true that very few did. But a public reaction justifiably flared up. A man may be compelled to sign a statement under duress. But it is quite another matter to drink with those who threaten force. Not without reason Catholic public opinion was seriously outraged at Archbishop Czapik's act of pretended fraternization.

From that point forward everything else was simply a question of detail, a problem to be solved by both the AEH and AVO or, to put it more basically, by the AVO alone. Terror against the clergy now increased. Outstanding resistance pastors were either removed by means of pressure on their bishops and by the "peace" vicars or, if this failed to work, they were arrested. Many were compelled by the modern methods available to a terror regime to join the "peace movement." Priests were threatened with transfers to remote points of service, and, if necessary, threatened with suspension of their priestly duties or finally with imprisonment. The legal reason was usually the same, a reference to a "provocative" sermon or article written before 1945. In such cases the first cooperative act was simply to sign some innocent little article or utter a few words at a "peace priest" meeting. The alternative to cooperation was terrifying. In place of the resisting pastor would come a priest who, although disliked by his parishioners, cooperated with the regime, and the outward appearance of life as usual would be the same. The recalcitrant pastor would simply disappear.

Thus, the fairly large parishes were gradually filled with members of the "peace priest movement." At the same time, many decent priests who were faithful to their vocations were pensioned and humiliated, for example, by transferring a pastor to some smaller parish as a curate, remarking that he may choose between this and the AVO's "guest room" or perhaps sentencing him to silence with the privilege of saying Mass and hearing confessions only or, in special cases, forbidding him totally to exercise his priestly functions. By the fall of 1952 this was the fate of most of the members of religious orders who had been transferred to diocesan service in 1950.

Terror was increasing. Only attendance at religious services was unhampered and even that to a limited extent. One could certainly not call this complete freedom of religion. In 1952, bible lessons and religious instruction for adults, which had been given afternoons, were prohibited. Operation of the only course for female teachers of religion, in Ward College, was also discontinued. More and more priests were imprisoned for teaching catechism outside the church and for caring for youth "illegally," as the communists said.

The first Imre Nagy cabinet in July 1953 introduced a considerable softening in the approach toward the Catholic Church. Deportations and internments were discontinued for the time being, concentration camps such as the ill-famed ones at Kistarcsa and Recsk were liquidated. One could breathe with somewhat more ease. There were fewer spies in the churches, permits to hold processions and non-routine devotions were easier to obtain, pressure against those who enrolled for catechism was not as great. The importation of bibles and prayer books from abroad was once again permitted. Governmental pressure upon clerical appointments was also somewhat lessened and occasionally bishops were actually able to fill vacancies with anti-regime priests. Occasionally also priests were released from prison with partial amnesties.

However, in March 1955, as a direct consequence of a change in Soviet internal policies involving a return toward Stalinism, terror reclaimed Hungary. Religious instruction was again restricted, priests were again arrested, to cite one tragic example, twelve disbanded Jesuits were imprisoned because they had maintained contact with each other. Several nuns who had been working as industrial laborers, clerks and domestics were also arrested for "illegal" religious instructions, since during their spare time they had given religious instruction to small groups of school girls in their homes.

By June 1956, the aftermath of the 20th Soviet Party Congress had made itself felt. Return to the way of legality was frequently stressed by the communists in the throes of self-criticism, the policy of sheer force was openly condemned, and thus the situation became easier even for the Church. Fairly large groups of priests were now pardoned, courts inflicted milder penalties compared to earlier sentences (by western standards judgments were still drastic), and a certain sense of relaxation was felt to be in the air. Serious criticism was heard from all sides. The Party had to defend itself against "leftist" and "rightist" deviation and critiques until finally the ferment, suppressed for so long, spontaneously and irresistibly exploded into the revolution.

Religious Life Under the Communist Regime

After the temporary climax in 1948, the development of Hungarian religious life was squeezed into an extremely narrow frame. From 1949 on all measures tended to empty freedom of religion of its real meaning and to replace it with the Marxian conception of religious freedom, which is nothing but a restricted freedom of worship in churches.

Closer investigation reveals that to say Mass in a church was generally allowed, and so was administration of the Sacraments. But this was only part of the picture, since those who went to church were checked and observed, they were pressured at their working places and received notations on their "cadre-files" as being under clerical influence. From time to time, sermons were closely checked and spies and provocateurs went to confession. However, it was not difficult to identify them because of their manner of speaking and their line of questions, crudely designed to spring traps. Because the faithful realized they were being watched, they simply went to Mass in churches on the opposite side of the city, wherever the size of the city allowed it. On major holydays, such as Christmas and Easter and the traditional feasts of the Resurrection and Corpus Christi, processions were so impressively attended that it could be called an open manifestation of faith and confidence in the power of God against the terror of a communist minority.

Contact between the clergy and the faithful outside of the churches was much more difficult. With the exception of the administration of the Sacrament of Extreme Unction, the regime definitely disapproved and found means to prevent a pastor from visiting his flock in their homes. And since no pastor wished to involve his parishioners in an awkward situation, this essential priestly function had to be discontinued.

Religious instruction was greatly hampered. It was completely interrupted in the upper grades of secondary school and in the lower grades as well as in the general schools it was subject to special registration. In many provincial towns the Government was helpless in the face of mass registration. But in fairly large cities most pupils dropped out. "People's educators" went from apartment to apartment, disseminating propaganda against religious instruction and terrorizing parents with the prospect of serious consequences if their children were permitted to be enrolled. Since there is no positive binding obligation for anyone to learn catechism in school, many parents thought they could make up for it by private instruction. The problem was intensified by the fact that only the unpopular "peace priests" obtained permission to teach catechism. Technical obstacles were also introduced. In Budapest, there was only one school in each district where catechism was taught, and courses were at noon following the normal morning school session. By the time the pupils had gathered from their schools, the hour for the lesson had expired.

Priests needed a permit to enter hospitals to administer the Sacraments to the sick and dying. But such a permit was only given when the end was near, if the patient's relatives applied, and a doctor approved it. Thus priests were compelled to don civilian clothes, hear confessions and administer the Sacraments in secret during visiting hours to those who not only were dying but who felt the spiritual need for divine assistance.

Operation of religious societies, including the entire organization of Catholic Action, was completely prohibited. Retreat houses were sequestered; the Catholic press was limited to one controlled weekly newspaper and one periodical; censorship was extremely strict, sometimes the press was required to publish specific articles, thus robbing these papers of their main objective. Further, a scanty allotment of paper restricted editions to a small group of readers. Any serious ideological education applied to everyday life under communism was completely impossible.

The number of seminaries throughout the country was reduced to five, less than one to each two dioceses in Hungary. Admissions were strictly limited, the staunchest teachers were either dismissed or paralyzed by controls. In one seminary the "moustached bishop" inspected the seminarians' belongings, and if there was found any printed matter other than official textbooks and prayer books (for example, typed translations of papal encyclicals), this was cause for discharge.

Religious orders were disbanded in August 1950, but, so as to permit the regime to boast of freedom of religion, eight monasteries were permitted to remain open throughout the country. Each monastery housed 35 monks or nuns with a school attached to each, six for boys and two for girls. This meant that only a fragment of the three leading male orders in Hungary, Benedictines, Franciscans and Piarists was allowed to operate. Doubtless there was an undeniable advantage in that the major convents of the teaching orders were maintained, among them the

Benedictine priory of Pannonhalma, dating back to St. Stephen's time. However, this was offset by the great burden of having to teach according to a Marxist curriculum and Marxian principles. Of course, both parents and students felt that this was an emergency situation and that, despite controls, a few hundred students were still being brought up in a religious environment. Their prospects for admission to universities upon graduation were poor, but the students of religious schools usually came from parents who were "class aliens," members of the former middle class, whose fathers in many cases were interned, deported or imprisoned and these students could not look forward to university careers in any event. The work of these religious orders, furthermore, was seriously handicapped by the regime regulation that only two novices per year could be admitted. In the normal preparation for the priesthood only a portion of those who request admission to an order remain to realize their religious vocations. Admissions were unable to make up for the drop-outs let alone the loss through death.

Today the majority of the members of religious orders, and especially the thousands of nuns, live and work as laymen in the world. A small proportion of the monks are engaged in scientific research and teaching, but the greater portion toil in factories as workers or clerks, many in unskilled jobs. A small number of the nuns are nurses, but most of them serve as workers such as streetcar conductors or domestic servants. It is only human as a result of this dispersion that some are lost to their orders, but many of them, by mingling among the people, have acquired great esteem through their diligence and their devotion to the Church and Christ's ideal. It was rather hard to employ in factory or household nuns who were accustomed to the solitude of the cloister, but their traditional discipline, modesty, faithfulness and honesty soon helped them to overcome the initial difficulties. And nuns who said their rosary by the kitchen range or a factory machine were heart-rending signposts of God's world, of spiritual life in death struggle against the shallowness of communist materialism with its accompanying terror.

What was the effect of this anti-religious policy upon the faithful's devotion? The influence of anti-religious propaganda in the press and in the seminaries, which charged that religion was only a superstition as opposed to the world of progress and science was by far less effective than the communists had expected.

On major holydays, great groups of the faithful attended Mass and took part in processions as manifestations of their opposition to the communists. If only for outward reasons, the people expressed their solidarity with the Church and with the ideals of religion and nation. And how moving the papal and the national anthems sounded when sung after Mass on solemn occasions. These were heartfelt spontaneous declarations of faith which the free world can never fully understand. No one who was not there can possibly understand. Many Hungarian men returned to the practice of the age old Christian customs of greeting priests with "Praised be our Lord Jesus Christ," thus professing their faith, even if today some of them do it only to show their opposition to the regime, and lifting their hats in front of a church, while the woman made the sign of the cross.

The effect achieved by the regime with its "peace priests" was disturbing, if not for everyone certainly for many. Those priests who surrendered certainly did not increase the Church's authority. Many people openly avoided these priests as they tried to carry out their ecclessiastical functions. For example, many faithful left the communion rail if a "peace priest" administered the Sacrament. Although the anti-regime clergy disapproved of this attitude and chose to make no distinction before the altar between priest and priest, it is an undeniable fact that public reaction was an expression of the simple faithful's *anima naturaliter christiana* outrage against those who had no backbone and accepted a compromise. Naturally, the faithful did not direct their disgust toward passive quiet priests who occasionally and with constraint appeared at peace meetings, but rather toward the influential and leading "peace priests." It often happened that parishioners refused to speak with new regime appointed pastors selected to replace devoted and beloved servants of God. When episcopal letters were read in church, recommending the delivery of agrarian products, or stressing peace and unmasking "the imperialists who scatter explosive fountain pens," the congregation instinctively felt that the voice was annoyed and strained. Nor did parishioners refrain from caustic remarks if a curate read them with conviction. Regime inspired statements frequently contained agricultural terminology which urban priests did not understand. Many times sober-faced peasant parishioners would remark aloud in the middle of a sermon, "Please do not talk about that, for it is something we know much better."

Another technique which had a harmful effect upon worshippers was the well-known spy system among communist officials and Party representatives employed by the AVO. It is only human, even if not indicative of strong character, that people who were Christian in name only and not willing to bear the cross faltered under pressure. Unfortunately, the same principle applied in certain cases to Hungary's priests, because the flock is merely a reflection of the shepherd. To be sure no open apostasy was required, the individual only had to take one barely noticeable first step toward the regime and the Party. The practicing Christian should not go to Mass openly on Sunday, should not go to Communion publicly too often, since the Church's law itself does not require it but once a year. He should not contact his priest. Or if the man were a priest, he would only have to attend just one peace meeting without participating. He should sign only one protest against the warmongers. Did not the grave consequences resulting from refusal seem quite out of proportion to the regime's small request to do "such simple innocuous little things."

Three very essential features must be emphasized to show how the life of the Hungarian Catholic Church has been maimed and paralyzed. First came the seizure of office by "peace priests" and the "moustached bishops" in July 1951, whereby the Church's system of government was literally paralyzed. Bishops were unable to contact their priests without hindrance. Both the "peace priests" and state officials foiled the bishops' directives and instructions. Loyal priests were removed. If a bishop refused to sign a communist-originated directive, he was either arrested and his deputy signed the order, or he was commended to the tender mercies of the AVO, who either interned or imprisoned him. In some instances, bishops suggested that priests particularly identified by the AVO as undesirable to the regime should resign their ecclesiastical posts and accept—temporarily— lower positions. It is hard to imagine what it meant for the bishops not to be allowed to open their own mail, except in the presence of "peace priests" and civilian AEH executives. Most of the priests refrained from writing to and visiting their bishops. Bishops' chancellories were empty, there was scarcely anything to do. The emergency powers delegated by the Holy See, the war-time relief measures which had arrived in December 1950, could not be proclaimed because the AEH prevented it.

The communists, in addition to assuming the power of Church government, also fell into the possession of Church archives, thus furnishing material for denunciations and disciplinarian actions by the AVO; there was now literally no end to the possibilities for exercising pressure and attacking the clergy and laity alike.

Finally, the Church was deprived of its facilities for education, since the schools and Catholic Action had been prohibited and the religious press were restricted, drab and limited to a small readership. Enthusiastic priests tried to organize a clandestine form of Catholic Action, but it soon turned out that this was physically impossible under police rule. Even the most innocent meetings in private apartments became well nigh impossible. All that was left was the church, a rare handshake, a reassuring silent look, a murmured bit of encouragement or admonition to hold on, souls' secret solidarity with each other and with Christ hoping for a better freer future.

Basic Attitude Toward the Regime

There were four basic types of religious attitudes toward communism.

The first group consisted of those persons who rejected communism completely opposing it every step of the way. The model was furnished by Cardinal Jozsef Mindszenty. The strength for such action is found in Holy Writ's warning, "What hath the faithful to do with Belial?" This is why the primate refused compromise with the regime. He well knew the Hungarian proverb, "if we give our little finger, they want the entire hand." This group included persons, among them many intellectuals, who willingly risked the loss of jobs, the threat of forced labor, even internment or prison, but refused to recognize communism. They did not accept responsible jobs or any kind of role, refused to take an active part in Party seminars, dodged the "transmission belt" front organizations such as the Democratic Women's League, the Association of Democratic Youth and the Hungarian-Soviet Society. They neither read the communist press nor listened to its broadcasts, instead they turned to Radio Free Europe, the Voice of America, French, Spanish, and even Turkish transmitters, although the latter two used rather inflammatory language. This was not the only course of action the extremists pursued. To youth this group urged passive resistance since "it is not worthwhile to study for communists." For workers they advocated as a principle sabotage and its execution as a duty which was at times justified and necessary. There was a consciousness, however, of the danger of accepting the principle of sabotage as a *modus vivendi*. Without proper ideological education, without practical propagation of the faith, it was feared that this course might make more difficult the understanding and solution of problems created by communist anti-religious pressures.

The second group followed the example of the early Christians in the Roman Empire and they sought consciously to dodge the pitfalls of extremism. They wanted to realize the principle: "render unto God those things which belong to God and to Ceasar those things which belong to Ceasar." They refused to accept the regime as a matter of principle on an ideological and religious basis, but they tried to be scrupulously proper in their duties as citizens and in their work. "We cannot give the state what rightfully belongs to God," they would argue as they steadfastly remained out of the Party and all its splinter groups just as did the members of the first category. They did not accept anything from the state that God and His Church could provide, namely faith and ideology. But from the civic point of view they condemned sabotage, were good workers, paid taxes and contributed their compulsory loans. From the standpoint of the Christian Commandment of love they condemned any manifestation of hatred. They repudiated communism within the meaning of the famous Augustinian principle: "inimicus causae, amicus rei," but approached individual communists with brotherly love, looking upon them with sympathy as misguided souls, spiritually color-blind. Accepting humiliation, suffering, and persecution, this group followed the recommendations of Pope Pius XII, who had repeatedly pointed out that the early Christians broke the power of paganism, not through spectacular victories, but with blood and tears under patiently borne blows. The regime realistically sensed that this was an extremely dangerous attitude, amounting to an infiltration of their "new society," as they called it, and mercilessly persecuted all those who overtly professed this viewpoint, be it from the pulpit or otherwise, but the communists were helpless against those who tacitly lived according to these principles.

Due to human frailty with its fear of suffering and in no small part to the passive nature of Hungarians, there developed the third group of the "passivists." They were satisfied with refraining from contact with the Party and its fronts. If they were priests, they did not take an active part in the peace movement but made small compromises, such as attending its meetings. Let us keep quiet, they rationalized, we still must live. The priests were by and large absolutely irreproachable men who in ordinary times performed their duties in a model way. However, there were those who lacked heroism and a fighting nature and these men were more easily persuaded to cooperate, realizing that if they refused cooperation they would be replaced by another man who would cooperate. Their reasoning was simply that more could be done in this way than if the churches were locked and the best priests arrested. This, however, was a grave error of reasoning doubtless dictated by human weakness, since the regime carefully avoided closing churches. As it turned out the knowledge that priests were imprisoned for their courage was a much greater moral aid for the Church than if they had shunned their imprisonment through silence and intellectual compromise.

Unfortunately, the more the terror increased, the larger became the number of those who, although being anti-communist in spirit, were outwardly totally passive and even cooperated in small matters. Final judgment of this group is up to Him who sees our souls, Who measures secret motives and Whose judgment is not only just but also merciful. No court will ever judge these "passivists," but Hungarian society tacitly condemned their posture, and certainly in that distant future when the evil has passed, they should be humble and modest and not expect to assume leading roles.

Finally, there was and is the group of overt collaborators. They largely comprise those who were Catholic in name only. The regime succeeded in winning over to the Party even practicing Catholics, who were motivated by a strong desire to succeed, distinguish themselves and achieve advancement at any cost. While these actions were not motivated out of conviction, unfortunately it turned out in practice that ideology follows attitude, as a sort of justification. A French moral philosopher once remarked, "if you do not live as you believe, you will soon believe as you live," and this argument was amply proved in Hungary. Such collaborators soon professed their new found philosophy with such vehemence that they outshouted old Marxists, and their own consciences. Many of them did not have to wait for the revolution to find out the mistakes they had made, when old friends as well as recent acquaintances ignored and cast them aside. Talented youngsters were fairly easily won over, because it is in the nature of youth to be ambitious, to wish to make its own way, to rise, and to acquire position. It cannot be denied that the regime offered great material prospects to youth through free education, scholarships, generally favorable professional placement. It sometimes happened that the sons and daughters of families who represented ancient Christian and national traditions went to communist-directed colleges and tore themselves away from the obsolete "bourgeois"

environment; rural youth for its part could partake of materialism in the people's colleges and thus climb the ladder of success.

This group also included the "peace priests," most of whom
entered the movement through compulsion. The communists
very thoroughly catalogued their every weakness so as to compromise them at the propitious moment. There was, in addition, a small group of priests who collaborated because of a
desire to succeed. This group justified itself by claiming to prefer a year's confinement in a disciplinary monastery when the
Church and Hungary would be free again than a year in an
AVO prison. That more priests joined this camp under pressure
than for reasons of cowardice and ambition is generally borne
out by the fact that prior to the bishops' conference in July
1951, which was compelled to approve the peace movement,
the membership of the "peace priests' movement" did not reach
5% of the total of Hungarian priests. A distinction should also
be made between those priests who were the prominent leaders,
who helped to restrict the proper exercise of the bishops' power,
who became communist tools against their more courageous
fellow priests, or who were the beneficiaries of sizeable remuneration in return for which service was rendered, and those
drab overanxious "passivists," who rarely turned up at peace
meetings, who faithfully read out from the pulpit regime circulars, and who in due course secured their tenure and safety.
The hierarchy was aware of this distinction and after the uprising Church authorities deposed only the leaders and most active
members of the peace movement. It does great credit to the
Hungarian clergy that there was only one priest who opposed
the Church's decision and turned to the regime for help, thus
bringing on himself papal excommunication.

It cannot be said that the collaborators would ultimately have
curbed respect for the Church. The idea of religious and national resistance was embodied in Mindszenty who had become
a symbol. Everyone recognized that a church-state agreement
had been achieved only through the arrest of a second prelate,
Archbishop Groesz, and through the exploitation of Archbishop
Czapik's condition, sick and fearful of suffering, and finally by

the use of sheer force. A great number of priests had been interned and imprisoned in the rough ratio of fifty Catholic priests to each non-Catholic clergyman.

Evaluation of the Regime's Influence

What harmful influence was exercised by the communist regime upon the Church? Were there any favorable effects? In treating this question it is more important to rivet attention not on the external institution but rather on the Hungarian involvement in the Mystical Body.

There is no doubt but that communist ideology completely changed all standards of conduct and introduced revaluation of all values. Everything which had been held sacred and possessed prestige was profaned: God, religion, country, family, womanhood, Christian love and charity. Not only were these targets attacked but their sacred existence was denied and they became objects of mockery. Belief in God? Unscientific. Religion? Superstition. Love for country? Nationalist fascism. Parental authority? We do not care for old class-aliens. Chaste womanhood? "To bear children is women's duty, girl's glory." Love? Principle of the weak, ours is to hate our enemy! Our peace is a militant peace and can only be achieved if the enemy is finally destroyed.

This destruction of values was propagated by diabolical sheer force; it attempted both to influence and to mold public opinion and to reach the soul. All totalitarian systems breed the same propaganda, lies and weapons of calumny. This belongs to Satan's realm. And this devilsh effect, this atmosphere of lies, slander, and terror obsesses the soul, these nightmares make life a hell.

In this atmosphere belongs that constant feeling of insecurity, of complete physical helplessness. The firm believer knows the enemy has power only over the body, but who willingly accepts separation from his home, his family, his loved ones, his work? This pain of fear hung over people like the sword of Damocles. This feeling of insecurity was principally generated by the network of informers. "Everybody who lives is suspect" was a truism people understood. Late in the forties a volume published by the *Études Carmelitaines* pointed to these satanic symptoms and quite aptly remarked that probably the most terrifying manifestation was the systematic destruction of personality, the constant forcible intrusion into the innermost reaches of man's being. One need only look to the big communist show trials where broken, transformed personalities looked out at reality from the masks of their former egos, fearfully and strangely jabbering charges against themselves without the slightest attempt to translate the rigid formalism of the Marxian jargon into language which sounded natural for the wretched defendants.

These features: the destructive redirection of all values and the adoption of all the satanic means of the lie and violence include the damage, destruction and curse of communism.

Adoption of violence as a method of statecraft, in addition to causing the overwhelming majority to live in a constant mood of insecurity, also deprived people of the very basis of a truly human life conceived in freedom. Plants and animals require only air, sunshine, water, and food in order to survive, but man requires freedom to live, to develop his own personality, to work and to create. One of the great lessons taught by the revolution is that human masses who are compelled to live for a long time without freedom and who suddenly are set free, become so intoxicated with happiness that they literally forget themselves and their concern for their lives exclaiming, "I would rather die than live as a slave one day longer!" This is the answer to the question repeatedly asked of Hungarians who fled to the West: Why did the Hungarian revolution not stop at a moderate, Gomulka-like solution?

If the basic prerequisites of natural human life are thus denied, it is obvious that the necessary conditions for a religious supernatural life cannot exist either, since the supernatural world, in God's grace, is built upon natural life. Serious damage was done in the religious sphere. Tens of thousands of young children could not attend catechism and religious instruction in senior high school was completely discontinued; hence, no religious instruction was given to the youth during the most formative years. What it means to be exposed to militant atheist propaganda during one's primary school education, when one knows and understands little about religion, is not hard to imagine. At minimum the result is complete apathy and indifference toward religion. This may be a shock to the faithful living on this side of the Iron Curtain especially those who happen to meet such youngsters among the refugees. It is no great wonder that the number of Sunday churchgoers among them barely reaches 10%. First one has to develop in them an interest in religion preferably by pointing out the positive attraction and productive features of the religious life as opposed to the doctrines of atheism.

The religious ignorance of large masses of the people is directly related to far-reaching moral indifference. As mentioned earlier, the communists first tried to encourage youth toward moral licentiousness and then to gain influence over them. During the years of adolescence it is particularly difficult to resist sexual temptation and this would be especially true, as the communists well knew, for those who profess materialism devoid of religious ideals and grace.

From this attack on the moral code it followed as a sociological axiom that the masses would grow coarse in every respect. The greatest torment for cultured persons under prison sentence or suffering forced labor was to smart under the control of the dregs of society and to hear their vile obscene conversations, their swearing and cursing. "This is how hell could be," remarked one prisoner in a mine to his fellows when he overheard the obscene conversation between the guards and communist civilian miners. I heard of a tragic and unfortunately characteristic case. Among the guard personnel of one mine there was a married couple, the wife was also a uniformed member of the AVO, and they had a sweet looking five-year old daughter. As she walked one day outside the barbed wire, several political prisoners standing inside the wire spoke to her in a friendly gentle way, thinking doubtless of their own little girls. The child turned upon them with a flood of foul, unrepeatable language starting with "stinking fascists." The prisoners looked at each other, paralyzed with shock. This is what satanic education may do to a sweet innocent child. And one who is so coarse and uncouth at the age of five, what could become of her as an adult?

Legalization of extra-marital relations indirectly aided in the destruction of the religious concept. Mention has been made of the communist principle "to bear children is the glory of woman." Orphans and delinquents were brought up in state-controlled "janissary training schools" as the people called them, to make them willing soldiers of the regime in this goal of increasing the birth rate. The poet Attila Jozsef's sad words applied to them, "I have no father, no mother, no God and no country . . ."

One may well ask is this the way to live a normal human life?

Under ordinary circumstances proper pastoral supervision could have accomplished a good deal coupled with a functioning Catholic press and social and charitable organizations cooperating with Catholic Action. But how could the Church struggle against this deliberate destruction when pastoral activities were maimed, when religious instruction was sheer fiction, when the Church was deprived of its free press, its retreat houses, its social movements, when the ranks of its priests were decimated? "How can they believe in one of whom they have never heard? How can they hear without an evangelist?" This plaintive cry of St. Paul became timely behind the Iron Curtain.

It almost seems paradoxical to ask what advantages the Church gained from the pressures exercised by the regime? Only those lacking faith will not understand. The faithful know and feel the contrast between the supernatural and the natural world, with the differing sets of claims and attractions. Truly, those who are persecuted in the natural world rejoice as inhabitants of the supernatural world. They take the cross with Christ and will be resurrected with Christ.

Thus we can easily understand that when persecution maltreats the human appearance of the Mystical Body of Christ—the cross will help advance the triumph of His eternal Divine Being. And, according to St. Paul, everything will be to the benefit of those who love God.

The first group of favorable effects may be described by the motto "action breeds reaction." After long years under a terror regime the desire for popular freedom broke out with elemental power. The revolution wrote into Hungarian hearts with bloody letters the natural law and freedom.

In many people the godless state aroused a desire for a posi-

tive belief in God. They experienced the heresy of communism,
they were disappointed by the idols. Souls felt the idolatrous
emptiness, then felt a desire and demand for positive values,
for God. They longed, many of them, for love. Unfortunately,
this was more true of the aged than among the youth. But youth
was not unrepresented.

Communist attacks against the Church were mounted in the
knowledge that the Church was the core of the greatest resistance, and were doubled in fury as the regime learned it was
unable either to break or to overcome it. This opposition of
religion amazed many people and the Church gained their admiration. Many were the questions asked as to what constituted
the real nature of this Church on which even communists broke
their lances. The more disillusionment and, ultimately, hatred
against the regime grew, the more sympathy was felt for the
regime's stepchild, the Church. To cite only one example: during the years of common oppression within and without the
prisons old social democrats, true Marxists, the anti-clericals
of bygone days, approached both the faithful and the clergy
with brotherly respect and reverence.

Another group of favorable features may be characterized as
contrast-effects. Generally speaking, the fanatic activities of
Party people, the organized work of these "sons of darkness,"
pricked the consciences of many clerics and ardent believers.
"If we, having eternal truth and supernatural assistance, had
worked with the same resolution and persistence, if we had
been less proud, since it has been written that 'the gates of Hell
shall not prevail against us,' how many age old problems would
we have solved, how many indictments could we have avoided?"
Many people felt this argument strongly, and not without
reason.

There was also the general popular revulsion against any
form of state church. The decorations and awards bestowed on
"peace priests" reminded us that decorations and church offices
had also been given for political services earlier in Hungarian
history. The pendulum had swung first toward the right, and
now it had ironically moved to the left. Hungarians finally
realized as true what Montalambert had declared a hundred

years ago, "The Church's real support rests in the millions of its faithful, not in the princes' doubtful and short-lived assistance which may be withdrawn overnight." The Hungarian people today definitely reject any close church identification with the state power which in any way involves dependence. They also despise and deride politics carried on from the pulpit, priestly activities in the politics of the day on behalf of the state. All of this, we fervently believe, belongs to the Hungarian past.

It is generally true that every heresy includes a grain of truth. This applies to communism. Those grains of truth, mixed with errors, are often proclaimed with such force and exaggeration that they almost turn into their opposite error. But what *de facto* is a grain of truth, still remains truth and exercises positive influence.

Basic in the nature of things there is the concept of community. The Church in Hungary proclaimed this idea, but realization through Church membership was not enforced strictly enough. Yet it should have been done, especially since "they will recognize you to be My disciples from the love you bear to each other . . . whatsoever you do to one of the least you have done unto Me . . ." This is why Pius XI woefully complained that the greatest scandal of the twentieth century was that the Church lost the working class.

The communists, for their part, focused general attention upon the social question, although they pushed the problem to extremes and exaggerated it, distorting it into a collectivism where plurality is valued over the person, and where the individual is not considered as a free person but only as an instrument. Even if they did it mistakenly, distortedly, and forcibly, the communists did kindle the concept of solidarity in many people, reflecting that the true value of man develops in serving the commonweal, that one cannot live in individual unrestrained selfishness.

Even if forcibly and at a high price, communism helped to focus on and solve such problems of social welfare as old age pensions, tuition-free education, children's aid, which was their only achievement for the benefit of families, and paid vacation trips for workers. None of these labor innovations and benefits had been realized in Hungary earlier when other means were available, in the so-called "Christian" era (1921-30), when a priest moreover was minister of social welfare. It is a surprising fact that while before the war no old age pension plan for the clergy existed, the first steps were taken in the last decade and there are now eleven homes for old priests and monks, seven of which are subsidized by the state and four supported by the Church from gifts of the faithful.

Another practical step in the social sector was the collapse of social barriers. The storm of history approached and mixed the children of various social classes who had once been separated by artificial barriers. Now common misery brought them together. Before the war certain careers were generally reserved for the sons of the upper classes, while by unwritten agreement they refrained from entering others. In the thirties under the influence of statesmen and public educators like Count Pal Teleki, and as a consequence of the spirit of the times, many Hungarian educators strongly urged children of the middle class and intellectuals to enter upon commercial and industrial careers. But it was useless. The budding upperclassman strove after security and prestige in positions which meant safe livelihoods, toward careers which entailed social esteem whether it was officer, judge, doctor, or engineer. Under communism, the old upper class was compelled to take jobs as workers, while the sons of workers and farmers entered professional careers and filled leading positions.

Among the deported and imprisoned of the internment camps the same phenomenon occurred as a continuation of sorts of the process which had begun in the air raid shelters during the war where people who formerly lived in isolation found each other, recognized each other, and helped each other. We saw wonderful manifestations of this spirit during the revolution. Streetcars and buses ceased running to assist the general strike but trucks and passenger cars stopped as a matter of course and picked up waiting hitchhikers. During the first few days of this practice some people asked how much they had to pay? But acceptance of money was disdainfully refused, and later on no one even so much as thought of paying anything. The feeling of

"I should like to confess to you," the youngster exclaimed, "because I am sure that you are no 'peace priest' if you work here with us."

Another positive feature of communism which undoubtedly had a favorable effect was its contempt for empty formalities and its interest in true meanings. And in this connection communism did differentiate between main and side issues. This is the logic and style of simple men who work at machines and whose minds are not profound. A Hungarian Catholic periodical wrote as far back as 1948 that attention to the essential features of Christianity was a characteristic of the time. The most serious mistakes had been made along the line of the two most important commandments: to serve God with all one's heart and to love one's neighbor selflessly. Pope Pius XII declared that the basic principle of the struggle against materialism was to return to the roots of the early Christian Church, to recover the spirit of its essential foundation, which has sometimes been covered by subsequent layers of history in a way to make us forget its essence. The anti-clerical trend logically powered the Church's mills with water from its own mills. It is interesting to note that the first striking difference observed between the Hungarians who went abroad after the war and those who escaped following the uprising seems to be that the revolutionary youth does not appreciate empty formalism at all but curiously seeks the essence of their problems.

Strangely enough, as a result of the numerous seminars the communists held in the factories and offices plus the discussions, evaluations, and inquiries conducted in Party schools, people at large, and especially the youth, grew accustomed to a strange measure of independent thought. Due to the serious consequences events might bring, people began to ponder carefully what they read in the newspapers. And most importantly they began to read between the lines. They listened to political comments on the radio and made up their own minds.

This right thinking was reflected in the revolution. During the first few days workers and the youth acted with incredible common sense. They were not misled by slogans, although communist leader Ernoe Geroe's speech, October 23, tried desperately to ignite two explosive themes. The first was the question of anti-semitism and the second nationalism. But Geroe was mistaken. The common sense of Hungarians prevented them from swallowing the bait, thus maintaining the purity of the uprising from the outset. It is my feeling that the youth and the workers showed more reasonableness and discipline in their behavior than did the intelligentsia, who favored the idea of immediately creating or re-creating a group of political parties. True enough, the workers and youth had lived as one in communist Hungary, suffering alike, while the intellectual, conformist or rebel, lived apart separately in and out of prison and doubt, thus creating for them an atmosphere divorced in degree from the local realities. There was no doubt, however, as to the purity of the revolution when we but witness shop windows which were broken but not pilfered, and the hundred forint notes spontaneously collected in open boxes on street corners for the widowed and homeless.

The final positive effect bestowed on Hungarians by communism was the admiration for the virtue of heroism and scorn of philistine ideologies. The common positive feature of a corresponding sense of scorn for this century's totalitarian systems is what Mussolini postulated in two words, *vivere pericolosamente* —to live dangerously. While a philistine life paralyzes man's fitness to struggle, while it tries hard to avoid the cross, an attitude in complete negation of the Christian ideal which tends only to breed a hotbed of passivity and compromise, the stressing of heroism favors attainment of a truly Christian way of life. Hence, the very existence of a "Church of Silence" gives the faithful opportunity for a deeper, more sincere, warmer religious life than is normally present in a Church living on this side of the Iron Curtain, in peace and a free atmosphere.

Life behind the Iron Curtain not only furnished the air and opportunity to brandish the flag of heroism, but through persecution and through the necessity to take up the cross it forced many people generously, devotedly, and with extreme self-sacrifice to follow Christ, to be a heroic Christian. Hundreds and thousands daily had and continue to have such opportunities through suffering, degradation, and prison to become completely one with God as only few may achieve voluntarily. It is no human invention, but Christ's truth, "Blessed are those who suffer persecution for the sake of truth." Nor was it human invention when St. Paul declared, "If we suffer with Christ we shall be resurrected with Him." The cross is the symbol of suffering, but also the symbol of Christian victory. And again, as St. Paul admonished us, "Christ washes the Church in its own blood to make it holy and immaculate . . ."

Herein is the secret of religion, for even if the communist regime defiles and destroys the externals, the human face of the Church, its divine essence is renewed, and thus even cleans and beautifies its human face.

This is the final question. Did the regime achieve its purpose? Was it able to break the Church; did it paralyze Christian influence upon souls, thus overcoming the strongest obstacle to communist domination and so constitute itself as master over the entire nation's soul, giving credence to its totalitarian claims?

The answer is obvious from what has been said before. The regime was neither able to destroy nor to break the spiritual power of the Church which lives invisibly in men's souls. Undoubtedly much is destroyed on the surface, organizations broke down, members who had only loose outward ties with the Church fell away and went astray as leaves in the autumn wind. The Church decreased in numbers since it was unable to reach thousands of young souls, but not for once has the Church abandoned hope for their ultimate return. On the other hand, faith increased in many souls, and hearts warmed to Christ and His Church under the weight of the cross; persecution rendered respect and sympathy for the Church in many non-believers. Priests found it possible, on a restricted basis, to conduct serious pastoral work in the parishes, especially in the care for the sick and the poor. Around the pastor and the sanctuary of the Church cloistered the core of faithful who today are the Hungarian Church's primary support and treasure. Priests also experienced the fact that self-denying work for the benefit of souls provides an enthusiastic flock, devoted cooperation and even financial support, while service to the enemy regime and surrender entails contempt and deprives a priest of his flock's esteem and confidence.

The revolution created a new situation. The regime's basic internal weakness came to light. Its grip on men's hearts is much looser than even the staunchest reactionaries thought. That their own disciples, their pampered children, did not like it was clearly proved by the long and desperate struggle of the workers of Dunapentele, Csepel and Miskolc. Many secrets of the regime's terror and violence came to light, revelations which certainly did not make communism more attractive to the masses. Moreover, the servants and tools of the regime began to realize that when the critical moment arises communism would be unable to protect them from the serious consequences of their deeds.

There is no doubt that a certain change will occur in the people's attitude in this post revolutionary situation, since the essential weakness and evil of the regime are manifest and the dangers of cooperation easy to see; these changes will also affect the attitude of the regime. It is conceivable that due to their experiences many opportunist collaborators will reconsider their views and it might even be that many people who were formerly passive will now gain a portion of courage. It will be needed. For Hungary is witnessing the full brunt of communist blind fury and regime sanctioned violence has become the order of the day.

An essential feature from the point of view of religion is that Rome had spoken. The religious collaborators were condemned, they were suspended and one priest who sought regime refuge against Church authority, as well as encouraging his colleagues to do likewise, was excommunicated. Those priests who were placed in pastoral and ecclesiastical positions without reference to Church laws were called upon to vacate their posts. Moreover, clerical collaborators, even after they realized their mistakes and repented, will find their punishments prevent them from obtaining leading ecclesiastical positions as they stand exposed and compromised. This became a serious warning to the clergy which forced many to revise their attitudes. Those concerned will have to declare themselves, and those who do not obey will hardly be tolerated by any bishop, even if the regime should so demand. Communist duress will be necessary. It is probable that in the long run the Government itself will drop those priests who served the regime earlier for they have become

personally expendable, as the communists have repeatedly done
before. But even if this is not so, Hungarian priests will refuse
to cooperate with them precisely because of the recently learned
lessons of the revolution. Current signs seem to indicate that the
Hungarian clergy prefers the Church's eternal fate, to follow the
cross-bearing Christ, not to compromise with the atheist enemy.
The Hungarian Church is now, more than ever, what it essen-
itally should be and what its divine Founder prophesied, "a
sign which is contradicted." This is its power and glory. We
who today live in the free world may well be proud of our broth-
ers and help them in solidarity, not only by prayer, but also by
example.

So we come to the end of the Hungarian story of religion, but
what of the Free World's obligation toward the "Church of Silence?" What are the duties of the people of the Free World
toward their fellow men behind the Iron Curtain?

The lesson which the Church learned is obvious: to proclaim
the faith strongly against mistaken, heretical ideologies, to offset hatred with love, to foster serious religious discipline against
Party discipline, to replace loyalty to Moscow by faithfulness to
God, to counter feverish Party activities by organized and con-
sistent work and effort on behalf of the Kingdom of God. Despite all the material temptations of a state church, abide by the
opinion that we cannot give to Ceasar what is God's. When
clergymen are enticed to play a political role, they should adhere
to the Pauline principle that a priest is Christ's servant and the
steward of God's mysteries. When the religious believer is enticed to avoid his cross and to compromise and to be passive, he
should unflinchingly follow the way of Calvary. And the more
impossible it is to conduct spiritual education outside of the
Church in the press, on the radio, and through societies and
retreat houses, the more must the clergy intensify and exploit
their pastorate, care for the poor and the sick, and direction of
their flocks with a zeal contrary to the former complacency and
trust that "the gates of Hell shall not prevail . . ."

All this is a stimulating lesson for the religions of the Free
World since no one can safely say that all is well, there is no
room for improvement. The more we here in freedom take les-

sons to heart, the better will we brace ourselves for the battle against communist materialism and the more helpful will we become for the "Church of Silence," in our prayers, unselfish example, spiritual, moral, and material aid.

Such a positive posture will be much more to the point than the former practice which limited itself to discussion, mockery, attacks against communism, and exposure of the sins and errors committed behind the Iron Curtain. We must also point up the consequences of a practical adoption of communist ideas; but this negative approach is not enough, it is only a secondary, albeit an important side. The positive side must predominate.

Everything is not necessarily better in the West. And if we wish to defeat communism, we must realize all its positive features without losing our perspective.

The West must keep its eyes upon the world behind the Iron Curtain. The world's conscience must be kept awake.

These are the practical lessons which one may learn from the observation of the persecution of religion. The future is not especially bright, but for one brief moment the light shone and we saw the price the "Church of Silence" in general and the Hungarian Church in particular pay. If the western world really wishes to help and to protect itself against the danger of communist materialism, it must not fail to observe these lessons.

THE MIND

There is something diabolical about the manner in which the communists seek to breach the sanctity of the human mind. As Paul Landy reflected in his Orwellian remark "ignorance is strength," and so it must seem to the communist mentality. Deprive your opponents, your enemies of their critical judgment, strike down the channels of creative thought and close the means to objective truth. Then you have literally the captive audience. We have no doubt of communist thoroughness in this area. We have seen countless examples of Marxist morality justifying the means for the obtainable end of heaven on earth. We know their "brainwashing," we know their amorality, and now we shall come to know their techniques which brand them here and now as philistines, bent on intellectual destruction.

In this section the shocking story of the death of free communications is told, the callous suppression of a country's right to write as well as the right to read. This humiliation is compounded by the record the communists accrued in just one of the score of intellectual areas they entered—the field of music. For the general reader it is hoped that this case study of music under the heel will be both illuminating and alerting. For here we see the workings of the communist system in a sector not often subject to the glare of exposure.

Authors Paul Landy and Peter Budai are products of communist environment. Journalist and musicologist, both had reasonably assured futures if only they accepted communism fully. It was not possible for them to do so. Read, then, their stories, and ask yourself, "what would I have done?"

Mass Media:
"Ignorance is Strength"

BY PAUL LANDY

"Nineteen eighty four in practice" would be perhaps the appropriate title of this chapter concerning the mass media of press and radio in communist Hungary. The Hungarian October uprising revealed to the world the resounding collapse of Orwell's final argument. The "proles" did in fact revolt against "Big Brother." The slaves won the battle, but lost the war in the face of the overwhelming material superiority of the Soviet Union. Nevertheless, all the other features of the Orwellian nightmare might be applied to Hungary. Years of suffering, prison, concentration camps have injected into us young and older intellectuals the fatal dangers of the "thought crime," of the mere fact that one dares to think or talk freely.

The outer and inner Iron Curtain hung over every single step of our lives. The first, the Iron Curtain of hate, separated us with the help of the barbed wire and minefields from the West, and the second, the inner curtain of lies, the "ignorance is strength" theme, meant the complete separation of the people

* Paul Landy is a former Budapest journalist.

from the truth. The main components of this inner curtain
were the press and the radio.

The leitmotif of the communist way of life in terms of service
was to deny the truth. The cautious, calculating bureaucrats in
the apparatus of the Government, Party and trade unions
watched their steps, looked over their shoulders, loudly professed loyalty, and monotonously repeated official propaganda.
Yet many of them even in the darkest years wavered emotion-
ally, intellectually denied seeing in everyday life the appalling
contrasts between facts and claims, between realities and illusions.

The organizers, the effective directors of propaganda, consciously applied and worked out the theory of half-truths. They
distorted facts in so devious, subtle and twisted a manner that
the people no longer knew whom to blame. At the same time
the agents, the tools of this policy, the journalists, writers, radio
commentators were constantly subjected to a deliberate mental
and moral pressure. What every genuine intellectual cares most
about is spiritual freedom. But communism was in fact the
denial of this basic right. After all, argue communist dialecti-
cians, why should anyone want to think for himself since it is
universally agreed that everything is for the best in this the best
of all possible worlds.

To illustrate this unique technique I shall relate a typical
story. At the time of the slight American economic recession in
1949 the economic bulletin of the MTI (official Hungarian
News Agency) published a despatch stating this year half a million fewer cars would be produced by American motor car factories. Some Hungarian papers prominently featured this news,
which, in the opinion of the editors, confirmed the communist
analysis of an impending economic crisis in the United States
much the same as is being done today in Hungary with the current U.S. recession. But the top directors of the propaganda
apparatus thought and argued quite the other way. Julia Kenyeres, the editor in chief of MTI, and a Moscow trained female,
severely punished the editor who, when he was eventually arrested, was the target of a cross-examination concerning this
incident. His arrest, incidentally, took place three years later but

the Party security officer at MTI had naturally recorded the case in his personal file.

After all, what was wrong with this news despatch?

The reader's first reaction might be a good one from the communist view, but, on closer examination, the reader might also reason that if car production merely decreases by half a million cars what must be the actual production figure, and a country which is able to produce so many cars is most probably in an immensely strong economic position. One may argue, as the unfortunate editor did, that the high level of American car production is an established fact. In this you will miss the basic point, namely, in a communist country it is standard for every subject—whatever may be the issue—that there can be only one opinion, the right one. And each morning in Hungary, as throughout the entire "socialist camp," Moscow's *Pravda* tells the people what they need to know and believe and think. If the Party paper *Szabad Nep* says that a big slump will come and the facts make a mockery of this claim, then they must alter the facts. Therefore, to deny the truth is an act of service to communism since the means justify the end.

These and similar things which must sound utterly fantastic to western readers were matters of life and death in a communist country. Everyone knew, for example, that hundreds of thousands of persons regularly listened to western news broadcasts patiently playing a cat and mouse game with the jamming stations. In spite of this fact, the Government tried to wrap the news in complete secrecy. An ordinary person couldn't buy western papers or read them. Even editors and journalists were not able to bring western newspapers home. It was strictly banned and severely punishable if anyone made an exception to this rule. In 1953, a young journalist Istvan Friedrich who worked for the Budapest evening daily *Esti Budapest* was sacked because he tried to take western journals home.

All these preliminary remarks serve to introduce the famous words of André Gide in his memorable *Soviet Journal*. "There can be no question of harmony when the whole choir sings in unison."

There has never really existed in Hungary a completely free

press in the western sense. But despite its shortcomings, one could read numerous courageous sensible pieces in well-informed papers even in the darkest periods of the Horthy era. Moreover, during the second World War, until the direct Nazi occupation of the country, there appeared many outspoken articles and strong hints about the actual situation could be read between the lines.

After the war we experienced a short but extremely lively press renaissance. It was perhaps never before so free, so colorful, and so interesting. Even *Szabad Nep,* the Communist Party daily paper, was in a journalistic sense relatively well done. In Budapest alone twelve dailies were published plus numerous weeklies and several periodicals. In those days there were no barriers to free writing and editorializing and further there was keen and free competition for readers' favor. Nevertheless, while I was then working on the staff of a social democratic evening daily we could hardly see the menacing clouds on the horizon.

It was the summer of 1948. Through the forced merger of socialists and communists and by the excommunication of Tito, the press was already approaching an untimely death. Rakosi, Geroe, Revai and other Moscovites had correctly sensed the immense importance of a free press and realized likewise the urgent need for taking over the mass media. The political merger of June 1948 gave the *coup de grace* to the social democratic press. *Nepszava,* formerly the principal socialist paper, became the mouthpiece of the obedient, communist-run trade unions. Two other socialist dailies simply vanished from the scene. Formally they were merged with "brother" papers, but in practice communist staffs increased by a mere handful of former socialists. Step by step all socialists were either fired or imprisoned.

After the show trial of Cardinal Mindszenty there was in fact only a one-party press in Hungary. The Smallholder and Peasant Parties, it is true, each continued to publish a newspaper but they obtained less newsprint and somewhat later both papers ceased to exist. The dictatorship of the proletariat slowly, but with deadly precision, completed its suppression of every last remnant of a free press.

"Bread of Hundreds of Thousands"

With this slogan *Szabad Nep* began a recruiting drive. In a few months the paper was printed and sold in 700,000 copies. Everyone under the control of the "apparatchik" was obliged to subscribe to the paper. In every single *curriculum vitae*, in every personnel form one found the questions, "Which papers do you read? Are you a subscriber of *Szabad Nep?*"

There remained only four other dailies all communist dominated: *Nepszava* (50,000), *Magyar Nemzet*, the most popular paper (70,000), *Esti Budapest*, the afternoon Party paper (60,000) and from 1952 on *Szabad Ifjusag*, the youth paper, extremely popular, (150,000). These papers, however, had only secondary importance for *Szabad Nep* was the official organ of the Party, and was the first to receive important news or artificial leaks.

A reader may ask how in practice could the press be controlled? Firstly, the state owned all publishing houses and all printing plants. The state gave the initial permission for a paper to exist. Secondly, the Party had the last word in selecting the editors and for that matter even the ordinary staff members. Thirdly, there was the invisible censorship.

To give at least a few glimpses into the organization of the communist press we must naturally first cast eyes on *Szabad Nep* itself, since for a long time this meant *the Press*. The staff consisted of two hundred men. Technical personnel alone occupied a spacious building in the center of Budapest. This building was built by the "spontaneous" donations of Party members. At the entrance you found a miniature Iron Curtain, equally inpenetrable. After tearing through this dike successfully you smashed into a new wall. On every floor sat a telephone operator who kept a watchful eye on each visitor. It rather resembled a citadel more than a newspaper office.

By paraphrasing the oft-quoted words of the revolution's

Radio Free Kossuth "For many years the radio has been an instrument of lies. It lied day and night; it lied on all wave lengths," I am inclined to say that for many years *Szabad Nep* was a gigantic factory of lies, producing deceit everyday in every column. But it was a well organized factory of lies with workers, foremen, inspectors, executives and directors. It was a state inside a state with extraterritorial rights. Its leading body was the editorial board varying from seven to nine members. The head of this board and his two deputies were as a rule either members or alternate members of the Party's central committee. From 1945 until 1949 the editor-in-chief was Joseph Revai, the chief theoretician of the regime. Later it was Marton Horvath, son of one of the wealthiest property owners in pre-war Budapest, Frigyes Schiller. In 1951, he was replaced by Oscar Betlen, the *eminence gris* of the communist press, one of Hungary's most sinister figures, but Horvath returned again in 1954 although Betlen remained as his deputy.

Every day an executive session of the editorial board determined the Party line of the paper and decided the use of feature articles. Very often the chiefs of different departments also took part in the discussion. They in turn held meetings, each with a part of his staff. There began the production of lies, half truths, half lies.

The chiefs had direct telephones to Rakosi and other top men and they were in constant touch with them. They were informed about pending changes or dramatic events. When, for example, Laszlo Rajk was arrested in 1949, *Szabad Nep* began a series about the Titoist and Trotskyist menace two months before his trial. Soon readers themselves could sense peculiar straws in the wind, repeated sharp attacks always meant that we were on the eve of dramatic events.

Towards the end of his rule Rakosi personally supervised the publication of his speeches in *Szabad Nep*. In the spring of 1956, speaking at a provincial meeting, Rakosi unexpectedly called Rajk, who was framed and executed on his orders in 1949 a "comrade" and announced his "innocence." The text of his speech was published only on page two. Rakosi thereupon went personally to the paper's office, dramatically appeared in the printing plant, and supervised the printing process rectifying this error. In May 1956 Rakosi engaged in a sickening example of self-criticism at a mass meeting and that very night he was in touch with the editors on how to handle the story. Many times he personally instructed the paper what to emphasize in his speeches and how. When Khrushchev flew to Belgrade in 1955 the Hungarian press was perhaps the only bloc press which did not print even a single picture of the event. The Politbureau had decided against it and therefore despite the protests of editors pictures did not appear in the press.

It was natural that the phone system at the *Szabad Nep* building was connected with Communist Party headquarters. Every journalist on the paper was an employee of the Party. They used the same exclusive hospital and resort spots and they enjoyed priority in obtaining new apartments. The Party cell at *Szabad Nep* was not responsible to any higher body as other Party cells were, it was linked directly to the central committee.

With its 700,000 copies, with its immense budget and Party prestige *Szabad Nep* was a gigantic organization. All other papers were in fact simply its branches and its servants. Nevertheless, the other papers had a peculiar importance in several respects. One might, of course, raise the question why other papers were necessary at all? First, the communists wished to create the impression of a many-sided lively press. Second, all the papers had definite assigned tasks. The leaders knew very well that large segments of the population did not read *Szabad Nep* at all and it was common knowledge that even subscribers did not read it. These papers had limited scope so as not to steal the show from *Szabad Nep. Magyar Nemzet,* an old paper especially popular among intellectuals and the middle class, was allowed to exist because it reached important segments of the population. Later the paper became the organ of the communist conceived People's Front.

Szabad Ifjusag, the youth paper, spoke to the youth, and *Esti Budapest,* after the pattern of a Moscow evening paper, faithfully interpreted the Party line for afternoon readers. Among the contributors one found many non-Party men, but the editor was always under firm Party control.

Overall control of the press and radio was divided between the press section of the Ministry of Culture and the agit-prop department of the central committee. Selection of staff and direction of policy was handled solely by these organs. In the organizations which nominally owned these papers the trade unions, the Union of Youth, the People's Front, Party members controlled the top leadership. So in effect these papers had double supervision.

No paper could break a story before *Szabad Nep* set the pace or line. The pre-eminence of *Szabad Nep* was a constant source of irritation to journalists for only *Szabad Nep* men got the important news and minor officials constantly treated the other papers in very high-handed fashion.

Each paper plus the radio network had an overseer in the press section of the Party. These "apparatchiks" were responsible to the central committee. These men decided every important problem. If you were chief editor of *Magyar Nemzet* you were not able to hire a cub reporter without the permission of your special overseer. These men without exception never visited a printing plant, never worked on a news desk and, as cautious Party die-hards, never trusted their own journalists.

I might single out a typical case, the special overseer for radio. For years this man, Laszlo Balassa, who originally practiced medicine, was the watchdog of radio. Almost every day he toured Radio Budapest and played a central role in factional struggles. At the time of the memorable Twentieth Congress of the Soviet Communist Party Balassa personally edited the commentaries and speeches. For example, he did not want to broadcast the important speech of Mikoyan sharply attacking Stalin. He also personally compiled lists of those persons who, even as free lancers, were not considered reliable enough to write for radio broadcasts. He had special agents in every section. The same problem also faced every newspaper.

This build-up, control, and triple supervision of the press in its merciless crudity was surprisingly effective and for a long time completely stifled original thought and incentive.

One is haunted by the unforgettable memory of Orwell's Ministry of Truth in writing about the propaganda apparatus in communist Hungary. The "inner Party members" in propaganda terms meant the actual directors of lie-production, and the "outer Party members" were the mere executors, the more or less able intellectual slaves.

At the top of the propaganda hierarchy we find the agit-prop secretary of the central committee, who is a Politbureau member. The actual specialists are the middle men, who occupy the layer between the top leaders and the intellectual slaves. These men are as a rule dedicated, thoroughly reliable, lifelong communists, the organizers of the permanent purges. A portion of them know the West, another segment merely the USSR, but in the end their methods are basically the same.

For almost a decade Oscar Betlen has been perhaps the most sinister figure behind the scenes of the communist press. He is an able but ruthless old-time communist who has never hesitated to wipe out either human life or career lives in assuring his personal position or the interests of the Party. Even in the dreary history of *Szabad Nep* Betlen held a singular place. First, he was an efficient editor and simultaneously a reliable agent of the AVO. He had a direct phone to Gabor Peter's office, a former director of the AVO, now a semi-crazed inmate of his own prison. On several occasions he boasted of the fact that he personally informed the AVO about staff members. He had special informers on the paper who patiently collected "facts" and then suddenly, quite unexpectedly, he shattered his victims to pieces. He even sent his spies to coffee houses and night clubs in search of journalists. He kept a check on their every action, word, or gesture. In personal terms he acted the same as the Party, trusted no one and bit by bit ruined former favorites. As a man who belonged to Rakosi's inner circle he always succeeded in staging comebacks following temporary defeats. In 1954 when he worked as Hungarian overseer to the Cominform paper in Bucharest *For a Lasting Peace, For a People's Democracy* he drew up weekly critical studies concerning the issues of the paper. He had a hysterical hatred for the nonconformist, anyone whose remarks or behavior vaguely resembled originality or reflected harmful western influences. When another bureau asked for a reference about some ex-staff member, Betlen personally dictated his opinion. In some cases he hounded his victims until they were near to death. He followed them from job to job, everywhere making it impossible for them to work. He literally killed men and families in this way. After the revolution he disappeared, but he has already staged his latest triumphant return as the current editorial director of *Nepszabadsag*, the new name for the hated pre-revolutionary *Szabad Nep*.

For more than six years Julia Kenyeres was editor-in-chief at MTI, the official Hungarian news agency. She is an ancient life-long communist, who lived for decades in the USSR and possesses dual citizenship. Her husband, who was chief of TASS in Berlin in the thirties, defected to the West. From that time Mrs. Kenyeres became the living symbol of the Party line, an uncompromising persecutor of any ingenious original mind, which, in her opinon, was slightly deviationist (her daughter-in-law fled to the West following the revolution). Haunted by the memory of her defected husband, she refused to send anyone abroad and through the years she managed to dismiss every one of her responsible editors. She severely punished staff members for the slightest political mistake. A girl translator was once fired because she wanted to lend several western magazines to a friend. As a result of her dismissal she was forced for years to labor as an unskilled worker yet she possessed a perfect knowledge of three languages. Kenyeres also fired an editor on one occasion because he cut a Russian text leaving out some insignificant sentences. Only by her permission could her editors use western material. Every news item had to be based on Soviet sources. When there was no Soviet source, she phoned Moscow and held up MTI wire service until she had documentation even if it was a world famous event. At the time of the eventful Togliatti speech when the Italian communist leader sharply criticised Moscow, Julia Kenyeres prevented publication of the speech in all Hungarian papers for an entire week until *Szabad Nep* printed doctored fragments of the text. When Stalin, Molotov, Malenkov or Khrushchev made a speech, she personally and laboriously compared the original text with the translation word for word. Each year she spent her vacation in the USSR. Even during the peak of the Stalin cult no one could surpass her adoration for she had five different pictures of Stalin plus two statues of him in her office.

A third leading figure is Istvan Szirmai, a leading press chief of the Kadar regime. He also is an old communist, was formerly organizational secretary of the central committee and later became director of Magyar Radio. In 1953 he was arrested, although his brother-in-law was an AVO colonel. During the period of rehabilitation Szirmai was released and soon thereafter the colonel was arrested because of his alleged torture of rehabilitated prisoners. Szirmai, an Epicurean, likes pleasant western things, women, liquor. He always had several mistresses. He dressed well and frequently took himself abroad. After his release he became appropriately enough the director of the central state pawn shop. There followed a stint as editor-in-chief of a Party paper, and most recently president of the information office of the council of ministers. Contrary to many others, he knows exactly what it is all about. But using "doublethink" and the meager consolation of having no other choice he continues to serve the regime. He is the cynical type who realized that his personal fate is tied to that of the regime and accordingly clings rather desperately to the pleasant privileges accorded his position. He despises those who are serving under him and sacrifices those who are intellectually superior to him. He persecutes the dailies realizing perfectly well that he is wrong. He does not know a word of Russian, but *Pravda* is his official bible. Moreover, he is always on guard to defend himself against his unscrupulous opponents who are more skilled in "doublethink" than he is.

These then were the overlords of Hungarian propaganda at Radio Budapest, *Szabad Nep,* MTI. From this top level the word drifted downward to cover completely all manner of written and spoken word. Now we must look to the lower ranks of propagandists. Who devised, produced, and analyzed communist propaganda at the working level?

Step by step all able, talented, and honest men were screened out of the press and radio. The main requirement was no longer ability but rather political reliability, a suitable Party past, and unswerving devotion to the daily changing Party line.

The main bulk of these intellectual slaves consisted of three groups. The first was comprised of those who were long time pre-war communists, the second of those who were either converted to communism or bribed to work for it. The third and far the biggest group was composed of young persons who were either brought up or began their professional careers under communist rule.

As to the first segment, these men were almost in every case the directors or deputy directors of propaganda work from 1945 to 1949. After this date which coincided with the Rajk trial there began a permanent purge resulting in a constant struggle among the leading propagandists for position, influence, and higher income. Some of these men were former veterans of the Spanish Civil War and, accordingly, after the Rajk trial, having become tainted, they were summarily removed from their jobs. To fully understand the situation it should be noted that the press chiefs of the Foreign Ministry and of the Ministry of Interior were always former Spanish War fighters. They all vanished. In 1951 in connection with the arrest of Geza Losonczy, Janos Kadar, and Gyula Kallai, another well known and influential group disappeared from the scene. One could find only Muscovites in responsible positions, those who without hesitation followed every switch in the Party line.

Simultaneously with this process a new group emerged bit by bit from among those who had been schooled under communism or who had played renegades' roles in the other parties. There was a special university for journalism where selected young men, mainly Party members, found newspaper positions after one or two years of study. However, the "professors" were not journalists or editors, but Party ideologists or functionaries. They had to learn Russian, they were required to master every single fact about the history of communism and the USSR, but, in the majority of cases, they were not required to master the writing of articles. After this influx of new cadres the level of the press rapidly deteriorated. These newcomers, together with recruits directly from Party schools, played the role of informers, the "apparatchiks." These people were the capable watchdogs in every newspaper office, they denounced those who allegedly held revisionist or bourgeois views. Having direct access to the personnel chiefs they possessed a unique opportunity to destroy a man's possibility for promotion. Because of their general lack of ability these men naturally suffered from acute inferiority complexes and eagerly took revenge on their more talented colleagues. Certainly by these methods the Party deprived itself of the most valuable, most skillful persons. There is almost no really able journalist throughout the entire press of Hungary who by 1956 had not been punished, sacked, purged, arrested, or sentenced to long prison terms.

I might single out the case of Miklos Molnar, one of Hungary's ablest journalists, to reflect this general trend. Miklos Molnar worked on the staff of *Szabad Nep* from 1946 on as a cultural editor. Later he married the daughter of one of the most respected communist scholars, Laszlo Rudas. Everything went smoothly for him as an accepted critic. However, he was fired from *Szabad Nep* because be took a too severe sectarian line in cultural matters. He became one of the members of the editorial board of *Irodalmi Ujsag*, the literary weekly. Step by step Molnar became convinced of the utter sterility of communist propaganda, of the failure of the cultural revolution. Openly he began airing his dissenting view, and when Imre Nagy became prime minister in 1953 Molnar became one of his most ardent supporters. When the tide of political fortune turned against Nagy and he was ousted from office, Molnar did not become an opportunist. At a memorable reception in the Writers' Union there was heated debate between him and Mihaly Farkas, the notorious minister of defense who was later arrested. Farkas severly condemned the line of *Irodalmi Ujsag* threatening retaliation if it again published pessimistic poems or articles opposing the Party line. Next week, *Irodalmi Ujsag* published the now famous Tibor Dery article, praising the poem of Laszlo Benjamin which was the very poem severely criticized by Farkas and other Party leaders. At noon the day of publication Rakosi personally phoned Molnar, expressing his anger. Molnar calmly replied, "I do not agree with you, Comrade Rakosi." That was the first time that an editor openly disagreed with the Party chief. Everybody was breathlessly awaiting Molnar's arrest. The next day he was removed from his editorship because he "had lost the Party's confidence." But Molnar remained free, and he did not repent. He was sent as a student to the Lenin Institute. Just before the revolution he was named director of the Hungarian Institute in Rome. When the revolution broke out, Molnar wrote a final article in the last number of *Szabad Nep,* sharply refuting the charges hurled by *Pravda* that Hungary was in the throes of counter-revolution and defending the revolutionary character of the uprising. After the Soviet intervention, being threatened with arrest, he fled with his family to Yugoslavia. He was the first and for a long time the only Hungarian journalist who tried to take a stand against *Pravda,* the oracle of world communism.

The case of Miklos Molnar is not a unique one. There are many, many Hungarian ex-communists who have chosen his way after recognizing their mistakes, and who fought in the front ranks during the pre-revolutionary period as well as during the revolution itself. Later I shall speak in more detail about the revolt of the intellectual slaves against conformity, and against the oppression of Soviet domination.

All in all, we can say that the second group of those persons who were either reared under communism or became journalists after 1945, with the exception of a few "apparatchiks," became a completely lost asset to the Party.

As for those who were converted to communism or were bribed to work for them, the overall picture is less rosy. The very men, who for reasons of career betrayed their former allegiances and thus betrayed their past, became the most fervent and open admirers of communism. These men not so strangely were the first to collaborate with Kadar in November, 1956. Why were they more firmly tied to the regime than the young communists themselves? Their betrayal set in motion an unending and vicious circle for they were more hated than any other group in Hungary. Moreover, they had to prove their new allegiance, their reliability, their unshaken faith day after day.

They sank so deeply that later without any outside pressure, simply under the impact of events, these former non-communist renegades became the most reliable and most uncompromising pillars of the regime. In the lower ranks these neo-communists eagerly informed the police and the Party of every deviation. Camouflaging themselves as non-communist fellow travelers they tried to deceive the West and particularly those nations with socialist governments. They were the apostles of the ill-fated peace movements. Of the numerous examples, I would like to single out one which is perhaps the most degrading.

One is rarely so blessed with talents that he is able to hold ten jobs simultaneously. Well, in Hungary we have such an extraordinary man. He was at the same time chief editor of a weekly, deputy minister of culture, a deputy in Parliament, head of the university for journalism, deputy president of the Peace Council, general secretary of the People's Front, president of several other bodies, including a religious one, and even his wife was arts editor of an illustrated weekly. His name is Ernoe Mihalyfi and he is relatively well known abroad for he belonged to those exceptionally favored sons of the regime who were allowed to travel. This very busy gentleman, in spite of his numerous positions, always found time to make a trip every three months or so, representing Hungary at UNESCO meetings, at the UN, at the World Peace Council. It was a splendid life indeed, with three full salaries, three cars, several mistresses. All this might be surprising for Mihalyfi was not a professed communist. But as a "non-communist," Mr. Mihalyfi was the confidant of every communist leader from Rakosi to Kadar, with the exception of Nagy who despised him. This man, who before the war had been a member of the conservative Small-holder Party and editor of a daily paper, earned all this by denouncing to the Party literally everybody, including his best friends, his co-workers, his superiors, and subordinates. In the crucial period of the war between the Hungarian people and the Kremlin Mihalyfi chose the wisest solution. At the end of October he fled to Vienna as a refugee from the revolution and immediately after the 4th of November returned to Hungary, and with undisguised happiness flew into the arms of Kadar and Moscow. For this group a genuine democratic coalition would have meant political suicide, an end to a prosperous life. The brutal Soviet intervention rescued them and for the time being assured continuance of a luxurious but unenviable way of life.

There was never in the history of mankind such an intricately built, thoroughly prepared propaganda organization as under communist rule. Even Hitler's Germany had nowhere near such a vast and masterfully developed apparatus as the Soviet empire. The development and composition of the mass media served only one purpose: to promote communism, to accelerate the building of the new order and, last but not least, to sacrifice everything, truth, factual writing, honesty, morality to achieve the ultimate objectives of the Party. When we speak of Hungary, you must always bear in mind that the same has happened in the other Soviet-controlled countries, every national unit was only a part of a huge apparatus, physically and ideologically directed by Moscow.

We can follow step by step this process of control to get a comprehensive picture of the whole. First of all, in the Kremlin's textbook, news as such was extremely dangerous and contained explosive materials. The sole task of a big propaganda apparatus was to select, prepare, and distort the news and at the same time prevent the population by all possible means from getting the actual information. The news reported by TASS, Soviet official news agency, was the so-called general news. This category did not cause any specific substantive problems but to edit this TASS copy was a dangerous process. Everyone from the editorial directors to Party leaders had the possibility of comparing the tape sent by TASS and the copy edited by Hungarians. From time to time an unhappy paper was castigated or a news editor lost his job or even his liberty for unwisely cutting Soviet news. Everyone concerned kept a watchful eye on this and busily reported to the Party if anything, an important hint or an insignificant fact, was omitted from the translated text. So that towards the end papers published in full, completely devoid of change, the dreary lengthy speeches made by some Soviet leader or other.

At MTI a special desk prepared a so-called "confidential circular." This circular consisted of the controversial reports sent by western news agencies to which MTI subscribed, and the translations of important western press commentaries. This report was not published for the general public, but only in several hundred copies for the use of leading Party and Government functionaries. The editor was Julia Poll, a lifelong, Moscow-trained communist whose co-workers were absolutely reliable Party members. No one could enter this section except by special permission. Recipients received their "confidential circulars" in closed manila envelopes delivered by a special courier. Copies were prepared in a special room, where only the editor had permission to enter. Besides this daily bulletin of forty to fifty pages there was also a highly confidential report marked with an "X." It was prepared in only twelve copies and the recipients were the members of the Politbureau. For example, the tape-recorded Hungarian language broadcasts of BBC, the Voice of America, and Radio Free Europe were not published in the more general confidential circular but only in this edition. If a western paper wrote a critical editorial with personal remarks about Hungarian or Soviet leaders only the top Party leaders could read it. Then the Politbureau would instruct Radio Budapest or *Szabad Nep* to reply or to attack it. Their bulletins were sent several times daily by special AVO couriers to the central committee. In case of a very important event the director of MTI personally phoned Rakosi, Ernoe Geroe or Joseph Revai, the leading ideologist.

There was a special radio monitoring service consisting of twenty to thirty efficient translators. These men would listen to foreign broadcasts, make shorthand notes and then prepare bulletins. They could not see each other's material and they were under constant AVO surveillance and supervision.

This elaborate process was in reality a farce for in the end they harmed only themselves. The population was only theoretically deprived of the news. A majority of radio listeners regularly listened to western broadcasts. Of course, they were jammed, but with patience one could hear at least one news broadcast daily. So in point of fact only the backbone of the

Party, the middle-rank men, was kept in ignorance. At propaganda or Party meetings they were stunned to hear details of imperialist "lies" or "warmongering." There is no doubt but that hindsight reveals the scheme backfired completely. Even the "apparatchiks" did not know the facts, and consequently were not able to counteract western propaganda which was based on solid fact. The general public which officially professed total ignorance was completely informed about the most important events.

News editing itself was only the first step in the process. The second phase was involved in press comment. The trained columnists without need of special directives were always aware of their tasks of how to comment on an important Soviet declaration or speech. It was actually a ready made form one had to fill out since only dates and certain words had to be inserted. You could always find a dreary conformity. If Moscow proposed a new disarmament program, there was at hand the ready made mass of slogans: "The Soviet Union's new, unique contribution to consolidate and preserve world peace. It again proves the peace-loving intentions of the socialist camp. At the same time, the West is unable and disinclined to propose any serious or far reaching disarmament proposals." The text naturally varied slightly from time to time, but the basic principles were always the same. Moscow was always right, the West was always wrong or evil.

This method could not be applied in every single case. When there was a sudden, unexpected switch in Soviet policy, when something unexpected happened in world politics, the entire press was silent and waited for the golden words from *Pravda*. But the same silence often descended upon the news itself. If there was an American atomic explosion, and *Pravda* did not publicize it, the Hungarian press was silent and professed ignorance. When President Eisenhower made his "Atoms for Peace Proposal," *Szabad Nep* took three days before it published a distorted text based on the *Pravda* version.

There were also special instances when the satellite press preceded *Pravda* in commenting on the news. Take, for example, the Tito case. In the period between 1949 and 1954 the satellite press partly supplied Soviet papers with distorted information about Yugoslavia. Exile Yugoslav Cominform papers were published in Budapest, Prague, Bucharest, and Moscow. The Party set up a special section for concocting lies about Tito. Often the same article would appear several times in slightly altered form in every Hungarian communist newspaper. At MTI, editors had to plan when and where anti-Tito material would appear. If the news-wire did not put out something against Belgrade for a week, the editors were severely reprimanded. These materials consisted not of half-truths but almost completely of full-blown lies, and allegations without foundation.

Sometimes Moscow wanted to tell something through intermediaries. In that case, after a confidential message, *Szabad Nep* or some other satellite paper would be the first to publish the article. The Party leaders, Rakosi and the others, had special phones to Moscow. When they received an order in this respect, they instructed the agit-prop department of the Party, and, in turn, the editors were given their final orders.

Step by step the press and radio became a solemn oracle of the Party line without any originality, color, or life. It was very rare when Hungarian newspapermen were granted permission to travel. MTI had only one foreign correspondent in Paris. All other news dispatches were taken either from TASS or from other Soviet bloc sources. The Party never trusted journalists and only the loyal press "apparatchiks" were sent abroad.

The authorities by using a network of informers constantly kept tabs on the newsmen. In every newspaper office several informers or actual AVO employees worked as journalists. In the majority of cases it was not very hard to discover them as they were always conspicuous by their dilletantism and ignorance.

Besides the informers there were the direct agents of the AVO. These specially trained and selected men decided the fate of everyone concerned including the editors. The editor-in-chief was theoretically simply a servant of the Party and since he had higher and better contacts, he was to a useful degree above fear of these agents.

It was not at all surprising in the infrequent selection of foreign correspondents that the Party and AVO had the final word.

The editor would advance a nominee, but very often it was contradicted and persons were sent abroad who were unable to write a simple news story but enjoyed the full confidence of the inner circle. When the communist sponsored International Journalists Union held a meeting in Helsinki in 1956 the Hungarian delegation consisted of the leading Party editors, the leaders of the press section of the central committee, and certain other well known Party workers. The journalists were not asked their opinion, it was a matter decided by the communist authorities.

The same thing happened at the time of the Geneva conference. Men were sent who at the moment were favorite sons. Ability and knowledge were never decisive, political and security considerations governed exclusively.

Editors named from on high were responsible not to the readers or the staff but to the Party. This was due to the fact the state was the only publisher and since the Party leads the state it is only natural that the editors owed their allegiance to that body.

Coverage of news and editorial comment was determined not by practical considerations but by the needs of the Party. The so-called "pro domo" orders of the Party were sent weekly, sometimes daily, to the papers. It would be false to suppose that these were detailed instructions covering required articles. These circulars were confined to directives stating the tasks and duties in the industrial, agricultural or cultural fields. It was the task of the press to agitate for these objectives. There were, of course, some differences allowed in the style of the farm or youth papers but the basic principles were always laid down by the Party.

Sight should not be lost of the theory of half-truths the communist press used in its subtle distortion of facts. In addition to the silence surrounding important events, there were the open lies, and these techniques were very important weapons in the propaganda arsenal. Let me take as an example strikes and the economic situation in the West. The press always published in big headlines news about non-communist strike movements. When West Germany was swept by a wave of strikes, the Hungarian press naturally did not tell its readers that the basic cause of this was the unparalleled prosperity of the country. Commenting on the economic situation it would have been a cardinal crime to tell the true story. The papers published articles written by Soviets discussing only one side of the picture. You could read only percentages and decreases. When it was not possible to deny the upward trend of the economy then came the favorite slogan about a "temporary boom based on war preparations." At the same time columns on the "socialist camp" were filled with rosy descriptions of the new world where production and the standard of living were rising without interruption, where there were no strikes, and all was grand.

To treat the public as a child, was the guiding factor in this unique propaganda. Constantly repeating the old slogans, indoctrinating the readers day after day means that even those who know better tend to forget the real facts or make themselves forget. This is achieved by the comfortable method of stating that there is no objective truth. For if one innocent comrade stood up and stated his doubts he was told, "On the surface you are right, comrade, but don't you know that surface and substance do not coincide, the inner trends are the important ones." When he persisted he would be inundated by endless quotations from Marx, Stalin, and Lenin. And if he still remained unconvinced, which only rarely occurred, he became unreliable and risked imprisonment.

Communist propaganda campaigns are of interest. It is virtually impossible to recall how many different propaganda campaigns were started in Hungary during the course of one year. There was, for example, the campaign for the "peace loan." Annually the people were forced to donate to the state ten percent of their monthly wages. When it began in 1949, the State promised repayment in five years. The next year, however, the time limit for repayment was extended twenty years. Each year in September the press and radio began to shout the all too familiar slogans: "We are building a new world, you can see how infinitely better we live than in the past. We have built so many houses, so many factories from your loans. You give a loan to yourself, for everything is yours. But the state and the Party are magnanimous, for you have a chance to win huge sums on the state lottery."

After the publication of the government decree there appeared the usual stories about the happy workers who, listening to the Government and the Party, gladly give ten percent of their wages. After a few days the readers heard the customary announcement claiming that the population, as in previous years, again fulfilled the plan and gave even more money than the state requested.

The second regular annual propaganda drive was the celebration of Soviet-Hungarian friendship. Every year we celebrated a friendship month with the mighty Soviet Union. In every paper, on every wave length, this wonderful bond which tied together the two countries was praised.

Then came campaigns for youth, for a clean capital, every month we celebrated an anniversary either of the Party or of the Soviet Union. There was practically not a month went by when we did not have a chance for official joy and happiness.

All of this was naturally not mere propaganda for the sake of propaganda. It was a conscious well planned operation to make the masses forget their present misery and to indoctrinate the youth.

As to the political line it was clear from the outset that there could be no difference between Hungary and the Kremlin. But that was not all. There was also a thoroughly developed system of cooperation in the field of propaganda.

This cooperation had certain outstanding features. First of all, the bulk of the materials used by the press and radio came directly from Moscow. The main source of news was TASS. Besides this, MTI published several times weekly a collection of articles from Soviet newspapers. Moreover, the Soviet Information Agency issued special bulletins covering foreign countries. All these materials were forwarded to the press. Government press offices kept statistics of that portion of these releases used by the papers.

Newspapers had to make norm plans similar to every factory. There were daily, weekly, and monthly plans. You had to state how much Soviet material, anti-imperialist material, and people's democratic material your paper intended to use on any particular week and in any particular month.

So in fact editing meant filling and fulfilling norms and quotas. Every propaganda organ had a special Soviet department which regularly prepared material for publication. There was in addition the organ of the Soviet-Hungarian Friendship Society, a weekly which printed materials solely from Soviet sources on or about the USSR.

On the radio one could listen to Russian language lessons each day as well as reports about the Soviet Union; further, three times a week you had had the splendid possibility of listening to Radio Moscow's Hungarian broadcasts. All in all one may say that the bulk of printed material was either written by the Soviets themselves or supplied by them. The task of the press was to provide local color.

Every month selected trade union delegations, peasant groups, worker groups, women's delegations visited the USSR and after their return the papers published their accounts of the marvellous Soviet life under the headlines: "Meeting with Soviet people," "Two wonderful weeks in the Soviet Union," "An unforgettable journey," "Dreams coming true."

Press propaganda had to follow every switch of Kremlin policy. With the exception of the above mentioned special cases, Hungary always awaited the voice of Moscow before commenting on any important western diplomatic move or international event. I still remember how MTI awaited the word from Moscow on important events. In February 1950 the Soviet-Chinese agreement was signed and almost immediately western radio reported this fact. But in Hungary everyone awaited the TASS announcement. TASS finally began to cable the material twenty four hours later. Morning papers were two hours late and subscribers never did receive their copies. But this was not important for only one thing mattered. No political mistake was made. It often happened that copies of the papers were on the street only late in the morning because of delayed TASS cables.

The editor in chief at MTI held special lectures for new staff members explaining that one must not trust western news agencies, since they cable provocative and false stories designed to trap good socialists, thus one can rely only on TASS. For a long time the press published western dispatches only when they were quoted by TASS or by Soviet papers.

The Abortive Return

In June 1953, four months after the death of Joseph Stalin, Imre Nagy formed his first government and from this date Hungarians count the period of "thaw." The same press which for years had repeated Moscow's voice began to destroy the old and thoroughly rotten principles of Stalinism. It was like awakening from a nightmare. I was in prison at the time of the death of Stalin and during the formation of the Nagy cabinet. When I was set free in September 1953 my first impulse was to reread the papers. It was a thrilling and unique experience to observe step by step the changing tone of the press. It was only the beginning, but in fact the intellectual and spiritual preparation of the October Revolution began at this point.

From June 1953 we lived in a period of sudden switches, dramatic upheavals, intricate and complicated political battles. Looking back there is no doubt but that the immense majority of the former intellectual slaves had revolted against the physical and mental oppression of the Soviet communist strait jacket.

Breaking the ice of Stalinism was a slow and dangerous operation. The first period ran from June 1953 to early in 1955. During Nagy's premiership a special government press office was set up under the leadership of Zoltan Szanto and Miklos Vasarhelyi, both of whom were deported to Rumania together with Nagy by the Soviets in November 1956. This office was the focus of the ideological battle against Stalinism. However, the Party press department existed simultaneously. This group played Rakosi's cards. While the two bodies clandestinely waged a bitter struggle, the press slowly began to slip out of the hands of the Party bureaucrats. The "apparatchiks" were increasingly isolated and real journalists began to gain a certain influence.

For the first time since 1948 the press again assumed a measure of popularity. People once more read newspapers. At the outset the change was hardly perceptible for the average reader. When *Irodalmi Ujsag,* the famous standard bearer of liberalization, was started as a bimonthly in 1954 it did not sell well. The most important factor was the rapid change that took place in the political outlook of writers and journalists. They were the most enthusiastic followers of Nagy largely because they began to recognize the basic failure of communism.

There was a revolt at *Szabad Nep,* the Party propaganda stronghold, in 1954. At a stormy Party meeting almost every leading communist journalist including the majority of the members of *Szabad Nep's* editorial board delivered a slashing attack on Party leadership, condemning it for sabotaging Nagy's policy and demanding a complete break with the past. A few days later the same happened at Magyar Radio and at the other leading newspapers. The top directors of the propaganda apparatus, the untouchable upper class, was fiercely attacked.

The change was less marked, however, in the press itself, although it was recognizable. *Szabad Nep* published many stories exposing the stupid merciless persecution of individuals by Party bureaucrats together with scandals in the higher Party circles.

As to the personal side, it would be a separate story to tell of the metamorphosis of the intellectuals, who did understand their responsibility toward the vices of the past, who wanted to make a clean breast of it, and who, for their part, sincerely broke with the past and solemnly swore "never again."

The honeymoon did not last long. The fermentors of dissent at *Szabad Nep* were removed and severely punished. The Party had lost an intellectual elite, but had won a temporary victory. When Malenkov fell from on high, it was the sign that the new course was doomed too, and by February 1955 there were definite signs warning the public that Rakosi would strike back with a smashing blow directed against the Nagy group and its supporters. The blow fell in March and the curtain of silence descended once more. The most outspoken critics were expelled from the Party. At *Szabad Nep* alone twelve leading journalists were dismissed and new Party commissars were put in charge of press work. The government press office was dissolved. Party functionaries eagerly accepted the mantle of revenge and a new purge began.

The purge was short and unbloody, but it was enough to crush scores of talented newsmen replacing them with Party hacks. The times of purge had changed and those affected were not threatened by direct physical annihilation, but they were not allowed to write or to work as journalists or even as free lancers. But the purged this time did not bend the knee before Rakosi. Nor did the authors. *Irodalmi Ujsag,* as the *enfant terrible* of the literary world, held aloft the banner and waged an effective rear guard action against Rakosi. In the summer of 1955 the crucial hour came. For the first time in the history of communist Hungary a paper was confiscated by the police. This unheard of occurrence was a sensation and the few thousands copies which had already been sold created a black market of its own where the prices of the confiscated edition reached near fantastic levels.

To protest against this new repressive measure seventy eight outstanding intellectuals, writers, journalists, actors, musicians, composers, and sculptors presented a memorandum to the Party demanding spiritual freedom and rehabilitation of their discredited colleagues. The Party retaliated in December 1955 by condemning the "revisionist, anti-Marxist" views held by these men and singled out leading communist writers and journalists like Tibor Dery, Gyula Hay, Zoltan Zelk, Tibor Meray, Tamas Aczel, and others for attack.

The Party then organized a propaganda campaign against the writers and journalists. Meetings were held in factories where Party functionaries demanded severe punishment and the press was forced to publish articles attacking Nagy and his followers, who were meanwhile removed from the Party.

Nevertheless, everyone in Hungary felt that Rakosi and the Kremlin had won only a battle but certainly had not won the war. It was obvious that the intellectuals were supported in their courageous struggle by the entire population. Poems of resistance were copied and passed from hand to hand. Thousands knew the text of the intellectuals' memorandum.

The Twentieth Congress of the Soviet Communist Party in February 1956 played a vital role in the anti-Stalinist "thaw" in Hungary. The open attack on Stalin and his debunking in Khrushchev's secret speech gave a tremendous spurt to the demands of the intellectuals, the youth and the masses. The congress and its aftermath struck hard at the Party bureaucrats and die-hards. At the same time rebellious intellectuals and students began an offensive for the dismissal of Rakosi and for the complete rehabilitation of Imre Nagy.

Bit by bit the press regained courage and some of its former energy in attacking the past and present, unmasking the horrors of the regime. The beginnings were made in cautious form. There was a pretext at hand, the Twentieth Congress. This was the "trojan horse" of satellite liberalization. With the exception of the Party papers almost all other publications and last but not least the radio literally flooded the public with articles and commentaries emphasizing the historic importance of this congress. *Irodalmi Ujsag* and *Beke es Szabadsag*, both weeklies, were in the first ranks of the assault.

This ideological struggle was coupled with practical political steps, including the creation of the highly vocal Petoefi Circle. After years of silence it was for communist Hungary a wonderful and respected intellectual forum for the exchange of opinions.

Nights at the Petoefi circle were literally sensations in Hungary. The historians, economists, agricultural specialists, held their meetings and the press reported accounts of the meetings prominently. Meanwhile, the Stalinist old guard waged a desperate fight against the irresistible demands, trying to keep Rakosi in power. On the night of May 27, 1956 a momentous meeting of the Petoefi circle was held in the Budapest Officers' Club. Hours before opening not only the building but the neighboring streets were overflowing with enthusiastic listeners. From 5 P.M. to 4 A.M. Hungary's leading writers and journalists in a tense atmosphere made sharp attacks on the Party leadership, demanding political liberalization, freedom of culture, dismissal of Rakosi, rehabilitation of Rajk and Nagy. The members of the central committee present tried unsuccessfully to defend

solidarity and unity had become a real factor. And this is something indeed.

Human solidarity increased understanding for those who had
different opinions and whose viewpoints were somewhat contrary. People had learned to hate the lasting terrorism, the internal struggles and wars, and a great desire for peace filled their
souls. Extreme nationalism lost the footing it formerly enjoyed,
revisionist aspirations to regain lost territories based on revenge
and violence disappeared. The Hungarian nation wants to live
in peace and freedom with all of its neighbors in the Danube
basin. People long for a solution permitting contact with adjoining nations without passports or tariff controls; they long
for close ties with states organized on the basis of the human
right of freedom with borders becoming nothing but symbols,
and after a temporary era of a central European bloc similar to
the Benelux States, the idea of the United States of Europe
should gradually develop.

Moreover, certain barriers crumbled even with the Church.
The members of different orders who barely knew members of
other communities, their spirit and their rules, met each other
in deportation and prison, got to know each other, thought less
about differences than about their common vocation and fate
and felt more genuine solidarity than ever before. During the
years before the dissolution of the orders, the superiors of these
various Church bodies met at conferences and acted in close
cooperation. And when some of the members of religious orders
who were transferred into dioceses mingled with diocesan
priests, former existing differences disappeared and seemed ridiculous. And when diocesan priests had only the laity's help
and aid to rely upon in both the spiritual and financial sphere,
they included laymen more in their work and the faithful knew,
esteemed, and loved their priests more than before. Many many
friends were made especially among workers by priests and
monks laboring in their ranks. During Easter 1956, one worker
was heard to ask a priest who labored at his side and who had
been forbidden by the regime to exercise his priestly functions,
"May I see you tomorrow?"

"Of course," said the priest, "you are perfectly welcome."

the top leadership, but the audience sneered at them. It was doubtless to date the most powerful demonstration in post-war Hungarian history for democracy, freedom and a decent life.

Three days later Rakosi made a desperate, final attempt to save the situation. Having just returned from Moscow he and Geroe called together the central committee, sharply condemned the bourgeois demagogic demands of the Petoefi circle and forced the committee to issue a resolution criticizing the Petoefi circle. They particularly singled out Imre Nagy and his associates for attack. The population, fearful of the past, awaited the arrest of these men. Actually, Rakosi and his son-in-law, AVO chief, General Istvan Dekany planned to arrest 402 intellectuals, army officers, youth leaders, and only last minute Soviet intervention prevented it. This final tactical victory of Rakosi lasted only six weeks. On July 18, in the presence of Mikoyan, Rakosi was fired and Ernoe Geroe was promoted to the coveted post of Party first secretary. At the same time the Politbureau went through a shakeup. Kadar, Revai, the ideological dictator, and former social democrat now a hated renegade, Gyorgy Marosan, became members of the highest Party body.

From this date forward there was no barrier which could have halted the attack by the writers, students, and journalists. Papers closed their ranks and with the exception of *Szabad Nep* a concerted drive against Stalinist communism began. The Writers' Congress was a new occasion for an all out attack. Now nearly everyone was demanding the posthumous rehabilitation of Rajk and the complete rehabilitation of Imre Nagy and his political platform of national communism.

There were signs before October that the laboriously built edifice of Party control and censorship was crumbling at its foundation for the writers and journalists themselves were revolting against Party tyranny. Party leaders were unable to grapple successfully with the intellectually superior writers and journalists. Day by day there appeared the passionate poems, articles, stories of injustice, vice, corruption all demanding punishment of those responsible for this lost decade.

The eerie but thrilling Rajk reburial was the prelude to the final prerevolutionary move. The day following the funeral a new outspoken weekly, the *Hetfoei Hirlap,* appeared publishing articles written by men standing close to Nagy or reaching the last steps of rehabilitation. It was the first paper which openly attacked Matyas Rakosi. At this time *Irodalmi Ujsag* published a satire by Gyula Hay on Party functionaries with the result that other papers followed suit. Meanwhile, to take the play from this inner and outer Party opposition, Geroe decided to arrest Mihaly Farkas, former minister of defense and chief of the AVO, together with his son, an AVO colonel, and other high ranking security officers. But public opinion demanded an open trial, the granting of which could have been equal to a condemnation not only of Rakosi but of Geroe himself. Miklos Gimes, a well known communist journalist and former member of the editorial board of *Szabad Nep,* wrote an extremely sharp article which tore to pieces the weak arguments of the Party leadership in this and other issues.

Freedom and After

During the revolution even the screened loyal staff of *Szabad Nep* revolted against the leadership. All papers faced the facts of the uprising and accepted Imre Nagy as the new prime minister.

During the short lived revolutionary period from October 30 to November 4, 1956 not less than seventeen completely different papers were published, among them new ones, like *Nepszava* (social democratic), *Kis Ujsag* (smallholder), *Fueggetlenseg* (organ of the Dudas group), *Magyar Vilag* (independent), *Igazsag* (revolutionary youth), even the newly organized Socialist Workers' Party (communist) had its *Nepszabadsag.*

This lively and colorful press was one of the chief weapons of the revolutionary government. Unfortunately, because of the fluctuating situation, the papers were read only by Budapest readers and did not generally reach the countryside. Nevertheless, the revolutionary press had a tremendous influence and audience and every paper was sold out in minutes.

The Party-made journalists suddenly disappeared from the

scene. Newspapermen, who for years had been forced into silence, began to write. Old and new journalists, Catholics and
communists, all who had turned against Moscow had a place
and opportunity to write. This brief thrilling period lasted
only four days but it was enough to show how a genuine free
press would have been born in Hungary had Moscow not
crushed the emerging democracy.

After many years of silence the papers had had a unique
opportunity to unmask bribery, corruption, and cruelties committed by AVO men. Hungarians will never forget the reports
telling of Rakosi's 40,000 forints monthly earnings, his luxurious villa, and the torture chambers of secret AVO prisons. No
one directed journalists what and how to write, they followed
nothing but their consciences.

A review of the revolutionary press refutes the Kadar regime's
arguments about "counter-revolution." These papers differed
in political outlook and aims, but they were in spontaneous
and fundamental agreement in deciding to preserve certain
features of post-war Hungary, for example, land reform, and
nationalization of basic industries. No paper made a campaign
for the return of the old pre-war feudal type aristocracy, no
paper advocated a fascist program. Naturally, there were right
wing papers, for example, the *Fueggetlenseg*. But at the same
time, in the same building the communists edited *Nepszabadsag*. There was a real competition for readers. Later, perhaps,
hard financial realities would have forced a number of papers
to cease publication but even this would not have altered the
fact that it was a genuinely free democratic press.

Let us take for example *Igazsag*. This paper was the authentic
publication of the revolutionary youth. Its editors fought at
Killian barracks and sent reports from the battleground to the
desk. They were young students, communist and non-communist journalists, enthusiastic followers of Imre Nagy, sincere
social democrats. Not one of them dreamed of the return of the
old days and they were equally determined to fight against both
Stalinism and foreign domination.

After the 4th of November the picture changed fundamen-
tally once again. A few days after the fourth all journalists and

writers solemnly took an oath not to write under the new oppressive regime. *Nepszabadsag*, official Party paper, was no longer edited by its former editors who published it during the revolution. They had gone into the first ranks of the intellectual resistance. The paper now appeared under the pens of Party hack writers, by those who disappeared or were fired during the revolution. *Nepszabadsag* was and is the most despised newspaper in the history of the Hungarian press. The people burned it, and threw it away.

Towards the end of November there reappeared *Nepakarat*, organ of the trade unions. Shortly before Christmas *Esti Hirlap*, a former "independent political daily" came into being. Besides these three dailies several weeklies and periodicals had reappeared following the initial consolidation of the Kadar regime.

Nevertheless, this press was similar to the pre-revolutionary press. The Party once and for all was convinced that its most dangerous adversaries are and were the journalists and recognized the tremendous importance of a free press. Therefore, Kadar conducted a ruthless campaign against journalists and writers. Those very journalists who before October and during the revolution were the standard-bearers of democratization were forced to hide in the underground or to flee. Former leading communist pressmen like Miklos Gimes, Pal Loecsei, Sandor Novobaczky, Miklos Vasarhelyi and many others were either imprisoned or deported. Many outstanding intellectuals fled abroad to escape the fate of their friends and comrades in arms.

In the first stages of the post-revolutionary period it was not easy for Kadar to wipe out immediately all traces of the former freedom. *Nepakarat*, the trade union paper, which sometimes sharply and outspokenly criticized Kadar's policy and supported the concept and actions of workers' councils was sold out in hours and was widely read.

There were debates and discussions in Party and regime circles about the press and radio. There was one school which advocated that the mere fact that papers were published helped to consolidate the situation for Kadar. The other faction, and this view carried, flatly stated: we must strictly control the press for October showed the fatal consequences of relative press freedom.

The turning point in control was the *Pravda*-Tito dispute. Budapest papers published the arguments of both sides. A number of the staff at *Nepszabadsag* wanted to reply to *Pravda*. Kadar flatly refused to permit this. Whereupon there took place the first strike in the history of the Hungarian communist press. The anti-*Pravda* group refused to work and accordingly *Nepszabadsag* was unable to appear the next day. For the next week the paper was put out by Party hands and pseudo-journalists. Toward the end of December several former contributors returned to their desks and tried to turn out a popular paper printing big headlines, saucy pictures, sex, and crime stories. A few days later Kadar fiercely attacked the paper for this effort and as a result *Nepszabadsag* today is an odd compromise between *Pravda* and a western style evening daily.

Nepakarat, having been threatened with severe punishment because it questioned some aspects of the regime's policy, has become a well disciplined regime paper. Several journalists, who protested against this reimposition of controls, were either fired or fled to Yugoslavia.

Just before Christmas *Esti Hirlap* was founded as a non-party newspaper. It was born during the temporary lull when there were still talks between Kadar and representatives of other parties. Its staff consisted mainly of non-communist or formerly jailed journalists. The editors tried to present a non-political informative newspaper. It was very popular and sold well. After a few days, however, the regime began to exert pressure on the paper and quickly transformed it into a Kadar organ.

Actually within a matter of weeks following the Soviet crackdown the press had lost even the remnants of a fictitious liberty. At first it served the interests of Kadar to permit sharp attacks against Rakosi and his reign. But since January 1957, coincidental with wiping out of the opposition, the press and radio have become once more regime weapons in trying to turn back the clock, to return to Stalinist methods and communism.

Bit by bit many of the former directors of communist propaganda returned to their posts. Today in the radio and in the papers we find the same figures who were leaders in the darkest

Rakosi days. The government press office and the press department at Party headquarters again control all newspapers. They do not permit any criticism of the regime and the main task of the dailies is to attack "counter-revolution and imperialism."

At the same time there are ruthless and permanent purges among the intellectuals. About 400 journalists were removed from their jobs, and journalists' and writers' unions were banned. The Party set up a special commission to investigate what each journalist did during the revolution. At *Esti Hirlap* seven journalists were removed, at Magyar Radio about sixty newspapermen and commentators were similarly fired on short notice. Simultaneously their places were filled with reliable former AVO men and old Party functionaries. At MTI, an ex-Army political colonel was named news editor, at the Radio, a former police colonel became propaganda boss.

The control of the press is even more severe today than in the heyday of Stalinism. The same propaganda methods are applied in a country where only two years ago the whole structure of communism was shattered by a revolution which was supported by the entire nation. It is incredible but it is true. Never underestimate the resilience of Party organizational controls.

There are, however, some important new features. Now everyone realizes that the communist press and radio have nothing in common with the truth and these media are simple factories of lies. Today there are no able intellectual slaves left to the regime. The elite of former communists are either in prison or abroad or refuse to write. The remainder represent the compromised, the traitors, the cowards. The Party has undoubtedly lost its intellectual elite and I doubt seriously if a new generation will provide candidates since communism as a philosophic force is forever dead in Hungary.

So ends at least for the time being the sad story of the Hungarian media. But it proves to the whole world that it is impossible to stifle the ferment of ideas, to lead astray for long the youth and intellectuals of a nation, that sooner or later, the unwitting accomplices of a monstrous inhuman regime will awaken and break again and again the bonds of tyranny of which communism is a willing handmaiden.

Music and Communism

BY PETER BUDAI

Communism and music may seem a paradox. In fact, they are, but only in so far as one takes into consideration their very essence. Music is an art of expressing deeply human feelings and thoughts, while communism is a doctrine and a practice to suppress, avoid, eliminate every sort of special feeling and thought. Communism, on the other hand, as a system of government existing throughout the Soviet bloc, has been greatly interested in musical affairs, just as in any other field of cultural life, sponsoring the so-called progressive, and denouncing so-called hostile trends in music, on the basis of its Machiavellian policies.

"Music is a state affair," was the *vade mecum* of every communist functionary involved in the musical life of Hungary during most of the past decade. Music as a state affair dates in Hungary from 1948. There were, of course, some patterns to be copied in Nazi Germany and Soviet Russia. Both Hitler and Stalin were of the opinion that music, like any other type of art or literature, is nothing but a technique to increase political activity, or to deepen and to broaden the adherence and enthusiasm of the masses.

* Peter Budai is a former drama and music critic for the communist controlled daily, *Magyar Nemzet*.

Nineteen forty-eight marked, as communist terminology usually had it, "the year of the turning" or in other words the date when the Hungarian Communist Party took over complete control of the country. Thus, when surveying musical developments in the last decade in Hungary, we have to differentiate between those years before and those years after this turning point.

Music and communism obviously had contact both before and after this date of takeover, but the nature of the contact was different. After the liberation of Hungary by Soviet divisions in 1945, the Communist Party led by Rakosi displayed an extremely liberal and lenient attitude toward music as well as toward the other cultural fields. The line changed in 1949 after power had been successfully seized by the Party. Thus the period before the "year of the turning" might be characterized simply as a prelude to what was to happen later.

Prelude

.Let us first look briefly into the notes of this prelude of communist musical policy. To get a clear picture, I had better mention in advance that the Soviets and their communist forerunners in 1945 had to face a special situation as regards music and musical life in Hungary. Hungarian music and musicians were never on the whole influenced by fascist trends. That is why in 1945 nothing could be destroyed as a remnant of nazi days. On the contrary, there existed a high-level of musical culture with a considerable tradition, good orchestras, numerous first rank artists, and a musical public opinion which had been used to European horizons.

The Party, aiming at a maximum influence on cultural patterns, could do nothing but show a friendly face and declare its readiness to assist in the reconstruction of Hungarian musical life. Hence the liberal programs of the opera and concert seasons as well as that of the musical broadcasts over the radio during that early period. The Budapest Opera House, for example, started the postwar era by reintroducing such modern European musical pieces as Stravinsky's "Petroushka," then

Darius Milhaud's "French Salad," Benjamin Britten's "Peter Grimes" and also Stravinsky's "Play at Cards." Moreover, the Budapest Opera House performed the premiere of a forbidden piece, which had never been given before on any Hungarian stage, Bela Bartok's famous ballet, "The Miraculous Mandarin." A genuine small scale renaissance of Hungarian musical life flourished in those days with the appearance of such famous guest artists as Yehudi Menuhin, Georg Sebastian, Erich Kleber, Otto Klemperer and with Mihaly Szekely and Sandor Sved on the opera stage, both of whom returned from their American tours in order to take part in this musical revival.

A very fruitful collaboration between Hungarian musicians and their American, English, and French colleagues took place, the result of which was a number of Hungarian concerts and visits abroad while many a foreign masterpiece was performed in Hungary. It was during this period that some outstanding Hungarian composers of the second generation, that is after Bartok and Zoltan Kodaly, had the opportunity to make their mark by successful performance of their works. Laszlo Lajtha in France and Sandor Veress in England were typical of these bright new names.

The Communist Party meanwhile was very busy organizing its ranks, training its cadres in the musical field and patiently waiting. During this period the activities of the Party in the musical field concentrated on popularizing Soviet music. The communist sponsored mass-organization, the Hungarian-Soviet Friendship Society, which enjoyed no mass support, tried to produce new musical pieces, published Soviet authors and composers and organized concerts with Soviet participants. One had to go to some of these concerts if he wished to avoid being charged with a "hostile attitude" toward the liberators, and through such devices the communists managed to mobilize some Hungarian artists and musicians.

One should never forget that in those times of the late forties and under those circumstances the Communist Party itself, and the leading communists personally, appeared as very tolerant partners, as the loyal opposition to some "decaying trends" in European culture. They constantly spoke out for a new "popular realism" as the Party put it.

In Hungary, few musicians heard the news announcement that in Leningrad comrade Zhdanov had spoken about musical questions and a new era of intolerance had been inaugurated. They had to wait a few months until communist control of Hungarian political life was completed and then the new era in Hungary also began. Penetration of musical life coincided, of course, with the political developments which resulted in complete communist rule over Hungary's social, economic, and spiritual life. Seizure and control obviously had their projections in the musical sphere. After proper preparation, the Party had begun its attack. This period lasted more than five years, five years of a stubborn, cruel, and brutal assault against everything human, national, outspoken or modern. The theme was always the same; the forms changed, developed and returned again. Hungarian musicians had a term from their nomenclature for describing musical life from 1948 to 1958: it was called variations on a theme by comrade Zhdanov.

With communists, it is always of first importance to build an organization. This they did in the summer of 1949 after the Rajk trial and the local council elections which they forced through immediately, exploiting the atmosphere of countrywide shock caused by the revelations of the mass show trial. As for the musical field, the Party quickly pushed its men into the key posts. In Radio Budapest, for instance, after the arrest of the former vice-premier Paul Justus (one of Rajk's immediate code-fendants) the Party delegated Istvan Szirmai, a Party central committee department chief, as director. The former opera director, Pal Komaromy, was placed under constant attack and criticism and soon resigned. The country's only concert manager company had been nationalized and a Party delegate was put at the top. This process repeated itself in the music publishing houses as well. According to typical communist doctrine concerning Party tactics, in those places where there was no actual key post to be taken over, the Party created one and the state apparatus filled it. Very soon at this rate offices, institutions and organizations found their leading posts occupied by a communist, or some fellow traveler. It must be admitted that the thoroughness of the communist-sponsored reorganization of Hungarian musical life left no untouched areas, it covered the whole. It would be very practical for us to see just how such an organization grows, as well as to examine its form and its aims.

Allegro

The core of the organization, as in all other things under communism, had to be the Party center itself, or in the case of music, the cultural department of the central committee. Here the general Leninist outline of "what is to be done" plus all important personnel affairs were handled; directions were given to the second echelon office, which was the Ministry for Public Education then headed by the notorious Joseph Revai, the Stalinist ideologist. The ministry's musical department was led by a former brother-in-law of Rakosi, Miklos Coillag, who before the war had worked in a country theater. This man had a dictator's authority and power over Hungary's entire musical life. His department controlled all of the musical organizations, orchestras, theaters, the films, concerts, as well as the education of young artists, involving such famous old institutes as the Budapest Academy of Music founded by Franz Liszt. The organizational system consisted of the appointment of an overseer for each area (in the majority of cases those responsible were renowned for their lack of any musical education and it was agreed that their general level of knowledge did not reach that of the average moviegoer). The leaders of the different musical institutions, including the State Opera House, had to make long and detailed periodic reports to the responsible communist overlords. The artists were also obliged to follow the directives given by the multitude of ministerial representatives. It became a tragic joke in Budapest musical circles that Zoltan Kodaly had to submit his new works for censorship before printing or performance to one of his former pupils who, not long before, had attended Kodaly's lectures at the Academy.

The musical hierarchy which had been built to make possible complete Party control really acted rather dialectically in that this organization of Party thought-control later became that of rebelling thought, that of the anti-communist revolt. But this belongs to another chapter of our history. The present topic treats of musical organizations and what the Communist Party did with them.

Since the most important factor in musical life was the composers, their association was planned to be the vanguard of communist penetration into Hungarian culture. The Hungarian Composers' Association has been from its foundation to the present communist-controlled. In its leadership the Party always maintained a majority unlike the membership which, of course, was constantly in opposition. From the beginning, the political officer of this Association was Ferenc Szabo, a multiple Kossuth prize winner and parliamentarian, as well as a central committee member. A former Moscow emigrant, Szabo appeared in Budapest in 1945 wearing a Soviet major's uniform. While a close friend of Rakosi as well as other leaders, Szabo was completely isolated from the main body of Hungarian composers and musicians and knew no other methods but force and threat. Being himself a composer, and objectively not a bad one, he used his post and his powers to suppress the works of others more talented than he. As a Party secretary of the association, Szabo never missed an occasion to brand Endre Szervansky, Pal Jardanyi, and others, among the best men of Hungarian music today as "right wing" and as "reactionaries" in his attempts to challenge their political opposition as well as to crush them as competitors.

The second important musical institution, also based upon the communist pattern, has been and is the music foundation, which, like the analogous literature foundation and the fine arts foundation, held total control over musicians' financial affairs. This institution had been ostensibly developed as a welfare organization, a salvation for every artist who had to face grim financial problems. In reality, the organization secured the complete subordination of the artists, who might have been made rich men as well as beggars by a simple order from the Party or from the ministry. These orders, of course, matched the attitude of the composer. If it was positive, the fees paid the composer or musician showed a favorable upward trend; if the attitude was negative, payments decreased or were totally absent. Apart from this practice, there had been introduced the system of "premiums." Certain politically leading composers, without respect for their creative activities as such, received a stipend amounting to 100,000 forints per year, an enormous sum—considering the normal annual income range between 12,000 and 18,000 forints—while others, far more gifted and productive, received but two or three thousand forints.

To the ministry-directed and Party-supervised musical life belonged the system of "state tasks." It was called a "state task" since it involved the mobilization of composers in order to write cantatas and oratoria in praise of Stalin, Rakosi, the Red Army, the 4th of April (Hungary's liberation day) and other such stirring communist feast days. If a composer fulfilled one of these "tasks," whether on a rather low artistic level or not, he received a tremendous fee. Thus in 1949 Pal Kadosa composed one of the most all time expensive Hungarian musical pieces entitled "The Oath of Stalin." This system of rewarding artists led to a partial corruption of the composers, since this was the only way for musicians to overcome financial difficulties. Let me underline that in those days any other field of remuneration such as foreign publishing royalties, phonograph record sales abroad, etc., had already been shut off.

But there were other means of control of musical life. I might mention the use of passports or, to be more accurate, the nearly complete suspension of travel abroad; the prohibition of any kind of contemporary music except Soviet; the elimination of all modern concepts such as are found in Stravinsky's works, as well as the banning of all west European composers from Debussy to Britten, who, however much he might have been praised as a "peace fighter," his "Peter Grimes" was nonetheless purged from the Budapest opera program. All this was nothing but the administration of the Iron Curtain policy applied to music.

The Question of Principles

How did the Hungarian regime translate the Zhdanovian cultural policy? Zhdanov stressed the importance of what is national in music. He, of course, meant Soviet music, not that of the satellites. For the satellite nations it was a nationalist deviation to maintain their special musical mother tongue, to tell their own national legends.

Here is a characteristic example. Bela Bartok was very popular among Hungarian music lovers. His three works for the stage "Bluebeard's Castle," "The Wooden Prince," and "The Miraculous Mandarin" were included in many Budapest repertoires. His concertos "Music for Strings" and "Divertimento" were consistently among the most popular pieces of the concert season. In 1949 there came to Hungary a man from Russia. It was stated he was a composer. However, his name Choulaki was not recognized in musical circles. Yet this name became notorious in the recent history of Hungarian music. Comrade Choulaki brought authority with him not from Soviet composers, but from the Communist Party to supply Hungarian cultural leaders with direction. He fulfilled this task. As a first step, he went to the broadcasting studios in Budapest where he listened to recordings of contemporary Hungarian music. Then he announced his views concerning this music. "Bartok is cosmopolitan and decadent, in his early works he is a narodnik (nationalist)." Choulaki summed it up like this, "Bartok nje otchin charosh" which means that Bartok is not very good. If this had been a private opinion of a Soviet comrade, Hungarian communist leaders would have also accepted it, but it was far more, it was an official declaration that outlawed Hungary's greatest musical brain in his own country. Ferenc Szabo, Miklos Csillag, and others including Istvan Szirmai, who was then Radio chief, later to become Kadar's press minister, cheered. From that moment on, Bartok's works disappeared from radio programs. The "Mandarin" was purged and never again performed. One year later a tremendous fight was necessary before permission was received for a solemn Bartok memorial concert on the fifth anniversary of his death.

So it was with Bartok and the same fate awaited the majority of Hungary's modern and esteemed composers. Sandor Veress, who had earlier migrated to Switzerland was, of course, prohibited, as was Laszlo Lajtha, the modernist composer, whose pieces were so loved in Paris. There was, however, a rather sizeable number of established musicians of the "second rank" after Kodaly and Bartok who faced a grim alternative: either they pretended goodwill and thus were allowed to remain composers, or they tried to oppose control and therein risked silence. Thus with Hungarian composers, one group *contre coeur,* one group with sincere socialist beliefs, both starting a new life as composers trying to reach a synthesis between the new esthetic requirements of the Party and their own endogenous musical conceptions.

Let us view these "esthetic" requirements of the "leading Soviet people."

The underlying basis for the esthetic requirements of the Soviets was the then recently inaugurated cold war policy, according to which music had to serve as a political weapon, constantly stressing the superiority of the socialist system. Thus western trends were prohibited and branded as decadent, cosmopolitan, and anti-democratic. The atonal music of Schoenberg or Alban Berg was detested as well as the other European musical advances as reflected in Honegger or Hindemith. Even Wagner was analyzed by the Communist Party organ *Szabad Nep* as a spiritual forerunner of nazi fascism. What remained the reader asks? There remained a part of classical music which was found popular and simple enough "to raise the cultural level of the masses." Plus, of course, every single piece of the Russian masters from Glinka to the military marches by Novikov or Alexandrov.

As for new musical works, composers faced harsh criticism. The hardness did not rest in unobtainable requirements, on the contrary, absence of transition in a musical piece from the basic tune, for instance from C major, made it more acceptable. The less harmonies were altered, the better. The less phantasy in music, the better. What was, on the other hand, extremely important was the optimistic ending, the fanfare "crowning" the last movement. "To what extent does this music mobilize the masses?" This question must always be answered. So a special favor was granted to certain musical forms, first of all, to those with choir. Solemn cantatas, songs of heavy praise, patriotic oratoria were preferred by the regime to those forms which could not assemble musical "mobilization" as in the case of sonatas, symphonies, string arrangements and piano pieces. During a plenary session of a 1951 communist plenum connected with first performances of new pieces of Hungarian composers, a very sharp debate took place between the Party representatives led by the notorious Ferenc Szabo and the opposing majority, which had been branded by Szabo as "the Divertimentists" with sarcastic allusion to their favorite form, the "non-political" Divertimento.

The Soviet Union, as usual, sent her delegates to the Hungarian musicians' plenum. The delegates, led by Hrennjikov, the Party secretary of the Soviet Musicians' Association, underlined again and again the importance of a permanent fight against western trends as well as against nationalist deviation in music. This remained the motto of Hungarian communist musical life. The result was a small number of bad vocal works sounding like military marches with lyrics by Party poets. The most characteristic of these mass-songs was "Weave the Silk, Comrade" by Bela Tardos who, and perhaps this is not by chance, was and is the general director of the State Musical Publishing House. Perhaps it is worthwhile to quote from these cantatas and oratoria as well as from the mass-songs, so that one may flavor the lyrics which are nothing but the rankest propaganda.

"Defend peace, youth, fight against the warmongers," were the opening words of a cantata which was awarded the Kossuth prize.

"Comrade Rakosi, thy name is blest by the world," echoed Szabo's march.

"Produce more than the machines," suggested a popular piece for the workers.

There were others outspokenly military, "If war comes, if you march, stand with us, you will be invincible . . ."

This was the music to prove the superiority of socialist culture over that of the "capitalist" world. This was the music which had to be "enjoyed" by the masses, instead of Stravinsky, Bartok, Mahler or Debussy, Brahms or Wagner.

One thing must be made clear. This shameful musical mess

was produced by a handful of careerists, and not by reputable and honest composers. The Hungarian composers have had two great old men, Bartok and Kodaly, whose example and authority were always so overwhelming that no real betrayal was possible. A number of very gifted and cultured composers lived and created in complete opposition to the inhuman and unjust communist political system. However, they were tolerated, and moreover, paid by the regime authorities under the necessity that there must be some sort of a genuine musical life under socialism. The opposition of the ranking composers, among them Kodaly, was not unknown to the top communists. In 1952, for instance, an important discussion of musical problems was held. Endre Szervanszky, one of our best composers, known for his sincerity and passionate nature, held a diatribe against the musical policies of the Party. Revai, then cultural commissar of Hungarian communists, surprisingly did not reject his views, but said, "we shall give you three years to think it over. I am sure the facts will convince you." Revai was wrong, Szervanszky firmly retained his opinions.

As we have seen, Marxist dialectics governed relations between the Communist Party and Hungarian music. The Party did its utmost to organize the artists, to get all musicians into one association, to control musical life. All this, on the other hand, helped the opposition to grow and strengthen. How these seeds of opposition brought forth their fruit we shall see later.

"The Grapes of Wrath" in Hungarian Music

On a hot July day in 1953, Imre Nagy, recently appointed Prime Minister of Hungary, described his program in the House of Parliament. This new Government program contained both shocks for the Party secretaries and some relief for the people. It was totally unexpected that he would with sincerity and conviction expose the failures and sins committed by the Communist Party and the Governments up to that day. The new Government program changed the country for a whole week into a free-thinking and free-speaking society. But only for one single week, unfortunately. At the end of seven days

Rakosi, the former dictator of Hungary, the most hated man of the communist regime, raised his voice. He did not argue with Nagy, in fact, he approved Nagy's statements, but in a tone which people might usefully refer to their hard bought experience.

Rakosi's speech, which marked the starting point of a new struggle between him and Nagy for power, however, could not stop a development pushed forward by elementary powers working within the social structure of Hungary, a development toward democratization, toward spiritual freedom, in one phrase: toward liberation. People on the street, in the old Budapest coffeehouses, and especially of all in the fashionable New York cafe, a traditional artists' club, began to speak freely about the intolerable unbearable conditions, about the fantastic crimes of the Rakosi administration. No terror was able to stop this long-range trend.

One had to live there at that time to appreciate what a tremendous change this was compared to those grim years before, when a unique Hungarian disease spread outward from the secret police, the so-called "bell-shock." You suffered shock when the door bell rang announcing your arrest. It would be, however, a simplification of Hungarian public feeling of 1953, if one limited this to a certain state of being terrified by the secret police methods of the communist regime. Public opinion was also horrified because of the chaotic economic situation, because of Party patronage in filling posts, because of official corruption, and because of the arrogant behavior of functionaries, as well as "bell-shock."

All this supplied the men of literature, music, and art with more than one reason to be discontented with the conditions of their homeland. And, as we have implied, the great men of Hungarian music, Bartok and Kodaly, were never uninterested in political affairs concerning their country. Thus, their former students, and those musicians who felt as their students, were also deeply concerned in what was happening to Hungary and Hungarians. The Hungarian musical world, just as with the writers, turned sensibly toward the policy inaugurated by Imre Nagy, despite its later denunciations by Rakosi and his adherents. Rakosi in vain tried again and again to reach an agreement with the writers and the composers, offering more and more to them. In 1955, Rakosi gave a party for the outstanding literary and musical figures in order to gain their support. Some people demonstrated by their absence, but those who were present also demonstrated; after having listened politely to what Rakosi said, they arose from their seats and left silently. Why, what had Rakosi said? In answer to the writers' appeal printed partly in articles and further developed at full sessions of the Writers' Association, he told them to keep lying, to give lip-service to the faults of the administration—as he put it—"to paint with pink colors." That was what those Hungarian writers and composers, who deserved the title, did not want to do.

Crescendo

A revival of freedom in the arts took place in spite of all the efforts of a weakening dictatorship to suffocate this rebellion of letters and musical notes. Freedom of the arts must not be considered as a formal one, limited only to the external shape of music, its forms, tunes, and style. This forced freedom of the arts brought with it a very interesting phenomenon. Artists now did what had been constantly demanded of them to do, they acted on the doctrines of comrade Lenin. They became tremendously realistic, they ceased writing "Divertimenti" and instead they wrote reality. This reality, of course, was not the reality the Party prescribed. It was, on the contrary, the sufferings and complaints and dreams of a suppressed, exploited, and colonized nation that was full of hatred and indignation against a way of living completely alien, unjust, inhuman, and vile, but enforced by a big power, the Soviet Union.

The first rank composers expressed their feelings in great musical poems. A common characteristic of these works was the reference to old Hungarian poetry, to the national traditions of independence, struggle, and liberalism. Pal Jardanyi, a young composer and professor at the Budapest Academy of Music, was first to initiate sharp debates between Party critics and

musicians with his symphony in honor of Vorosmarty, who had
been a leading Hungarian romanticist of the early nineteenth
century, often compared to Lord Byron, John Keats and Percy
Bysshe Shelley, and a brave fighter for Hungary's independence
in his time. Jardanyi turned for inspiration to his poetry. The
four movements of his symphony were titled after verses by
Vorosmarty. And what could not be told by music, was told by
these allusions. The final movement, for instance, the "Presto,"
had as title the poem "Battle Song," the words of which read,
"Hungarians, into the field, grasp thy arms, this dear soil should
be covered, with bones of the traitors." Jardanyi's music, apart
from this programmatic character, was a very fine, modern
work, written in a musical language nearer to that of Kodaly
than to Bartok, yet original and rich, having a certain musical
and poetic verve, maintaining throughout the whole its genuine pathos.

Rezso Sugar, another young composer, dedicated his powerful oratorio to the memory of the heroes of Belgrade who, in
1456 when the Hungarians led by Janos Hunyadi and St. John
of Capistrano, dealt a deadly blow to the Turkish armies. This
music, built as a monument to national self-sacrifice and Christianity, was prohibited for a long time. The authorities feared
that audiences would applaud too much. And when the "Heroes Song" was finally played, it was with tremendous effect.

The next work worth comment is a "Concerto" for symphonic
orchestra by Andras Mihaly. This piece was first performed at
the last plenum of Hungarian music in 1956. The title "Concerto" is an allusion to a musical opus of the late Bartok, likewise entitled "Concerto" who expressed in it his feelings and
thoughts about his country and the world, about his loneliness
and sorrow; you feel the same sentiments in Mihaly's piece.
One who is completely disillusioned and feels tragically alone
and lost, yet philosophic, writes music like this. The piece was
an instant success, in spite of the fact that its author used to be
one of the leading communist personalities of musical life in
Hungary from 1945 to 1949. But the more he evolved from his
Party prejudices, the deeper his music, that of a really gifted
man, developed.

As I have already mentioned, Endre Szervanszky is one of the better Hungarian composers and he is a man who tells nothing but the truth. A passionate fighter, he knows no compromise, neither in everyday life nor in music. His bitter fights with Szabo, "the Moscovite," as he called him, in the Musicians' Association, made Szervanszky a leader of the opposition to control and terror. The musician Szervanszky was no less brave and enthusiastic. Among his later works, a "Flute Concerto" was a tremendous success in Budapest as well as abroad. But the composer was not even granted a passport by the Hungarian Government to attend his Paris premiere. The "Flute Concerto" is a minor masterpiece; it gives the illusion of the cold and pure breath of high mountains, sings a wonderful song of simple souls, of people who know no hatred and treachery. In addition, it has a splendid melodic line which gives various opportunities to the solo instrument to show many colors and gallant movements. Nonetheless, it was not this work of the composer in which he spoke his heart. That came later, in 1955, when he composed his concerto "Hommage à Attila Jozsef." (Attila Jozsef was a Hungarian poet, revolutionary-minded, who became. a communist, but was later disillusioned. He was purged from the Party and finally committed suicide in 1938.) This piece was a declaration of war against the entire communist Stalinist world. An outcry of pain, a loud, unforgettable, and tremendous burial composition which left no doubt what the composer meant by it. The tragedy of man who has been made to believe and then had to face the grim reality which devastated his dreams, this is the moral told in his music. A world that is vile but yet stronger than me and I must live in it without any hope of being freed, this is the moral told by this music. Yet the music, although sorrowful and depressing, is filled with a sort of optimism, an optimism based on the only reality existing for the poet, beauty. The rather bitter truth of the Szervanszky concerto shows a certain affinity to Tolstoy's love of life, "which is God, and if you love God, you love life . . ."

The Szervanszky work has, of course, been sharply criticized within Party circles as indicative of a "typical pessimistic, petty bourgeois-influence." The press, including my paper, *Magyar*

Nemzet, reflected the opinion of the concert hall and of the radio listeners who were enthusiastic.

Szervanszky remained a target to be smashed by communist analysis. This is illustrated by the several efforts of some leading personalities who tried to persuade me to "withdraw" my press campaign in favor of Szervanszky. My answer was a joint article written with Szervanszky for *Irodalmi Ujsag,* the writers' magazine, concerning the most important problems facing Hungarian musicians.

The nature of this article can be described by its effect. Szervanszky received an enormous number of letters from readers, approving his complaints and charges against the regime, and, in addition, he received a telephone call from the Ministry of Public Education advocating his silence. He, however, did not give up, but fought on. At this time Szervanszky composed an extraordinary work. He again, referred to nineteenth century poetry and took two poems of the revolutionary poet Petoefi who himself fought as an officer against the Russians in 1849, and fell on the battlefield. Petoefi, to express his hatred of the opportunists and traitors of his time and his admiration of the heroic freedom fighters, had written two poems titled "The Song of the Wolf" and "The Song of the Dogs." To these pathetic and, at the same time, sarcastic poems Szervanszky composed masterful music. Almost for the first time in modern Hungarian musical literature, he succeeded in giving a splendid expression of sarcasm and bitter irony to choral music. This double chorus was performed in Budapest with immediate effect. The "Dogs' Song" became a symbol, and in many an amateur singing society it was speedily learned. Whenever it has been presented on the stage, the auditorium cheered so heartily that the applause turned into a demonstration.

This, alas, became a new method of lining up against the hated regime, "innocent" concerts with one or two pieces of this sort. The concert would end, in most cases, with an enthusiastic mass demonstration which, without words, was easily understood. This reached its zenith with two works of Zoltan Kodaly. The aged master (now 75) creates with his full energies, keeping his fingers on the arteriae of the nation, reacting to any trouble like magic doctors of past ages. He surprised everyone with his latest works. They were of a double importance both musical and political. Musically, they meant a summing-up of Kodaly's style including elements of his vocal music and of pure Hungarian folklore inspiration. Politically, they were a great appeal to the nation. "Hungarians, be alert," he seemed to say.

These two works of Kodaly were the "Zrinyi" and the "National Song." Both are based on medieval Hungarian poetry, the former revives a sixteenth century poet and military leader of Hungary, Count Nicholas Zrinyi, a champion of the 150-year war against the Turks, and Moslem imperialism. Zrinyi wrote several books, among them *Medicamen against Turkish Aphium*. The words of this archaic Hungarian prose were those of Kodaly's new vocal phantasy, a wonderful *a cappella* piece with baritone solo. The words told about a "horrifying dragon, the Turk" which "is plundering our gardens." The metaphoric text was not very difficult to be understood: who is plundering the Hungarian gardens now?

Although Kodaly finished his work in 1955, it was not allowed to be performed until the summer of 1956, when, after Rakosi's resignation as Party first secretary, a new liberal trend was introduced. Prior to this date, however, the radio choir had received the score and rehearsed the piece. The first performance burst into stormy demonstrations for Kodaly so much so that the musical department of the Ministry of Public Education issued a clandestine order that the "Zrinyi" should not be sung again. But they underestimated what Hungarian musicians dared to risk. At open air concerts—it was summer—the "Zrinyi" was performed and the Government was compelled to accept it. They simply could not initiate a trial against the grand old man of Hungarian music. The other Kodaly piece was a choral arrangement of the words of Petoefi's "National Song," a poem which has become a sort of national anthem in Hungary. The effect, as you might guess, was similar to that of the "Zrinyi."

I have so far described only the facts of music and composers in Hungary. There has been, of course, a broader field of music which would include the performing artists and musicians, and

Hungarian musicians as a layer of society suffered with the others and fought alongside the others. Hungarian musicians, except a handful of regime corrupted people, were underpaid and lacked the opportunities to go abroad. They were suspected and persecuted like other intellectuals. The best Hungarian pianists, for instance, did not realize the income of an average worker.

This is past. There came the revolution in which the musicians took their part, as did music. The first musical piece to be played by "Free Radio Kossuth" was Kodaly's "Zrinyi."

Since the fatal day of November 4, 1956, Hungarian music has been silent.

When in orchestration an instrument is silent for a while, there is written on the score "tacet." And so with Hungary today. But with countries, as with music, there comes a moment when the violins and horns and drums start to play again.

THE BODY

The nurturing of strong young bodies to maturity is one of the tasks and joys of parenthood. So, too, with the international communist movement. It is the conspiracy's objective to build a new society fashioned out of the youth, conditioned by special processes of education designed to remake the attitudes and mentality of tomorrow's citizens. In a very real sense both Leninist doctrine and the future of communism depend on the success or the failure of the weaning of youth made captive in those countries where the Party holds power.

The idea of a "Soviet man" is difficult for the non-communist to comprehend since for most of us it involves the destruction of our traditional norms and values. However difficult it may be to contemplate in abstraction the creation of a human automaton, we have but to consider the lessons of the next two chapters to judge the real meaning of such jargon as "socialist patriotism," "equal opportunities for both sexes," and "communist career planning."

Ilona Paul is the steady sure picture of the tested European lecturer steeped in history and culture, but with a keen eye for observing the world around her. To her teacher's mind communist education is indoctrination into something wrong, a far cry from the brilliance and renown of the old system of Hungarian schooling.

Pal Tabor speaks with special authority on youth under communism. Firstly, he is young himself. Secondly, as a communist youth leader, he partook of that great intellectual revival, the Petoefi Circle. He is able to draw together the threads of youth's activity in Hungary in expert fashion.

The Educational Weapon

BY ILONA PAUL

There must be cold frustration in the hearts of Hungarian communists today for the emptiness of their promises looms largest in the hearts and minds of the nation's critical class—the students. And the communists know it only too well.

"When I go into the common room," wrote a Party school teacher in the communist youth weekly *Magyar Ifjusag,* "all the other teachers suddenly fall silent. There is an ice-cold impenetrable wall between us . . . I am the only communist teacher in the school. I go about as if branded. The class staged a demonstration in the corridor and bawled at the top of their voices: 'We don't want to learn Russian.' I have to watch every word I say. There is such an atmosphere here that it is a crime to mention the name of Lenin . . ."

Why is it, you may ask, that the Hungarian bid for freedom had its roots in the demands of Hungarian students when these youth were the chosen "darlings" of the regime? How can it be that the carefully screened, pampered, and completely indoctrinated educated "class" of the future rejected all—privileges, career, material gain for a second of foredoomed glory on the

* Ilona Paul is a linguistics specialist, and a former Hungarian educator.

141

streets? This is the question, the answer to which may well contain the key to the ultimate disintegration of the communist boast of eternity and worldly paradise. For have you ever considered the present communist dilemma: the wave of the future depends upon the unswerving support of the young elite, tomorrow's hope. Therefore, a careful and thorough educational system must prepare in fact such an elite equipped in science, history and philosophy for its preordained role. In Hungary the process began in earnest in 1948 with the Soviet style revamping of the country's traditional central European school system. The process ended—in failure—October 23, 1956, when the students and school children poured forth their abilities and lives for such allegedly discredited ideals as God, freedom, and patriotism. Yet herein is the fascinating dilemma. What was and is the communist solution to this incongruity?

Incredible as it seems, the regime's answer was more indoctrination, a more perfect presentation of communist education, a more determined effort to force upon captive school audiences those Marxian precepts of life which were rejected spontaneously and bloodily at first opportunity. And is Red Hungary alone in this senseless effrontery of national sensitiveness? Not at all. We have but to look to Poland's youth and East Germany's universities to realize the satellite common denominator and its serious implications. For while a Soviet Russia can order massive programs of scientific and technical advancement within its monolith so as to reach parity with the Free World, international communism cannot infuse its chosen but dominated children with belief in Soviet invincibility and faith in the socialist system. And most important of all, the only alternative open to the communist leadership is apparently a dogged insistence that contrived and indoctrinated education is the solution, despite its complete bankruptcy throughout Eastern Europe. For us in freedom communist indoctrinated education may well be a streak of hope, a weapon so powerful in its operation that it will represent a real threat to communism in the years to come, an agent literally at work day by day in the midst of the enemy camp.

How can the communists expect to train and educate leaders

and scientists in the complexities of twentieth century technology without awakening the beginnings of creative and independent thought which has for all time been the nemesis of tyranny and dictatorship? How can the communists really expect to remake man in a Pavlovian mold, when, despite protestations to the contrary, man possesses a mind and a spirit immune to ultimate destruction by dialectic materialism? How can the communists in their egoism and arrogance dare to rewrite history in deceitful and shallow terms while memory and the forbidden fruits of objective truth remain? To a Hungarian no amount of learned falsity can eradicate such facts as the free Hungarian flag with its Kossuth emblem waving bravely, a symbol of genuine revolt; the spontaneity of nine million "fascist counter-revolutionaries," as the communists so frantically call us, overwhelming the wave of the future as if it were a mere ripple; the appearance of intellectual freedom creeping unwanted through the textbooks of class struggle, exploitation, and dictatorship of the proletariat.

What then accounts for such a seeming contradiction? What manner of education is this communist schooling which leads to the very ideals the regime seeks to destroy? Let us examine just how education in a communist state is carried on, and with what objectives and results.

Establishing Communist-oriented Education

To understand the current educational system in Hungary, it is well to recall that historically Hungarian school organization followed in the general tradition of European education. Hungarian schools were in fact based upon the Austrian model, largely as a result of the dual monarchy. There was the basic *gymnasium* with its heavy emphasis on a classical humanistic training. Of more modern vintage was the *realiskola* with its curriculum of modern languages and basic sciences. There was also the cross between the two types found in the *realgymnasium* where, for example, Latin and English might be studied as well as physics, geography, biology and mathematics. Finally, below the university level, there were the vocational institutes, those upper secondary level schools for applied drafting, engineering and the skilled trades.

In practice, children attended elementary school from ages six to ten. Then followed a sort of junior high trade school, the *polgaritskola,* for those youths not desirous of higher general education. Secondary school extended from ages eleven to eighteen. After this foundation students entered the universities. This system of education with its insistence on non-elective curricula was restored to general use in 1945 following the end of the war under the supervision of the national Ministry of Culture and Education in Budapest.

It was to this basic organization that the Hungarian communists early in 1948 directed their attention. From the first days of revolutionary Russia all Soviet planners have attached great importance to the development of a state-dominated and communist-oriented system of public education. And like Russia, the Hungarian regime was faced at the outset with the apathy and hostility of a substantial segment of the adult generation. Further, the introduction into Hungary of rapid industrialization, grafted onto a basically landed economy, created overnight a growing need for specialists and technicians, a commodity which Hungary did not possess in quantity The communists accordingly decided on a contrived program to weaken the authority of parents and bring children under the domination of the state and Party from the earliest possible age and to channel the greatest number of students into the careers most critically required by the regime. Private or sectarian education in any systematized form ceased to exist by regime decree with the notable propaganda exception of a handful of religious schools. The communist educational system which emerged from this pattern of endeavor was to become an instrument designed to educate the communist-dominated citizenry to a certain general level considered practical by the Government. From the schools would come trained manpower in the required numbers and specialities. And, most important for the future of communism, Hungary's youth would be imbued with loyalty to socialism and acceptance of the officially prescribed ideological, moral, and social mores. The goal was the hideous conformism of the "new

Soviet man," untiring worker for the state, unquestioning in his acceptance of Party leadership and selflessly ready to defend the communist motherland.

From the first day a child entered a nursery or kindergarten in Hungary, communist education began an unceasing campaign to indoctrinate him. Under this Soviet-sponsored system, the student was told:

Man's heritage is material not spiritual.

Toil, not leisure, is the privilege of communist man.

Individual thought and action must be subordinated to the collective will of the state.

Duty to the state transcends duty to the family.

The communist order is the only desirable economic and political system in the world.

Soviet world victory is inevitable.

Communism and its home—the USSR—is in danger until the final triumph.

The Soviet bloc must therefore hasten the day of victory. Thus it becomes the duty of every communist in the world to protect and strengthen the Soviet Union.

As a result of this stream of indoctrination the cleavage between education in the Free World and education in the communist sphere grew steadily deeper:

In a free society, questions from a student are a sign of awakened interest; under communism questions reflecting a spirit of inquiry brand the student as a potential subversive.

In a free society, the teacher reflects a sense of humility in the face of truth, knowledge, and facts still unknown; under communism the teacher becomes the absolute dispenser of all knowledge without qualification.

In a free society, educational institutions are guided and protected by respect for the principle of free academic inquiry, questioning and criticism flow naturally; under communism the institution of learning is a creature of the state without a mandate to question or to criticize.

This may seem strange to a reader whose instincts and convictions are closer to a Jefferson or an Aquinas than to a Lenin or a Rakosi. But consider the Stalinist definition of education:

"a weapon the effect of which depends upon who holds it and whom he wishes to strike with it." And who holds this weapon inside Hungary? Radio Moscow tells us, "the decisive role in the education of the younger generation belongs to the Bolshevik Party." As the communists themselves indicate, the purpose of education is to instill as narrow an outlook as possible and still permit a child to assimilate certain facts and develop special thought processes necessary to master a trade or profession. With this objective clearly in mind, communist educators developed their unique system.

Strict rules are laid down for the teacher to follow. He is told in detail what subjects to teach, what tests to use, what to include in course content, how to instruct, what extra curricula activities to promote, what norm of conduct to accept. There is little if any opportunity for discussion and improvement of educational techniques through cooperation among teachers, parents, and officials, as is so often the case in countries with highly developed school systems based in freedom. Since communist education denies the validity of ideas other than the Marxist-Leninist norm, it leaves its students ignorant of many of the great concepts that have motivated and still continue to motivate men in time and history. But to the communist, this matters little; the prime objective of education is not to spur the mental development of the student, but to graduate professionals who will advance the material interests of the state while remaining uncritical of its policies. This explanation, it seems to me, serves to clarify in part the posture of brilliant Soviet scientists apparently unconcerned by the ruthless methods and goals of their Government.

The Hungarian School System

One of the first actions which accompanied the communist takeover of Hungary was the nationwide establishment of a general elementary school system binding upon all children ages six to fourteen. This meant in reality that communist basic indoctrination covered Hungarian youth from age three, the usual entrance age into kindergarten, which was especially true of working class children, to age fourteen. A high school system prepared students of fourteen to eighteen for their *matura* examinations. This sector of the system covered college preparatory, technical specialization, pre-teacher training institutes, academies of commerce, agricultural high schools, and industrial high schools for textiles, machine building, electronics, and construction. In addition, there was available secondary level instruction in music, languages, and vocational trades. Upon successful completion of secondary school examinations, students were permitted under certain conditions and with Party approval to matriculate at a college or university. Ordinarily four years of work was required terminating most generally in a doctor of philosophy degree.

In 1948, the study of the Russian language was made compulsory for all students above the age of eleven. Almost from the beginning of this process of sovietization, in 1949 to be exact, the training of Russian language teachers was set apart from ordinary academic preparation of language instructors. There was good reason for this action. In 1947, when the Gorki Institute initiated the first Russian courses, any Hungarian who knew the merest smattering of Russian grammar was free to solicit a teaching assignment. But with the systematic glorification of things Russian, primarily through language, the situation changed in earnest. *Szabad Nep* editorialized on the publication of the new Russian-Hungarian dictionary in 1951 that "this language is one of the richest, most developed and expressive languages in the world. It has an almost immeasurable importance from a political point of view. Russian was the language in which Lenin and Stalin, leaders of the whole of progressive humanity, wrote, spoke and taught; it is expressive of the most advanced ideology, Marxism-Leninism, and of the ideas of scientific communism and the proletarian revolution. . . ." Obviously, ragtag teachers could no longer be tolerated, and the system of appointments gave way to a strict preparation designed to ensure proficiency. To guarantee a continuing flow of qualified lecturers for the future, the state established a Russian Institute in Budapest where a four-year university level curriculum was compulsory. Graduates were certified as secondary school teachers.

Coincidental with the introduction of Russian language study, the communists revamped the administrative organization of Hungarian education. The business of education was placed in the hands of a minister of education. He controlled approval of textbooks, instructional content of school curricula, a general inspectorate, faculty appointments and liaison with district and county school departments.

The whole educational system was overhauled, first the textbooks were screened, then the teachers, later the pupils themselves. A separate textbook publishing company was set up to direct the editing, publishing, and printing of textbooks. New, young reliable Party functionaries were put in charge of the "educational reform." This was an integral part of the much heralded cultural revolution. Anyone, old communists included, who gave rise to the slightest suspicion of being a deviationist infected with "decadent bourgeois ideology" was dismissed. But this did not immediately affect the bulk of the teaching staff for the communists had not enough newly trained "cadres." Inevitably, this led to the indoctrination of the existing teaching staffs. Old, aging teachers after a tiresome day had to visit scores of political schools where they took seemingly endless courses. He, who was labelled "politically backward," sooner or later felt the whip of the dictatorship. His overtime work was not recognized, he did not get any salary raises, and at the first convenient moment he was mercilessly sacked.

The education of all youngsters from six to eighteen years was in the hands of Mrs. Ferenc Vadasz. Her husband had been for years the general secretary of the journalists' union and as such his main task was to inform the Party and the security police of the behavior of prominent journalists. Scores of Hungarian journalists were denounced by him. His brother was an AVO lieutenant colonel. Mrs. Vadasz proved a true chip off the old block. She organized the ceaseless brutal indoctrination program in the schools. The "Vadasz-regime" meant the gradual and complete eliminiation of the liberal traditions, the national heritage, and the all-out sovietization of the schools. It is easily seen just how complete the ministry's powers were. But an examination of the school departments on local levels reveal an even more thoroughgoing overseership. Each county council school department contained a cadre or personnel section which represented Communist Party interests, a high school department which supervised secondary level instruction, a general school section which handled the various local, general and elementary institutions, a boarding house section which controlled students and apprentices living in dormitories and rooms away from home, a teacher training section which saw to a ceaseless round of indoctrination for the often hapless instructors, a parents' council section which, among other things, directed family indoctrination toward Party aims, and an inspection staff which covered all levels of schooling in the area theoretically twice yearly, including a special investigation of the state of Russian language training.

The director of these county boards was never a teacher, but always a Party member with strong training in political indoctrination. That this background was important cannot be questioned. Political indoctrination of both teachers and students was carried out to the extreme. All elementary level teachers, for example, periodically had to pass special seminars organized by the Teachers Branch of the Hungarian Trade Union Federation. The seminars were single minded in intent: the history and program of the Communist Party, Marxism-Leninism and current political topics. In addition, each summer teachers had to take Ministry of Education sponsored political courses organized by local teacher training sections. Those who failed to attend such regional summer schools brought on themselves the obligation to pass successfully a two-year correspondence course which was subject to a monthly audit by a county political director. This was not the end. Each month teachers on all levels were instructed to read assigned political books and pamphlets, sometimes *en masse* in collective reading sessions. The reading of the communist press was compulsory semi-weekly. After school Party lectures provided the occasion for county council political officials to check on the teachers' faithfulness to their

forced readings. Moreover, official Party meetings were scheduled monthly, and attendance was compulsory. In fact, teachers
were expected to take notes on the meetings. Thus, it was not
for irony's sake alone that county council school departments
were headed by politically trained non-teachers.

Once the communists had established a general school they
turned their attention to the secondary level of instruction.
The state maintained the "humanistic" *gymnasium* and the
realgymnasium. The former *realiskola* was turned into a technical school. Higher education was oriented toward scientific
and technological universities and colleges of social sciences
with faculties for fine arts, philosophy, etc. To this pyramid was
added the various military academies, including one for training political officers, and the teacher training institutes. Apart
from this formal system of school education, there were net-
works of high schools for workers, university evening courses,
correspondence courses, and school teachers' continuation
courses.

Parents had little influence on the selection of courses for
their children. The traditional Hungarian opening and closing
school prayers were forbidden and replaced by group singing.
On former holy-days and feast days and on Sundays the pioneers
(in effect the Party cadre for children from six to fourteen)
scheduled competing events designed to wean children away
from familial religious influence. Christmas day became the
holiday of the Pine Trees, St. Stephen's Day became a communist day of sports, and Lenin's birthday, January 21, became a
national festival.

Few, if any, classroom discussions were held in the general
schools. Homework was assigned in either the Hungarian or
Russian languages. Homework was carefully checked the following day. Written examinations were required in grammar
and arithmetic. Compositions and themes almost always were
of a political nature dealing with the Five Year Plan, Stalin, and
Soviet aid to Hungary.

Apart from normal homework, the pioneers in collaboration
with county council school departments periodically gave political themes to children to be written with the aid of the parents.

The purpose was obviously to educate parents and quite probably to detect political unreliability.

As aids to indoctrination, schools were littered with pictures of the USSR and its leaders coupled with propaganda bulletin boards replete with the latest Five Year Plan production statistics. Propaganda posters boosted zeal for Russian literature, geography and natural history. It actually became so ridiculous that the Ministry of Education issued instructions in 1951 as to how the space problem in the classrooms was to be handled. On the front wall one would henceforth find pictures of Rakosi, Stalin and Lenin, framed under glass. The other three walls were to be adorned with political slogans: "By learning well we contribute to the Five Year Plan's success." "Long live the leader of the Peace Bloc, Comrade Stalin!" "With Lenin's doctrine, with Stalin showing the way, and under Rakosi's leadership, we are marching toward Socialism." In one corner usually stood the "peace bastion" consisting of a primitive drawing of bricks on paper backing. Each time a pupil excelled a small red flag would be pinned to one of the bricks. The purpose was to encourage student enthusiasm but actually it worked the other way since so much time had to be spent maintaining it.

In general, the Hungarian elementary school curriculum was based upon eight years work grouped as follows:

First Grade: reading, writing, counting, singing, physical education.

Second thru Fourth Grade: reading, arithmetic, spelling, singing, physical education and in special schools Russian language six times weekly.

Fifth Grade: Hungarian language and literature, six hours per week; Russian language, three hours per week; natural history, three hours per week; art, two hours per week; mathematics, four hours per week; gymnasium, two hours per week; singing, two hours per week.

Sixth Grade: The same curriculum as the fifth grade with the addition of history, three hours per week.

Seventh Grade: The same as above with physics replacing natural history.

Eighth Grade: Physics is replaced by chemistry and geography by descriptive geometry. There also entered at this point a period of self-criticism ironically termed "constitution."

Teachers were required to tutor slow students twice weekly without added compensation. Lessons were planned very carefully. Curricula for the individual subjects were issued by the Ministry of Education. During summer vacations teachers were required to develop detailed plans for each lesson of the coming school year. The plans were to indicate the interpretation placed upon various topics. One description I particularly recall treated of "Shakespeare as the critic of dying feudalism and supporter of monarchy and the town bourgeoisie . . ." The communists have done their best to annex the greatest minds of the past to their cause, and it was the teacher's duty to maintain the illusion in exactly the prescribed manner.

Every child who wished to enter a high school upon completion of the compulsory general school had to report his intention three months before the end of the school year. He had to submit a biography stating, among other things, whether his father was a Party member, and his occupation before and after 1945. This information was then passed on to a commission consisting of the school principal, a Party official, a parents' council representative, a DISZ (the Communist Youth Federation— roughly comparable to the Soviet komsomol) or pioneer officer and a woman member of a communist front, the Democratic Women's Union. There a decision was taken relative to the applicant's acceptability. If the prospective student proved reliable, he would then be assigned to a vacancy in the vicinity of his home. The school year ran six days a week from early September to mid-June. Classroom capacity was limited to fifty students.

The communists had a completely controlled school system by late 1950. But if their paper organization was rigid and supervision all-pervading, what of its efficiency and product? There is no doubt that academic standards fell during the decade of control. This is perhaps especially true in Hungarian higher education. One need not look far for the reasons. The exclusion of qualified students on the basis of parentage and political reliability ranks first followed closely by the nerve-crushing demands by the regime on teachers and students alike resulting in a weariness and a negativism, hostile to learning. Prior to 1953, for example, students from working class families could not be failed. In the rush for quantities of graduates, quality suffered and trained illiterates poured forth from the campus. Pressure detracting from serious study was maintained on students to join Party and front organization units. To join was an enervating experience, not to join jeopardized your very status as a student. If this were not enough, the instructors stood in constant fear of classroom informers whose role was to incriminate teachers on behalf of the security officials conveniently set up in the registrar's office. Students were enjoined to study themselves sick, which many did. Compulsory courses in communism, compulsory attendance, compulsory group study of political issues, compulsory propaganda readings, all took a toll.

I have a brother who, before his escape to the West, was an engineer who had been trained at one of Budapest's universities. His story is typical enough of the Hungarian communist school system to be retold. He was a product of the communist crash program to train ten thousand engineers. His course of study was first cut from four to three years. Then many of his instructors, who were educated by non-Marxists in "non-Socialist" countries were declared "unreliable" and removed. Their replacements were not engineers or if they were they had never taught. To offset this deficiency the regime immediately created an engineering teacher training institute. To recruit a student body they drafted students who had failed in the engineering faculties. So my brother had the odd experience of seeing classmates who had failed their courses end up as the teachers. Paralleling the formal training went the indoctrination, usually given at night during an individual's free time. These classes were famous for the ignorance of the Party instructors. I can vividly recall my brother relating how an acquaintance of his asked the instructor one night, after a long lecture on political economy, how it was that most U.S. workers seemed to own automobiles. The instructor started off well, "The Party never deceives anyone. It is true that there are many cars in America.

But they are owned by . . . , they are mostly in the hands of . . . , exploited workers do . . . Class dismissed."

Discrimination in Communist Education

Complete equality of educational opportunity for all citizens is a proclaimed goal of the communist school system. However, an interesting number of factors have operated to produce real discrimination, both intentional and accidental, against various groups of Hungarian society. One of the contributing reasons for the decline in academic standards was the application of class criteria instead of scholarly aptitude as the determinant for admission to higher institutions. The regime's policy of favoring children from working class and peasant homes discriminates not only against the children of the "dispossessed" but against the children of professionals (doctors, lawyers, architects, etc.). This policy hurts not only innocent children who, by virtue of upbringing and ability would be normally acceptable, but denies their full talents to the Hungarian people. If proper working class background made university training possible and, in some cases, mandatory, Party-backed children and the sons and daughters of Party members had no difficulty in attending schools of their choice completely outfitted even to the highest grades. Since emphasis was on political loyalty, students who had not even graduated from secondary school but who were deemed reliable by the regime were often admitted to universities. Between 1937 and 1956 the country-wide percentage of working class children admitted to high school rose from 3.4% to 38.7% while the percentage among the peasants rose from .6% to 21%. Among university and college students the percentages increased from 2.7% to 33.1% in the worker category and for the peasant class .8% to 22.2%.

Social background, then, became the criterion over marks, intelligence, ability. The communists wanted, as they so oddly put it, "a nice percentage" concerning a student's origin. In the early days of communist consolidation of power, sons and daughters of professionals and intellectuals were expelled summarily. It even happened that the great grandson of Ignatz Semmelweis, the medical genius who discovered puerperal fever, was refused admission to the Budapest University medical school, although he wrote a brilliant entrance examination, simply because he derived from a family tree which included intellectuals and property owners.

Molding the Individual to the Approved Pattern

In its broadest sense communist education transcends the formal school system. Virtually all organized activity open to a communist-dominated youth was and is available only through groups sponsored and controlled by the state or the Party. Primary among these organizations are the young pioneers, the DISZ, and SZHSZ (the League of Fighters for Freedom). Among the many indoctrination and para-military duties of these organizations there was the unique assignment which in a very real way adjusted the future of many youngsters. Functionaries of these organizations assumed the rights of parents checking on school attendance, granting admission to schools, counselling, questioning, and lending political advice.

Indoctrination started early. For the communists "even the smallest child must know who leads the country to glory. We shall teach the young to love the Party. There must be more political education in kindergarten."

There is the shocking picture of what this purposeful drill did to children and their families. I had a particularly close friend who, together with her husband, watched their daughter's development with great anxiety. There were no prayers in her kindergarten. There was instead an emphasis on politics. Her first school song began, "long live, long live Comrade Rakosi." Attempts to neutralize the indoctrination at home were not successful. Partly, this was due to parental fear that the child would inform her teachers at school with the resulting dire consequences involving anything from loss of job to internal deportation. However, the real problem, if you can subdivide this horror, usually began when children were old enough to think and judge for themselves. One of the basic reasons why school children under the communist system so easily lost mental and moral poise was the intellectual jungle of lies in which they, as well as their parents, were forced to live. Students early realized that everyday life in Hungary was different from what they were taught in school, from what they read in their text-books and newspapers. Parents, if they did not want their children to adopt the objectionable moral principles of communism, were often compelled to tell their children what they themselves believed was right and wrong, still cautioning them to behave in school as if the indoctrination was taking.

Special forms of political indoctrination existed in the sec-ondary schools. Subjects not in line with communist doctrine had to be omitted, religion and ethics, for example, only to be replaced by courses in Bolshevik ideology. Other courses were drastically revised to exclude "incorrect" knowledge. As a result, teaching objective facts became both impossible and nightmar-ish. Insignificant events in Hungarian history would be blown up out of proportion so as to depict a devious communist point. In arithmetic, only examples connected with the Five Year Plan were given. In geography, while a study of the British Isles con-sumed one unit, Rumania was allocated six times that of Britain, and the USSR was discussed for half a year. No time was generally spent on the United States. During Russian gram-mar lessons careful attention was required of definitions. The words "right" and "left" carried precise political meanings and had to be recalled constantly.

Classroom activity was supplemented by the young pioneers which organized youngsters up to age fourteen and the DISZ which supervised extra curricula programs of youth to age twen-ty-five. Both organizations were patterned on Soviet experience although the Hungarian pioneers had absorbed the very active and highly regarded boy scout movement as part of the overall communist effort to destroy unwanted opposition. It was at times difficult to differentiate between these youth groups and the schools since teachers had to participate and only students who were members of these organizations could be usually certain of consideration for higher education. The pioneers met weekly in classrooms to read *Pajtas* (Comrade), the group's newspaper, to sing communist marching songs, and occasionally to submit to individual interrogation regarding their teachers' political views as well as their own.

Soviet achievements as a matter of standard practice were praised to the skies whereas Hungarian merits were practically ignored. The USSR was depicted as an earthly paradise, as the model for all the people's democracies to emulate. Textbooks and teachers alike credited most technical advances to the Russians. Students were often heard to remark "Oh, another Michurin." Michurin, the eminent Soviet biologist, was regarded as the communist example *par excellence* and became the butt of many Hungarian jokes. The USSR always had to be cast in the role of defender of the peace. Sharp witted students would inevitably ask, if this is so, why are the Soviets and Hungarian leaders speeding up rearmament. The stock answer that the communists wished to defend free Hungary against western imperialistic slavery usually brought sad smiles to many young faces. Teachers saw this with bitterness but they were powerless to do anything.

The Tactics of Communist Education

Under the communist system of education, the student in the classroom, like the worker in the factory and on the collective farm, becomes intimately familiar with a "norm."

A norm in communist language is a goal set by a planner for accomplishment by an individual or a group. In education, too, the communists felt that they must have some unit of measurement around which they could build a system of norms. So, rather than items produced or acres harvested, it was and is pages memorized, amount of homework written, or the number of books read. Emphasis is placed on collective action. Goals were collective. Class and school teams challenged each other to "study contests." A class often pledged itself to accomplish some task for the Party, for example, to reach the goal set for a fund-raising campaign. The student had to become a Stakhanovite of learning, pressing, always competing. The teacher, in turn, had a norm also, the number of passable students per year. The satisfactory teacher was the one whose students passed on to the next higher grade. Thus, once a teacher had established an acceptable percentage of failing pupils, he dared not fall below it. Consequently, each year the teacher had to manipulate carefully his pass and fail figures in order to produce his acceptable percentage yet not remove a safe cushion which might be required suddenly to show his rate of improvement.

Not only do the communists shape the line of study to be followed by the student, but they seek to fill each working hour with some form of approved Marxist activity. In the Free World, most educators believe that the student should have some time to himself to do as he pleases—time for play, sports, social activities, hobbies, spare time employment. By taking part in a variety of activities, it is felt that a student develops a well-rounded personality. However, in communist style education nothing is less desired than a well-rounded personality. Just the opposite. The goal is not an educated society of reasoning individuals, but a phalanx of unquestioning citizens. Jozsef Darvas, the Rakosi minister of education, bluntly indicated the communist aim: "They (the students) must be imbued with deep affection for everything that our building of socialism represents, and for all those . . . who have raised our fatherland to the highest peak it has ever attained in its history. They must be filled with the deepest hatred for all those who threaten our new fatherland."

Socialist patriotism became a constant theme in the educational process. Students were taught communist patriotism was inseparable from love for the Soviet Union which had realized and defended socialism, and now speeds the building of socialism in other countries. To facilitate indoctrination teachers were organized into collectives, described by the Party as social units based on the principle of socialism. At the heart of the collective was the need for absolute conformity in the teachers' political creed and a satisfactory level of vocational proficiency. By constituting collective units the Party reasoned that communist teachers would lead the waverers and would demand strict adherence to the goal of remolding society. To better prepare younger teachers for their state responsibilities, the regime established teacher training institutes. The curriculum was devoted to giving teachers "a deeper knowledge of dialectical materialism, while training them in the practice of communist morality and Bolshevik behavior and will power." For their efforts the teachers were compensated on a scale ranging from university professors (4000 forints per month—about $150 in purchasing power) to elementary teachers (1300 forints per month—about $50 in purchasing power). The school system in Hungary had become mere indoctrination centers dedicated to technical training, communist humanism, the class struggle, and the glories of the USSR.

But still the process did not end here. The communists sponsored a massive after school para-military program loosely justified from time to time as "athletics." This movement, known in Hungary as MHK—"Ready to Work and Fight"—required considerable physical prowess. Rigorous qualification tests were mandatory not only in the traditional areas of physical fitness, such as the obstacle course and cross country running, but the boys and girls had to display minimum proficiency in marksmanship, use of grenades, parachute jumping, and automobile handling.

Student Opposition

We are now able to discern the total outline of the communist tactic applied to education:

Control the youth and thus the future.

Control rigorously all levels of education.

Provide the citizenry with a usable level of general education.

Indoctrinate students constantly in Marxism.

Control firmly all after school student activity.

Sovietize the school system in the interests of destroying national traditions and patriotism except for the USSR.

Establish the "Soviet man."

Influence parents through their children.

Organize the students into supplementary physical reservoirs of labor.

Train the school age youth in military science.

But this is not the end of the story of communist education

in Hungary. By late 1954 the communists themselves realized something was amiss in their carefully laid plans. An attempt was made to popularize DISZ, the Hungarian youth organization. But the gambit failed. By 1956 student resentment had taken slightly more overt forms. The issues were coming into the open, centering upon the restrictions placed on student choice of advanced education or on the selection of the type of work preferred; the physical awareness of the contrast between communist theory and the harsh realities of everyday life; communist efforts to regiment leisure time in favor of "voluntary" work brigades; communist efforts to suppress Hungarian traditions and culture and to substitute humiliating reverence for everything Soviet; and deep seated bitterness toward communist persecution of parents and friends.

The summer and fall of 1956 provided a further stimulus to student feelings. The enthusiasms of the Petoefi Circle, the excitement of the general intellectual ferment, the poular concensus that political change and liberalization were around the corner, all added to the increasing student pressure for regime recognition of their complaints.

One week before the revolt itself a wave of student meetings swept over the country. University graduates held meetings to prepare a student's congress and adopted resolutions containing their most urgent demands. On October 18 the DISZ leadership was forced to accede to the demands contained in a seven point program which urged:

1. that the overloaded curriculum and compulsory attendance at lectures be abolished.

2. that language instruction be made optional and only one freely elected foreign language be required.

3. that more attention be paid to sports rather than formal physical training.

4. that instruction in Marxism-Leninism be given a correct ratio to the whole curriculum and that the number of lecture hours in Marxism be reduced.

5. that compulsory national defense education be re-examined.

6. that student food be improved.

7. that suitable and adequate buildings be allocated for student dormitories.

This spontaneous movement of students soon outgrew the framework of educational matters. For the first time the demands voiced by writers were openly supported by the future elite of the country, by the students.

Perhaps the most historically famous of the many student leaflets which appeared on the eve of the uprising was the multipoint ultimatum issued by the students of the Technical University of Budapest:

1. We demand moral and material appreciation for engineers. Beginners should be assigned to engineering jobs with starting salaries of 1500-1600 forints (purchasing power of about $55) and they should also obtain premiums.

2. Top career positions should depend on school training and professional knowledge.

3. We demand the abolition of compulsory attendance at all lectures, the optional teaching of languages and non-professional subjects and the teaching of one required language course voluntarily selected.

4. University students must be offered possibilities of undertaking both group trips abroad with state subsidies and also private trips independent of IBUSZ (state tourist agency) control.

5. It should be made possible for young engineers to seek employment abroad which is not subject to political or family prerequisites.

6. Overcrowding of student dormitories must cease.

7. We demand an increase in canteen allowances.

8. Dining halls providing student food should be subject to university control.

9. Restore the independence of universities.

10. We demand the reorganization of the university youth movement and the democratic election of new student committees.

11. We demand the return of a travel allowance.

12. Reduce the cost of technical literature for students and grant each student a textbook allowance.

13. We demand the training of a realistic number of engineers each year.

14. Students should be able to obtain scholarships for the periods covering preparation of dissertations.

15. We demand a public trial of Farkas and his associates (notoriously cruel secret security police director).

The story of the uprising and its suppression has been told elsewhere in this book. The effects of the revolt on communist education have been deep and, it appears, lasting. In Budapest, for example, according to communist admissions some 171 educational institutions and schools were damaged. In Sopron two-thirds of the entire student body of the mining and forestry college fled to freedom. In the Szent-Gotthard school district of western Hungary, thirty percent of the pupils were listed as missing. In the capital city *Nepszabadsag*, the Kadar controlled Party paper, complained late in January 1957 that in schools "books are burnt, demonstrations held, and there are schools where not even the elementary rules of order and peace are observed." Students were prone to receive their teachers with anti-Soviet slogans. Nearly all students dropped the Russian language and principals were powerless to prevent the staging of student strikes. At the end of the school year the press was forced to admit that school resistance still continued. *Magyarorszag* stated that in the biggest Budapest working class district, Angyalfoeld, only four of the thirty schools there had communist principals.

University youth was equally stubborn. When, for example, Gyorgy Marosan, the hated social democrat renegade, and minister of state in the present Muennich cabinet, visited Budapest University in April 1957 he was not able to deliver his speech. Hundreds of students gave him a "standing ovation," clapping and shouting again and again, "Long live the Party." Whenever he tried to begin his address, he was interrupted by this mocking ovation so that at the end he was forced to depart without having held his much publicized talk.

In August 1957, *Magyar Ifjusag* reported that "purging committees" were to be established on all campuses. The committees would be composed of Party, Government and KISZ (the post-revolutionary communist youth federation) officials. As a result of the work of the committees, many students were expelled from school or were forced to suspend their studies. This witchhunt reached the secondary schools, too. When twenty thousand young people indicated their desire to continue their studies, the Government allotted only five thousand places to the entering freshman classes. Chief conditions of admittance were political reliability, good marks, social origin. Special emphasis was naturally laid upon the "political past" of these teenagers.

The regime wanted to reform the university, where "the bulk of students committed grave crimes against our people and her future. The majority took part in the direct preparation of the counterrevolution . . ." In May, the Party cell in the Budapest faculty of law was dissolved by higher Party organs. According to *Nepszabadsag,* official Party paper, the Party became a hotbed of alien influences, even the leadership consisted of class aliens, people who were infected by "counterrevolutionary germs." That was the first time in the communist history of Hungary that a whole Party local had been dissolved because of alien elements having gained the upper hand. *Nepszabadsag* drew the obvious false conclusion, stating May 28, 1957, "it was only a dirty slander of the imperialists that the Hungarian youth turned against communism."

Before the new school term began this past fall, the regime wiped out the last concessions which had been granted some of them, as a matter of fact, before the revolt. The compulsory teaching and study of Russian and Marxism-Leninism were again reintroduced in all schools and universities. Where in the past there had been only one completely sovietized middle school, where the common language used was Russian, there are now five Budapest middle schools organized on this basis. Thus the situation is now worse than before the October revolt.

In September, a new formula for tuition and scholarships was introduced by the regime. The revised program directed that only politically reliable students with "appropriate social origin" would get any assistance from the state. In addition, tuition fees were raised to 2000 forints per semester (about two months income for the average wage earner).

The process of rebellion is not yet through, although the total repression of the nation by Soviet might, aided by Hungarian communist accomplices, is now complete. We have but to look to the regime's own admissions, in this instance, the Ministry of Education's *Koezneveles* (Review of Public Education). An article by the Ministry's chief of Marxist-Leninist education revealed that the number of university teachers of ideology fell from 500 in 1956 to 250 in 1957. He also admitted that the teaching of Marxism-Leninism had to be suspended during the winter and spring terms of 1957 and only now a cautious return to compulsory lectures in this area was contemplated for the 1957-8 academic year. The article was indeed candid in its admissions citing as reasons for the failure of Marxist indoctrina tion the dependence on the Soviet experience, the inability of lecturers to quote other than Soviet Communist Party history, the unprofitable vulgarizing of western economics and society, and the lack of facts inherent in the teaching of Marxism with its corresponding insistence on blind acceptance of the dogmas.

A full circle has been made. Indoctrination begets indoctrination, lies are compounded, and students who themselves mounted the barricades against Soviet tanks are told in their classrooms "it didn't happen! It was an adventure of the western imperialists."

Small wonder the students of Hungary today show no interest in politics. Small wonder too that the Communist Party is displaying signs of acute anxiety toward their educational system. The simple truth is communist indoctrination of a suppressed people does not work and no amount of "doublethink" will change it.

The Youth

BY PAL TABOR

On October 23, 1956, an entire post war generation emancipated itself from the established communist order with a violent wrench, determined to mold its own fate and future. This tormented generation, in less than a fortnight, virtually swept the air clean of Marxist tradition and relieved the strains of many years. Everyone felt that the age of promises had passed and the time had come to stand the test or to give up for good. Whatever the outcome of the present desperate struggle against Soviet domination and communist oppression may be, one thing is abundantly clear: Hungarian youth stood the test and challenged the neo-Stalinist regime. This was a youth that knew that it had been cheated and perceived that the same old gamblers of Party politics were turning the same old tricks in which our existence, our happiness, our times, and our future were at stake.

But the October uprising of the young generation could not be cut off from its source of power, for this was something more than a political upheaval; a tremendous inner revolution was

* Pal Tabor is a writer, and an ex-member of DISZ, the Hungarian communist youth federation.

in reality taking place. Observers who had watched the Hungarian scene closely had been able to see for a long time that under the apparently quiet surface of communist control the youth ebbed and flowed with rebellious undercurrents. But in order to see properly the political, emotional, and psychological ingredients of October, we must look back to the early post war years.

At the outset of the post war period there was certainly no lack of danger spots in Hungarian life. It was only after the smoke of war had lifted that the terrible destruction became visible: a crippled state, dwindling resources, soaring prices, a flowering black market, inflation of such dimension that printing presses could not keep pace with the get-rich-quick atmosphere. At the same time the intensity of the political struggle increased almost daily. After the folly of war youth felt that 1945 offered one of the greatest, if not the greatest, moral potentials of our history. The young generation looked with exasperation and contempt upon the former professional politicians who had done everything wrong and had miscalculated everywhere. Youth searched after new values. All in all this was an era of high ecstasy and ugly schemes, a singular mixture of unrest and fanaticism.

The Period of Searching

Every party and organization, Smallholder, Peasant, Social Democrat, Communist, even the tiny Radical Party had youth organizations. In the schoolrooms, at the universities, in the coffee houses, everywhere passionate debates were going on. The best organized group was, of course, the communist youth, trained after the Soviet model. In this period, however, even they behaved decently for at that time arguments and not naked power were still decisive. Every Party had a student circle where outstanding scholars and artists held lectures and gave performances. The fire and impatience of the youth led many to the socialists and even to the communists. Anything that gave hope of newer and greater experiences constituted the most luring trap. The haze of dizzy illusions and conflicting hopes blurred the real dangers looming up in the background.

In 1948, the impending *coup d'etat* of the communists chilled the atmosphere. Many devoted and sincere left wing democrats and socialists were led astray by lofty communist promises and thus helped to dig the grave of the young democracy. Having swallowed the Social Democratic Party, already weakened by internal strife, the Communist Party began to wipe out the independent and free youth organizations. Communist thugs replaced non-communists in positions of leadership in these organizations. The new leaders did not tolerate opposition. The idealistic supporters of the much heralded "new world" became bit by it deeply disappointed. The various youth organizations were then merged into huge superorganizations. During the first phase there were peasant, young worker, and student groups. Somewhat later, all these organizations were replaced by that administrative machine of colossal proportions, DISZ, complete with a central committee and rigid regulations. This mammoth organization comprised more than half a million members from all strata of society. In fact, it became in time the "little party."

From 1948 to 1953 was the period of uniformed youth, of ceaseless indoctrination by the Party, by the school, by the propaganda machinery, and especially by the "little party," DISZ. Soon, even the convinced idealistic young communists became tired bureaucrats, watching over hordes of suppressed youngsters. Fear rather than enthusiasm, intrigue rather than solidarity, suspicion rather than honesty became the principal features of this organization. Its leaders tried to imitate the parent party in every respect. The same unconditional obedience was demanded, the same periodical purges took place, the same constant indoctrination. In every factory, every office, every village cells were formed in local organizations. No effort, no money was spared to win over the youth. At the outset there were still some stirrings of hope within this new organization created with such publicity and promise. Later, however, the distance separating the leaders from the youth grew almost daily. What had

happened? The deceit of communism had once more been at
work. These leaders of youth, cynical though they were, were
themselves misled by the appearances of universal support, the
usual overfulfillment of quotas, the telegrams addressed to the
Party, and the artificial clouds of skillful propaganda. Obedience, centralization of power, strict discipline, inflexible loyalty, these were the foundation stones of the DISZ.

Let me present the life of a typical DISZ local organization
in any year at any given Hungarian factory or institution. There
would be two or three organized events weekly to evaluate the
work of the members, to lecture on books by Soviet authors
(among the most favored topics: Ostrovski, Fadyejev's *Young
Guard*, Assejev's *Far Away From Moscow*), speeches held by a
Party official or expert (the usual themes: How can we increase
our production? New productive methods. Let's learn from our
big friend, the Soviet Union). Every month there would be a
general membership meeting. The average monthly time one
was forced to spend at these meetings and lectures amounted
to some twenty-two hours. Besides this, DISZ, as the auxiliary
arm of the Party, its golden base of the future, had to help the
Party's general activities by all means available. At the time of
the annual "spontaneous" peace loan or other such collections,
DISZ received special agitational tasks. Members had to visit
scores of apartments in a given district and there to conduct
friendly chats with the lodgers about their wonderful life and
Hungary's even more glorious future. It was a dream of mutual
distrust, for visitor and visited equally exercised "double talk"
while visibly bored with the whole well-known but extremely
dangerous procedure. After having successfully convinced each
other of being solid, reliable, and enthusiastic supporters of the
regime, a similar scene would take place in the adjoining apartment. Nevertheless, it was not always so simple. In each organization, in addition to the great majority of completely indifferent
young people, there was always a handful of zealots pretending
to be filled with burning indignation against everything "un-
worthy" or "harmful" to the cause. They reported everyone who
was not cautious in his remarks, who did not greet them with
sufficient enthusiasm. So in a sense house agitation was a breed-

ing ground for potential informers, supplying them with splendid opportunities for exercising their future calling.

The basic local unit consisted of cells or groups comprising
ten or twelve members. At the weekly meetings the members
had to discuss the local political events of the week, the behavior
of the youngsters, report any disorder, harmful remark, inefficiency or waste and to suggest proposals for the forthcoming
monthly DISZ meeting. This meant in practice that from the
age of fourteen, or if you consider the pioneer movement too,
from the age of seven, every youngster was under constant
surveillance, under ever present watchful supervision.

In the darkest periods of the Rakosi rule few dared to challenge the authority of the DISZ. Practically every young man
had to be a member of this organization. So instead of becoming
an elite organization, it grew into a huge mechanism which had
nothing in common with the real problems, desires and dreams
of youth. It was intended to mold teenagers into the "robot
youngsters" of the Stalinist age, who had to follow with unan-
swering loyalty, without hestitation, every zig-zag and sudden
switch in the Party line. And the most able, most devoted of
these DISZ youths were educated and trained to become ideal
Party members, as the slogan put it, "DISZ is the school for the
Party."

The secretaries of the local organizations were old Party members, having the right to take part in the leadership sessions of
the local Party organization. The Party always maintained a
watchful eye on its youth organization. It had to be a model
organization. No one really cared whether DISZ won the genuine allegiance of the youthful masses, in an authoritarian
bureaucracy only the visible results, paper-statistics, counted. It
was as if a page had been taken from Chekhov—every local cell's
files were packed with "dead souls," paper members, while in
fact only a tiny fragment of this membership could be called
activist in outlook.

When the honeymoon of consolidation was over, even the
youth organization became the scene of purges. Hardly a year
passed after the merger of the different youth organizations when
the bulk of former non-communist allies were mercilessly thrust

out of the leading positions. The well-trained "young Turks" of the Communist Party took over the leading positions. At the time of the Rajk trial and still later during the liquidation of the former left wing socialists scores of youth leaders vanished without a trace, presumably into the cells of the secret police. Some were put into concentration camps without trial, such as Gyoergy Egri, former secretary of the Union of Young Socialists, Pal Jonas, former youth leader of the Smallholder Party, and many other non-communist youth officials.

In 1950, 1951 and 1952 scores of young men were thrown into prison for alleged anti-communist activities during the coalition period. Usually the chief evidence against them consisted in their reluctance to merge with the communists or in some cases their protest against communist doubledealing.

During the purges every DISZ member had to submit detailed personal history statements time and again. In 1952, a story circulated in Budapest about a twenty-one year old youth, who held a minor position in the economic planning office and who was forced to write not fewer than forty-two biographic histories in two years. This was not a unique case. When a periodic purge began, central directives invariably ordered the collection of new personal histories from the membership.

Youth in Disillusionment

"Communism is just around the corner" was the slogan of the Stalinist era. The regime by its use of every conceivable means of mass persuasion tried to rationalize the untold human misery and suffering in terms of the glorious communist future. For ten years the Party and Government tried to instill in the youth a spirit of selfless devotion to the task of building socialism.

This was a closed world filled with the incessant drumming of propaganda. Besides the DISZ and the pioneer organizations, education and indoctrination were the main weapons in the struggle to win the minds, souls, and allegiance of the youth.

From the benches of the elementary schools to the university rostrum one could hear the same basic theme played in numerous variations. After the communist *coup d'etat* new textbooks were issued by the authorities expressing orthodox Party views. The first reading material covered the lives of prominent world communist leaders. Even the mathematical samples were illustrated by examples such as "if the socialist cooperative produces so many tons of grain . . . ," "if the workers almost fulfill their norms, but ten percent is producing less, then. . . ." After the crushing of revolution a Budapest paper reported on a Budapest school where children had torn one page out of a textbook on literature. The textbook page had contained a remark that "the Soviet Union was the second homeland of Petoefi." The poet Sandor Petoefi, as you have read earlier in this book, was a hero of the 1848 revolution who was killed by Russian troops. He has since been a national Hungarian hero. No wonder that the children were upset for the demands of sovietization did not leave them even Petoefi.

The youth federation (DISZ) and the Ministry of Culture stepped up its ideological offensive against the "remnants" of alien, bourgeois theories, the influence of the church and youth's unsocialistic attitude towards the Party, state, and indoctrination. These efforts, however, were of little avail and at the beginning of 1956 the situation had not substantially altered. DISZ leaders met to discuss methods of restoring discipline among young people and on January 7, 1957, *Szabad Ifjusag,* the daily youth newspaper, wrote: "Political uncertainty, poor ideological activity, the low standard of work in DISZ and its lack of political emphasis, in many instances spurred the growth . . . of hostile elements . . . Are there such elements in our universities? Unfortunately, there are. Their presence is revealed not only by the erroneous views still prevalent, but also by open provocations and posters and leaflets slandering the Party and Government. . . .

"The elimination of ideological liberalism . . . and a determined stand against every erroneous view is our principal task. It is our task to convince advocates of erroneous views and misled young people that their ideas are wrong. In this respect we must not be impatient and must resist every attempt to replace educational work with administrative methods."

The discontent and unrest among the youth did not from

the outset assume political forms. Actually, it has taken many outward forms, ranging from hooliganism to political and intellectual apathy and later to political and intellectual unrest.

Hollow explanations and pat phrases could not hide certain basic facts. The numbers of high school and university graduates sponsored by the regime increased rapidly, but at the same time the general level of scholarship just as rapidly deteriorated. The effect of political influence on school life, the selection of pupils according to political criteria rather than ability and the attempt to let social background establish the admissibility of students to higher schools had appalling consequences. As Magda Joboru, deputy minister of education, then and at present, wrote in the September 1, 1957 issue of the educational review *Koezneveles*: "In 1955-1956 . . . the allotted percentage of peasant-worker university students was 66 percent, although we knew very well that among high school graduates there was a far smaller percentage of students qualified for more advanced studies. As a result, we were forced to admit weak students who most likely would leave in a few years, whereas we refused students of middle class background despite the fact that they were able. In the same way, we set the peasant-worker student percentage at 60 in high schools without making provisions for their board, while we rejected city students of intellectual or middle class background even though they did not require board."

I might add to these words the little known fact that hundreds of able youngsters had to choose unsuitable studies in which enrollment was still open as their only access to advanced education.

Neither dry statistics nor official admissions can give the full story. There are scores of sad, unfortunate stories of talented young people who were simply unable to get admission to higher schools because of their social background. The despair and hopelessness of such a situation caused many to commit suicide for having been refused permission to continue their studies.

"Communist upbringing includes the eradication of incorrect attitudes." This was a regime slogan. Accordingly, those, who in unguarded moments unconsciously revealed their real opinion of the Government, were deprived of the possibilities of learning. The school faculty, the parents' association, and the youth federation decided the fate of youth. Scapegoats for all visible faults and failures were to be found among the "un-repentant" youths who were infected by dangerous western ideas. In the vocabulary of the communists this disease ranged from western dances to approval of John Steinbeck.

An administrative apparatus of colossal proportions such as was the Hungarian communist school system produced tens of thousands of half-finished "products." As we have said, the pattern and organization of communist education was a nega-tion of planning. Viewed in economic terms it might be said that it was a typical case of over-production in a saturated mar-ket. The insoluble problems began in the elementary schools. Every year one hundred thousand children finished general school at the age of fourteen. But high school facilities were available only for some forty thousand children. In 1956, for instance, merely sixteen thousand students had the opportunity of learning a profession. So there still remained twenty-four thousand children who did not know what to do next. As *Mag-yar Ifjusag* asked in its February 23, 1957 issue: "What should happen with these children? Should they sit at home or will they become tramps, criminals, outcasts? Monthly, several hundred cases of 14-16 year old juvenile delinquents reach the police."

This merely meant that the regime must cope with the stag-gering problem of finding jobs for tens of thousands who were led astray by communist slogans. All this could not but produce unrest among both the educated and semi-educated. This grow-ing current of discontent had been evident for years, to realize its fullest expression during the revolt when these young people at last found outlets for their groping quest for a better life.

It must be borne in mind that the roots of this awakening of youth rest deeper than in the school or in the failures of commu-nist planning. Besides the inherent contradictions of the com-munist pattern of education three other basic causes should be re-emphasized, namely home, religion, and patriotism.

As to the home, it is common knowledge that school can only

to a certain extent influence the mental and emotional maturing of children. As the reader has learned from the chapter on family life, the immense majority of parents rejected communism as a political ideology, as a state religion, and as a philosophical force; even those who favored some vague sort of democratic socialism were repelled by the hated regime. Even the pioneer organization and the youth federation could not eradicate the underlying influence of the home and parents. When October 23 pulled the whole structure of illusions down it threw light on the immense strength of the links connecting parents and children. In the long run the climate of home mattered more than illusions, the satisfaction of childish vanities and the rigid discipline of communist youth organizations. The seething bitterness of the tired, worn-out parents against the stupidity, cruelty, and exploitation of the regime was bit by bit unconsciously instilled in the youth. They, themselves, saw the large gap between the lofty promises and the appalling reality. In the long run the permanent indoctrination could not cope with the permanent reality.

While down the course of the years communist propaganda dwindled into an area of popular resentment, the moral authority of the church and the influence of religion, as you have already seen, were rapidly increasing. In 1949 the trial against Cardinal Mindszenty was the signal for open warfare against all religion. This was followed by the imprisonment of Archbishop Jozsef Groesz, Lajos Ordass, head of the Lutheran Church and other outstanding religious leaders, including Lajos Stokkler, leader of Hungarian Jewry. During the height of the religious repression even those young people who were not churchgoers or religiously inclined soon realized what was actually at stake: freedom of thought, expression, conviction. They professed solidarity with the church for the same evil forces that suppressed the church suppressed liberal thought and public opinion throughout the country.

In addition to home and religion patriotism was the third decisive factor in the smashing defeat which communism suffered in Hungary. In prewar Hungary excessive nationalism and passionate chauvinism were among the dominant features of public life. From 1948 on however, to use a favorite expression of Hungarian political jargon, the communists "fell over on the other side of the horse," that is, excessive nationalism was replaced by shameful servility and an unconditional obedience toward everything Russian to the complete neglect and humiliation of the proper patriotic feelings of the people.

Youth was taught to praise the Soviet regime, the Soviet army, Lenin and, above all, Stalin in glowing terms. To be and to remain faithful to the great Soviet Union, that was the first commandment of the new faith. The textbooks on Hungarian history emphasized the peasants' uprisings and communist-led strikes, but, for example, said practically nothing concerning Hungary's legitimate interests in the Danube valley.

Using deliberate falsifications of important facts, even Czarist Russia was painted as an old friend of Hungary and a supporter of the various national aspirations of East European countries. The principal function of history lessons was to build up, preserve and foster the cult of "sovietization." Lies no matter how base were accepted as the absolute truth. The Party and state furnished a constant stream of new material to foster the "spirit of internationalism."

This revolting praise of everything Russian did not mold the youth to the pattern of a Soviet robot age. On the contrary, these officially sponsored campaigns actually helped to keep alive the spirit of true patriotism. When the regime celebrated the day of liberation, or the anniversary of the Bela Kun dictatorship in 1919, or of the Russian October revolution, but left unnoticed the most cherished Hungarian national anniversaries, such as the 15th of March, commemorating the war of national liberation in 1848, it profoundly injured the national feelings of the youth. The red-white-green national flags almost disappeared in a sea of red banners over which red stars shone and ancient emblems were replaced by the ubiquitous hammer and sickle. The people, and above all the youth, remained silent but they did not forget. First, the stifled feelings found outlets in the passionate acclaiming of national athletic teams. Each Soviet-Hungarian track or soccer match was preceded by frantic security precautions. In early 1956, the Soviet national team playing in Budapest was greeted with hisses and arranged in concert by the youngsters. Soviet films played before empty houses, while every play and drama which expressed national aspirations was an immediate hit. The same effects were observed in literature. While our best poets enjoyed unrivalled popularity, hundreds of thousands of Soviet books published in staggering mass editions remained unsold on the shelves. As early as 1952, it was considered impossible to sell either a used book written by a Soviet author or any prepared communist textbook. The storehouses of the nationalized bookshops were filled to capacity with unsold copies. Ironically, this phenomena affected even such great Russian novelists as Tolstoy, Chekhov, and Gogol for the new reading public, educated by the Party, instinctively rejected everything Russian. Probably never before in the history of Hungary have people read less of classical Russian literature than in the very period and in the midst of the much heralded Soviet inspired "cultural revolution."

As the years dragged on the young generation became deeply disillusioned. In its more extreme forms this revulsion from everything communist took startling forms. The press became alarmed seeing the numerous signs of discontent, laziness, waywardness, hooliganism. The very generation which was supposed one day to become the pillar of the new society "just around the corner" turned openly against communist reality. The rapid increase of juvenile delinquency was not the whole story. The behavior of urban youth especially alarmed the Party and the Government and, in a sense, parents also. The broad outline of youth's disorientation was visible: from the breaking up of family life to the forced imposition of a dreary state religion of materialism, from the mass-produced books which no one wanted to read to the evils of forced industrialization and collectivization, from the crowded schools to the influx of tens of thousands of peasant lads to the city only to find equally miserable living conditions and the arid sands of the Stalinist way of life. Who were these "hooligans?" The outraged indignation of regime authorities, the unending campaigns conducted by the communist press could not hide the basic fact that the immense majority of these youngsters were by no means criminal, but simply young people roaming the streets, parading in outlandish suits, drinking to forget, and dancing to American jazz. There was no widespread "hooliganism" in the Soviet sense of gangs committing violent acts. It was rather a permanent public parade of disoriented, disappointed youth in long, draped jackets in loud colors, with painted "American" ties, padded shoulders, tight trousers, and yellow or light tan shoes with thick crepe soles.

Their jargon was an incomprehensible language, their pathetic and wild enthusiasm for everything which they considered western ran from records to fancy ties and these symbols expressed their deep-rooted discontent with the dreary life and pitiful pleasures offered by communism. These youths were almost without exception members of working or lower middle class families. But the children of high ranking Party and state officials could also be found in their ranks. I might reflect that even children of the communist elite are not exempt from this disease of wishing to live.

The present Hungarian foreign minister, Endre Sik, is a well-known figure in the West. He had lived for twenty years in Soviet Russia and after the Second World War he was Hungarian Minister in Washington for several years, later deputy foreign minister. He is known as one of the staunchest Stalinists in the upper ranks of the communist hierarchy. His son, Igor, was born in the USSR, educated partly in Moscow, partly in Washington. He speaks perfectly both Russian and English. He has spent most of his life in fashionable villas in the Moscow countryside, beside the Potomac, or in the Buda hills. He has always had all the money he wished and ample opportunity to spend it. He wears western clothes. His life is a round of parties and visits to fashionable night clubs. He hobnobbed with artists, dancers, and other "dubious" characters according to communist writ. He was once arrested for creating a public disorder, but promptly set free. Even Rakosi warned Endre Sik of his son's "incorrect" behavior. However, Igor Sik is visibly bored with all the nonsense of the communist way of life and leads the life of a typical "golden youth." He has been in the past officially a pupil at the Academy of Theatrical Arts but that was merely a pretext to enable him to continue a leisurely existence. Igor Sik, as an example, is only one of many. In other cases, revolt against the regime takes still other forms, as with the son of the now deceased first post-revolutionary foreign minister, Imre Horvath, who fled to the West, choosing to start from the bottom rather than to lead the life of one of the communist elite.

To return again to the underprivileged majority of the youth, even the young "heroes of work," the celebrated shock workers, turned at sundown into youngsters flaunting western-styled clothing, made of poor material. Papers reported the startling discovery that in homes and dormitories the walls are plastered with pictures of actresses, in one youth hostel an investigator reported he found only one picture of Lenin. Young readers seek out and read old dog-eared mystery thrillers, paying fantastic prices for them in the peculiar black market of detective stories. A series of articles which regularly appeared in the communist papers gave gloomy descriptions of young people not caring about politics, but talking solely of sex, dancing, and mysteries.

However, there is still another substantial segment of youth, yet unmentioned, the educated, whose disillusionment found expression in more sophisticated and dangerous forms. A portion of this group was once enthusiastically communist, some were not Party members, but all belonged to the DISZ. From 1953 on, this educated young group became the most enthusiastic supporters and promoters of the thaw, following and acclaiming the writers and journalists who challenged Stalinism. *Irodalmi Ujsag,* the famous literary weekly, was bought by thousands of students. They helped start the Petoefi circle, the heart and brain of the liberalization drive preceding the revolution. Their attitude expressed active opposition to the regime, or more accurately, to the Rakosi-Geroe leadership. While the Party line followed the customary zig-zag, switching from left to right, issuing contradictory statements, the youth solidly supported the course of Imre Nagy.

Youth in Reaction

All during this period, 1953-1956, official spokesmen complained either about the political apathy of young people or their support of so-called hostile ideologists. On July 1, 1955,

the educational review *Koezneveles* listed a number of "alarming attitudes" prevalent among high school and college students. These included indifference, chauvinism, and "under-
estimation of the results of the efforts of the last ten years."
Similarly, the youth federation paper *Szabad Ifjusag* on August
27, 1955, charged that "imperialist propaganda" was aimed at
turning young people away from Marxist ideology and political interests. The slogan, "stay away from politics," *Szabad
Ifjusag* said, "is one of our most dangerous ideological adversaries today." The Party's inability to attract young people was
also indicated in a number of attacks on the survival and influence of religious education and on the growth of "confused
anti-Marxist ideologies" in higher educational institutions. On
October 4, 1955, *Szabad Ifjusag* revealed the extent of anti-
Party ferment in universities when it reported that only about
fifty percent of the students at the Budapest College of Liberal
Arts had attended the prescribed courses in Marxism-Leninism.

The decisive year of the "ice-breaking" was 1956. The resistance against the Stalinist old guard which was far from
dormant flared up renewed after the historic Khrushchev debunking of Stalin. Ironically enough, for almost a year before
the revolution, communist writers and student rebels had
spoken for the entire population in demanding a more liberal
rule and the Party in its omnipotence resisted these demands
and made concessions only slowly and almost always belatedly.

The latter day struggle against communist excesses went on in
three phases. The first phase lasted roughly from the end of the
Soviet Twentieth Party Congress to the famous press debate in
the Petoefi circle where the first frontal attack on Marxism appeared; the second phase took the country to the downfall of
Rakosi; and the final phase closed with the revolution. The
reverberations caused by the Khrushchev disclosures shook the
very foundations of communist faith in Hungary. At this stage
the struggle was mainly an inner Party and inner youth federation fight against the Stalinists, but increasing numbers of youth
were being stirred from their apathy. Communist writers, journalists, and students began to launch direct attacks on the policies and leadership of the Party.

The stronghold of this ferment was the Budapest Petoefi

Circle which officially functioned as an adjunct to DISZ. Beginning in March 1956, the Petoefi circle sponsored a series of lectures on such subjects as the Five Year Plan, postwar philosophical developments, pre-war labor movements, and the role of the press and information services. Soon huge crowds assembled at the meetings to witness the fierce attacks launched on communist blunders, failures, and crimes by lecturers and participants as well. Speakers proposed virtual abolishment of forced collectivization and the establishment of worker's self-government in factories. The internationally known Marxist philosopher Gyoergy Lukacs (later exiled with Nagy to Rumania but who has since been permitted to return to Hungary) declared that Marxism had become more unpopular than it had been in the prewar Horthy era. At another session, the widow of former communist leader, Laszlo Rajk, who had been executed in 1949 as a Titoist, denounced the Party's policy of brutality and demanded, together with the participants, the public rehabilitation of her husband.

The ferment reached its peak at the momentous June 27 press meeting. Some six hundred people filled the huge Budapest Officers' Club and outside thousands were listening to the debate through a public address system. The meeting began about 4 P.M. and lasted until dawn. The nation's outstanding authors and journalists with the full support of the audience denounced Stalinist policy and leadership and called for the rehabilitation of Imre Nagy.

Three days later Rakosi struck back. The activities of the club were suspended and a Party resolution was hastily drawn condemning the organizers and the group around Imre Nagy as being responsible for this shocking event which brought forth unheard of public denunciation of the Party. Meanwhile, Rakosi prepared for sweeping arrests. Protest meetings were held in factories where the participants demanded severe punishment for the accused. However, this groundwork was actually the death knell of the hated dictator. On July 18, 1956, Moscow instructed the Hungarian Politbureau to give way to popular pressure. In this short-lived second phase even the most diehard Stalinist became aware that short of massive reprisals nothing could save Rakosi's position. The organized drive against the anti-Stalinsts found very faint support even in the most servile Party circles.

After the downfall of the hated "Big Brother," Rakosi, the rebels, intellectuals and students were still dissatisfied with the appointment of Ernoe Geroe, an old Moscow hand, to the post of Party first secretary since it was felt he also represented a major stumbling block on the path of further liberalization. As before, students and young writers were among the leading fighters of this Hungarian "Operation Ice-break." While issues of *Irodalmi Ujsag* were being sold out regularly in a matter of hours, the Party and Government felt more and more anxious over the brewing storm among the youth.

The changing attitude of the Party was marked, among other things, by a memorable editorial in *Szabad Nep*, the official Party organ, on August 28. Referring to contradictions and shortcomings in Party work among youth, *Szabad Nep* said: "Lately, young people's interest in politics, their passion for debate, their tendency to criticize, their healthy impatience demanding progress . . . have greatly increased. Yet there still are many young people who are indifferent . . . and whose ethical outlook is lax both in their work and private lives. One of the chief factors contributing to this situation is the fact that we have not been able to relieve young people completely of the social burdens of the former regime. . . . In addition, our youth federation only lately has begun to champion just interests. The more DISZ breaks away from hackneyed imitations of Party methods and adapts its work to suit the genuine requirements and interests of young people, the more its influence will grow."

Then the paper added: "The DISZ central committee heavily criticized errors committed in the course of the past few years at its last session. It criticized the belittling of the masses of youth, the decline of spontaneity in its basic organizations, bureaucracy in leadership and use of administrative methods. . . . Most of the points in the resolution adopted at that session are correct and conform to the tasks set by the Party for DISZ. . . . We must point out, however, that the process of translating the resolution into practice was begun only with great difficulty."

In September the writers held their annual congress which was awaited with general interest and anticipation. The meeting was a sweeping victory of the Nagy forces who, joined by the non-communist writers, ousted Stalinists from leading posts. In fact, the election of the leadership was the first really democratic, completely free secret ballot voting since the 1945 general elections. After this momentous meeting the tide of the ferment swept through the nation with an irresistible force. First of all, the students started an all-out offensive against the old and thoroughly discredited communist forms of education.

Teachers and students alike launched slashing attacks on communist education and demanded radical and not merely superficial or minor changes. Startling demands and proposals were heard in October at the meetings of the Petoefi Circle, on university campuses, and at a convocation of high school students. The students derided the Party-controlled DISZ and pushed for its dissolution or, at the very least, its total reorganization. The former *avant garde* of the Party, the communist students, teachers, intellectuals dropped the remnants of their former ideological illusions. On October 13, the teachers held a meeting in the Petoefi Circle which became a unanimous demonstration in favor of a change. In the presence of Magda Joboru, deputy minister of education, they openly voiced for the first time their list of grievances and threw light on the basic faults of communist education. Deputy minister Joboru, succumbing to the pressure, promised the swift rehabilitation of unjustly dismissed teachers and major changes in the educational pattern and curriculum. Up to this point, only the most controversial issues had been debated at writers' meetings or in the Petoefi Circle and the debates had not been printed in the Party press. But suddenly it was out in the open. On October 19, *Szabad Ifjusag*, describing events at the Universities of Budapest, Szeged, and Debrecen, stated that the chief demands were for greater autonomy and the removal of "stupid limitations born in an atmosphere of dogmatism," and it added that other "issues were also at stake." The paper emphasized: "The fight is one for Socialist democracy, for realization of the Party's

July resolutions [announcing Rakosi's dismissal replete with promises of greater liberalization], for a happier and better Hungarian life. The fight is being intensified against advocates of sectarianism and restoration and a ruthless campaign has been started against the 'local bungler'. . . . Although there are several demands with which it is impossible to agree, the fight now being conducted is reminiscent of the glorious days of 1848. At that time, the whole of university youth rose to the pedestal of national respect. Today, it is well on its way to achieving similar heights."

It would be well to recall this quotation when we hear of the slanderous accusations directed by the communist press today against the youth and the intellectuals.

On the same day, youth achieved a smashing victory. The minister of education hastily announced the abolition of compulsory Russian language study, compulsory attendance at lectures, and compulsory physical training, that is, paramilitary training. However, these far-reaching but belated concessions could not quell the student revolt. For by this date student ferment was in essence a political revolt against the straightjacket of communism, against the very pillars of the regime, and not merely against failures in education.

"The truth is presented differently every day. We hardly have accepted one thing, when we must regard everything from a different point of view. We cannot become everything from a different point. We cannot become decent adults if we do not know the truth," said one graduate at a students' congress which convened October 19. A passionate searching after the truth was the real goal of the thinking and actions of an entire young generation supposed to have been educated and reared in the spirit of communism. They were no longer satisfied with clumsy explanations, cheap dialectics, or glib manipulation of communist persuasion. No Party functionary could possibly have replied to a young girl, who, speaking at this congress, challenged the world of lies by explaining: "Some higher authorities ought to give the teachers encouragement, because I see that they continue to live in a state of uncertainty . . . and are afraid to talk. We have noticed that whenever one of us takes a definite stand on any matter, the teacher stops us and is afraid to reply. And . . . even if we express our opinions freely now . . . it is obvious that the political trend can change. We fear that we shall again be victims of going one step forward and two steps backward."

But Hungarian youth was fed up with the disgusting political maneuvers and resolved to push forward. Looking back, the zero hour of the regime was signalled by a decision taken by the Szeged University students. On October 20, the students in this large city finally broke away from the DISZ and decided to form their own independent organization MEFESZ (United Association of Hungarian University and College Students). This was an undisguised challenge to Party strength by the youth. The hastily accepted acknowledgment by the authorities revealed the inherent weakness of the ruling Party. They pretended to be unaware of the real significance of the step taken by the Szeged students. The papers stressed the Marxist character of the new union and the fact that it affiliated with DISZ. The regime seemed unaware that nothing could halt the rising tide of youthful discontent and political unrest. Soon after its formation MEFESZ drafted a strongly worded twenty-point program which demanded among other things that "those responsible for crimes committed in the past be called to account, that the death penalty be abolished for political crimes, that the country's electoral system be reorganized on a democratic basis and that March 15 be re-established as a national holiday." The formation of MEFESZ and the drafting of the twenty-point program was the spark which touched off the general outburst.

The following day, October 22, student mass meetings were held throughout the country, including the universities of Budapest. The Budapest University youth took the occasion to proclaim its decision to affiliate with MEFESZ and to cut its connection with DISZ. The resolutions adopted at the meetings demanded an independent national and foreign policy expressing "the true interests of our country." The students asked also for the speedy reinstatement of Imre Nagy to a top Government post. The youth again and again expressed its fiery solidarity with the Polish people in their struggle for liberalization from Soviet control.

The entire nation, and especially the youth, had watched events in Poland with admiration and envy. There had always been a close friendship between the two countries, the roots of which rested in the common historic fate of these two European nations. The press published front page news about Polish developments and the initial, successful defiance of Moscow by Gomulka and the Polish people electrified Hungarian public opinion.

As tension mounted the resolutions became gradually more outspoken and intransigent. On October 22, the Petoefi Circle drafted a ten-point resolution based on previously issued student and intellectual demands. The resolution published in Budapest papers on October 23, called for an immediate session of the central committee and the return of Imre Nagy and his followers to leadership, the revision of the second Five Year Plan, the expulsion of Rakosi from the central committee, a public trial of the hated Mihaly Farkas, former defense minister and security tormentor of thousands, the publication of Hungarian foreign trade agreements, including information on Russian-Hungarian uranium deposits, and the placing of future Hungarian-Soviet relationships on a basis of equality.

These resolutions and their general popular acceptance prepared the ground for a proposed silent demonstration of sympathy with Poland planned for October 23. The resolutions also marked the full emergence of youth as a political force with which the Party and state had now to reckon. There was no doubt that the great mass of the population supported these demands. What had obviously happened was the unlikely prospect of the elites of contemporary Hungary joining together in an open and unequivocal stand favoring liberalization and barring the way against any eventual Stalinist counterattack.

The two weeks of the revolt touched off by the now famous march of Budapest's youth already belongs to history and need not now be recalled in detail. From three o'clock the afternoon of October 23 "we held the streets," as the first youth slogan put it. Enthusiastic students covered the city, from the statues of General Bem and Petoefi, to the Polish Embassy, Parliament and to Magyar Radio. These sober minded and proud young Hungarians did not realize at the time perhaps, that they were marching themselves into history, but when the first shots were fired by AVO guards at the radio building against the unarmed demonstrators, everyone, even the youngest among them, suddenly awakened to the fact that a death struggle had begun for the freedom of life itself from which no retreat could be made.

Let me quote a characteristic passage of a news report broadcast by Radio Budapest October 23, before the communists had conveniently discovered that these thousands of young people had decided to fight and die for the "restoration of fascism:" "National flags, young people with rosettes of the national colors, singing the Kossuth anthem, the 'Marscillaise,' and the 'Internationale,' this is how we can describe Budapest today. . . . Scholars, students from the technological faculties, students of philosophy, law, economics, along with students from other university branches, took part in the march led by their professors and leaders of university Party organizations.

"At first there were only thousands, but they were joined by young workers, passerbys, soldiers, old people, high school students and motorists. The vast crowd grew to tens of thousands. The streets resounded with these slogans: 'People of Kossuth march forward hand in hand'; 'We want a new leadership—We trust Imre Nagy'. . . . The shouts reverberate, the national colors flutter in the air, windows are open. The streets of Budapest are filled with a new wind of greater freedom. . . ."

After the first shots this "approved" demonstration grew almost immediately into a flaming revolt against tyranny. And the same youngsters, who were only hours before walking and singing, took arms to fight for freedom, independence and humanity. In spite of the passionate pleas of the Party-controlled radio, the AVO attacks, and even after the Soviet forces intervened, these patriots stood their ground. With a meager arsenal of old, new and a not inconsiderable supply of home made weapons they fought against an overwhelming military force. Scores of heroic and moving cases of courage and self-discipline could be mentioned. Hungarian youth remained true to the traditions of 1848 by its grim determination, ingenious methods of fighting, and pure unsoiled devotion.

Eyewitness accounts of the fighting have described in detail the self-sacrifice of this young generation. Teenagers put scores of Soviet heavy tanks out of commission and Soviet troops were able to crush the bitter resistance only at the price of heavy casualties and great loss of prestige. When the revolutionary coalition Government was formed October 30, the youth was jubilant. This tragic honeymoon lasted but four days when on November 4, 1956, Soviet tanks once again attacked the Hungarian capital.

The Spirit of Resistance Continues

However, even after fighting ceased, resistance was far from over. The youth and intelligentsia became the moving spirit of a fierce underground resistance. The buildings and walls of the city were plastered with placards and posters denouncing the puppet government. On November 12, the Committee of Armed Revolutionary Youth circulated the following appeal: ". . . In the name of the dead, in the name of the dead of the Hungarians and Russian peoples, we accuse Janos Kadar and call him to account, he and his superiors, the responsible leaders of the Soviet Government. As evidence of our strength, we will keep up the [general] strike as long as a single soldier is on our country's territory.

"For a neutral, independent, democratic and Socialist Hungary.

"There can be no more bargaining, no pardon, no excuse. We accuse and the accusations must be answered."

The Kadar government, installed and kept in power by Soviet arms, initiated a ruthless manhunt against the young people. Thousands of youngsters were picked up at random on the streets, in houses surrounding the scenes of battle, and almost immediately deported to the Soviet Union. A part of them was later repatriated, in the face of world revulsion.

Even today, no one knows the exact number of young people

still being retained somewhere in the USSR. Despairing parents face a stone wall of silence on the part of communist authorities. They inhumanly deny knowledge of the fate of these young Hungarians.

In retrospect, perhaps the youth has been and is the most stubborn adversary of the Kadar group. In January, February, and March 1957, the papers were filled with warnings against continuing counterrevolutionary activity in the schools. These "dangerous counterrevolutionaries" were six to eighteen year old youngsters who demonstrated their real feelings by attending almost *en masse* the newly reorganized school religious instruction. The few children of hard core Party functionaries who were forced by their parents to wear red pioneer scarfs or who refused to attend catechism lessons were severely roughed up by the other children. "The schools are not ours," complained the regime press. As late as July and August 1957, the papers vividly depicted the "harmful influences" existing in the schools. In February the students organized strikes. In March they lighted candles commemorating the anniversary of the revolution of 1848. They celebrated the revolution's anniversaries by silence and the wearing of dark clothing.

Even late in the spring following the revolt, the ruling group had to fight a frontal battle against youth. On March 15, the traditional national day, when the regime feared new outbreaks of violence, the universities and schools resembled beseiged fortresses. Scores of police were assigned to universities and regular government communiques claimed discovery of various secret arm caches. In the schools militiamen watched the teenagers and whenever small groups assembled they were dispersed and in many cases severely beaten by militia.

Over six thousand students fled abroad after the crushing of the revolution. Those who remained at home were subjected to a form of permanent purge. The entire leadership of the various MEFESZ organizations were arrested and subsequently imprisoned. The reopened concentration camps at Kistarcsa and Recsk were filled with hundreds of young people. Their parents were allowed to see them for a few minutes each month. In the overcrowded barracks three people occupied one bed, they could not write or read, and they lived in a constant state of uncertainty and anxiety.

At the same time, the regime set up a new shadow youth organization, the KISZ (Communist Youth Organization). In September 1957, it claimed a membership of 160,000. However, in fact, the KISZ numbered only a fraction of this number. At the Marx University of Economics the Party local had only fifty members in April, at the philosophical faculty in June only 100 members. *Magyar Ifjusag,* the weekly of the KISZ, complained as late as June 29, 1957 that in the big Goldberger factory of 1200 young people only ten percent registered in the KISZ, and of this group only forty took part in club days and indoctrination meetings. On July 6, *Magyarorszag,* a Government weekly, sounded an alarm that in many schools only a handful of children had become members of the newly set up pioneer organization. *Magyar Ifjusag* was further pressed to complain on July 10 that in the fifth district of Budapest "a fascist type terror movement is obstructing the expansion of the pioneer organization."

While some papers warned against the danger of underestimating the influence of the "enemy" among the youth, the main propaganda line asserted that the October revolt was organized by a handful of arch-reactionaries and imperialist agents. Rewriting of the recent past was initiated at a frantic pace. Gyula Kallai, the Kadar minister of education, declared April 10, 1957, "It is not true that the Party fell to pieces on October 23. We are convinced that a few thousand armed workers would have been sufficient to disperse the counterrevolutionary gangs together with their American journalists and photo reporters." A Budapest Party leader, Mrs. Ferenc Csikesz, said in the Parliament on May 9, "the youth was not the basis of the counter-revolution in Budapest, but hooligans and fascist elements released from the prisons."

Meanwhile, Hungarian youth in their bitterness and apathy found dangerous new outlets of expression. The regime's journals admitted the alarming growth of juvenile delinquency in 1957. More than six hundred youngsters were sent to corrective institutions. At the same time, illegal prostitution was said to have increased at an equally alarming rate. According to police files, there are today some 40,000 illegal prostitutes in Budapest alone. Thousands of young twelve to eighteen year old girls are regularly being charged with clandestine prostitution. The bulk of the young girls come from working class families and this degradation is partially attributed to an attempt to supplement their meager earnings.

The general mood of a caged, exhausted youth denied the respite and rewards they believed they had earned with their sacrifices during and after the revolution is that of anger, despair, and deep-seated apathy. This seething bitterness against an inhuman and cruel regime is generally expressed by praising everything that comes from the West or that criticizes the prevailing order even indirectly. Nothing would be farther from the truth than to suppose that this generation had today fallen into line.

The balance sheet of almost two post-revolutionary years shows that youth is irrevocably lost for communism in Hungary. Having shaken off the labels of Party praise, this heroic young generation testifies to the everlasting influence of humanism, decency, and heroism. The constantness of Kadar-controlled press attacks reveal the continuing nervousness of the regime over the reality that Hungarian youth still bears up under immense pressure and continues to stand for freedom and independence, rejecting the empty promises of communism.

These representatives of the generation of lost illusions, this youth did not fight in vain, for their heroic revolt which shook the foundations of world communism will forever live in the pages of history.

THE MACHINE

The payoff comes when the communists move in to strangle the roots of the civil and economic order. It suits them to do so, for in the resulting chaos and confusion it is much easier to prescribe and legislate changes before the populace quite understands their full significance. Precision, planning and cold ruthlessness mark the modes of political and economic penetration. It is a game for which the communists wrote the rules; and it is an uneven contest since the Party always plays on its own field. Yet, exactly at this point lies the opportunity for special opposition. If the communists are denied the use of their rulebook and are forced to play on someone else's field, the victory is generally not theirs. With the sure knowledge which comes from exposure of facts, the Free World may profit from the tragic example of Hungary. These final pages show precisely how the communists conquer a political state and how they place outmoded economic theories into operation only to bring about complete bankruptcy.

To conclude our investigation into the ways of communism, we have two expert participants in the trial of this small nation. Dr. Jozsef Koevago was the last free postwar mayor of Budapest, and for this distinction he was imprisoned for many long years by the communists. He was released on the eve of the uprising and courageously consented to resume leadership of his city during Budapest's few days of freedom. When the Soviets returned, his only recourse was flight. Fortunately for the West he brought his story with him. Dr. Bela Balassa, was a teaching fellow in Economics at the University of Budapest—and with the exception of two years of deportation—served as an economist with Hungarian state enterprises. Now he is working on problems of collectivist planning under a grant at Yale University. He tells us of the incredible extremes of thoroughness and inefficiency which punctuated the planning and economic controls of Soviet inspired centralization.

Establishment and Operation of a Communist State Order

BY DR. JOZSEF KOEVAGO

In World War II the Allies decided that, following the defeat of fascism, they would give the liberated countries an opportunity to exist as independent states under democratic governments, freely chosen. The fact that the Soviet Union conducted the war on the side of the Allies secured an advantage for them wherein Communist Parties in liberated countries were able to figure in election campaigns as "democratic" parties. They obtained a legal right to start and develop political activity far beyond the significance of their numbers, mainly because they were able to rely on the support of Soviet occupation troops.

By the end of the war the Allies had also agreed that "war criminals" should be prosecuted. In Soviet occupied territory this brought about a situation in which all functionaries of the earlier state order lost their security. The Communist Party was able to overwhelm its opposition with charges. And the Party saw to it that statesmen who had stood the test before and during the war, outstanding figures of political and economic life, either would be imprisoned or would simply disappear from the public scene.

In Soviet occupied territory, the organization of the political

* Dr. Koevago is the former Mayor of Budapest.

police commenced immediately. The political police were under the control of the communists and operated under the direction of the Soviet secret police.

The Communist Party arrived in Hungary after the war with a vanguard which, during its twenty-five years of enforced exile, had obtained excellent training in Moscow. The Soviet Union took exceptional care of their emigré communist leaders. They were not dispersed into well subsidized job. They had to prepare for the future of revolution. They attended various schools, studied a Moscow devised curriculum for taking over political power in their own country when the opportunity arose. Any Hungarian communist who had some talent was recruited for this vanguard. In Moscow, the vanguard had every opportunity for observing the development of Hungarian political life, and for compiling in giant indexes personal data on the entire top layer of society and leadership in Hungary. In their notes, the Hungarian communist leaders paid particular attention to the intellectuals of the younger generation who inclined to the left. The Moscow emigré group knew intimately those Hungarian writers, artists, scholars, physicians and politicians who had shown some sympathy for communist doctrines.

Accordingly, as soon as the Communist Party legally participated in political activity, it laid the greatest stress on winning over these intellectuals. Within the framework of the secret security police (AVO), the Party also cultivated and gathered together these evil-intentioned, blood-thirsty elements found among all people.

After these preliminaries it was only natural that the Communist Party, beginning in 1945, exerted more and more influence on the leadership of the country, until by 1948 it had seized full political power.

The Gradual Takeover of Power

In free elections held during the fall of 1945, the Hungarian people vigorously declared its opposition to a communist state. In this election the Communist Party obtained only seventeen percent of the total national vote. The remaining eighty-three percent went to the non-communist parties. But the presence of Soviet troops and Soviet threats brought about a situation in which the Communist Party, still a small minority, was accorded a significant role in the coalition government formed after the elections. I should note that the Soviet Union had agreed to hold these elections only if the various parties promised in advance to include the Communist Party in the government, regardless of the election results. The choice before the free parties was either no election at all, or communist inclusion in the government. The latter alternative at that time seemed more advantageous.

The Communist Party of Hungary sought power without the least moral inhibition. The communist ministers informed the political and military leaders of the Soviet Union, or their local emissaries, of everything. These communist ministers were mere tools in the hands of the Soviet representatives in pursuit of their power policies. The Russians prevented the Government from conducting an independent free Hungarian foreign or domestic policy. The Soviet Union gave every aid, often in substantial amounts, to the Communist Party so as to facilitate the full and efficient development of the Party throughout the country.

Under Soviet pressure, the two most important departments of government, Interior and Transportation, went at once into communist hands. Control of the Ministry of Transportation in those days meant actual power. In a country devastated and disorganized by war, whoever had the means of land and water transportation in his hands could act with an effect extending from the center to the periphery of the country's lifeline, and only he could so act.

The majority party responsible for the country's future, as well as the other non-communist parties, dedicated all their energies to solving the great problems of a country devastated by war. Meanwhile, the Communist Party placed its own men in the key positions of public administration and economic life. The country had barely begun to recover from the calamities of war, when the communists loudly demanded radical changes in the entire economic structure. Their aim was to destroy all the old institutions and customs. They knew that the Government would tend to lose its capacity to handle the affairs of the country if they succeeded in their course of action.

The political struggle was rather one-sided. On one hand, there was the Communist Party supported by the Soviet army and the secret security police; on the other hand, there stood the Hungarians, wracked by war, observing with growing anxiety that, in the eyes of the communists, every old traditional institution, custom, and belief was becoming suspect and subject to punishment. Such an attack directed at killing all traditions could not have been borne better and more steadfastly than it was borne by the Hungarians. The new, young, inexperienced non-communist leadership stood the test better than the communists imagined. Parties and determined individuals led the defense against communists attacks and there was a time when it looked as if the development of a stable democratic Hungarian Republic could not be prevented, even by the presence of the Soviet army. At this point, the communists decided to act with all force. A *coup d'etat* was initiated.

An avalanche of charges was directed against the smallholders, the majority party. The smallholders were literally forced to expel a number of its representatives. In such a manner, the Smallholder Party lost its absolute majority. From the representatives thus expelled a new and influential opposition group was formed, the Party of Hungarian Liberty.

But the majority party could not escape attack even at this price. A decisive blow was to be directed against it, and through it, against the country at large.

In February 1947, in bright daylight, Soviet soldiers surrounded the apartment of Bela Kovacs in downtown Budapest and arrested him. Bela Kovacs was the secretary general of the Smallholder Party which had obtained fifty-seven percent of the votes cast at the last general election. He had fought against the communists in their demands that they exercise majority control although they only enjoyed minority status. He demanded an inquiry to find out to what extent each party participated in the actual exercise of power, and he argued that this participation must be in conformity with the results of the elections. The entire country sympathized with Kovacs' logical arguments.

His arrest proved that the Hungarian Republic enjoyed but apparent independence. Every and any leader could be arrested by Soviet troops at any time. The non-communist majority could do nothing against Soviet power cast in a role which was obviously to support the aims of the local communists.

Fear and dread settled upon Hungarian political life from the date of Kovacs' arrest. Shortly afterwards, Bela Kovacs was falsely indicted on a charge of spying against the Soviet Union. It seemed obvious that further steps would bring a similar fate to the prime minister as well as to other non-communist leaders.

Under this barrage, the majority party fell apart. Many of its representatives were arrested, some leaders were prompted to flee and the party, thus bereft of its drive, lost the confidence of the people.

In conducting this insidious struggle, the Communist Party found allies, naturally but unfortunately, among the non-communist parties. They were attracted by the promise that collaborators would obtain a full measure of power, once the majority party disintegrated. To the Social Democratic Party, in particular, the traditional Marxian siren songs of "exploitation of labor" and "unity of labor" could be applied.

By August 31, 1947, the eve of new elections, the country was confronted with a restricted ballot containing a political field torn to pieces. The non-communist opposition had even been deprived of its legal existence. There were only six weeks before the elections within which new parties could be organized. According to the law, a voter's petition had to be drawn up before a new party came into being. It was common knowledge that these "sheets of presentation" went to the secret police by way of communist agents. Still, there were courageous people who formed new anti-communist parties. The Democratic People's Party and the Hungarian Independence Party were among those which were founded at this time.

The voters again testified to their non-communist views. In spite of the false voting papers manufactured by the communists, the result of the elections once again turned out to be a resounding defeat for the communists. They obtained but twenty-two percent of the vote. The remaining votes went to non-communist parties.

Yet the Communist Party had achieved its aim. By this election, it had become, relatively speaking, the strongest party, and it had smashed the non-communist majority into several disorganized parties with a consequent weakening of the opposition.

Following the principle "divide and conquer" the communists had succeeded in fragmentizing their opposition. Now they were in a position to make short work of the remaining parties, one by one.

The political struggle was now being fought on a much grimmer scene than in 1945. At that time, the Hungarian nation still had some hope that the western world would not stand by inactively while the Soviet Union penetrated European areas. But in 1947, the western world seemed to acquiesce in the fact that the Soviet Union had, in fact, established a sphere of privileged control by prohibiting communist European nations from joining the Marshall Plan. This sphere of control gave way directly to the satellite system.

The question of the Marshall Plan was a turning point in the fate of the satellite European countries. They had to reject the helping hand of the West. They had to accept the dependence of their economic life on the Soviet Union. Here, within the context of economic life, the various satellite Communist Parties obtained the key to foreign policy which opened for them the road to full power. They had already held the key to domestic policy for some time, locked up in the headquarters of the political police. The Marshall Plan was born of one of the most brilliant visions of contemporary history. It is a pity that countries with a humanistic tradition, historically fed with western ideas, were denied participation, through no fault of their own.

Communist Consolidation

The next important task of the Hungarian Communist Party was to liquidate the two strongest opposition parties. For upon completion of this task, there could be no constitutional obstacles in the way of the new order. The secret police conveniently produced the data, by means of which it could be "proved" that the opposition leaders were enemies of democracy and their parties a hideout for fascist reaction. By June 1948, the propitious moment had come to end the Social Democratic Party by the simple maneuver of incorporating it into the Communist Party. The other parties still existed in name but by this time their independence was totally gone.

Let us glance at what happened to the main branches of power. It was Montesquieu, writing in the eighteenth century, who distinguished the three branches of legislative, executive, and judicial power, and found the ideal solution in their strict separation. In more recent times some political theoreticians have added a fourth category: the power of the head of state or, according to the latest behavorial theory, the power of policy decision. Let me now discuss briefly what happened to these four branches of power under communist rule in Hungary.

Legislative power had been exercised by Parliament. The communists first had to put an end to the independence of Parliament. They had to obtain a majority in Parliament. In 1948, Parliament still existed in a formal sense, but its work was almost completely directed from the Budapest headquarters of the Communist Party. Parliamentary work was thus reduced in substance to the execution of communist plans. Since its very existence was jeopardized, Parliament no longer thought of controlling the activities of executive power.

Executive power was gradually transferred during the immediate postwar years entirely into the hands of the communists. Care was taken that communists or frightened fellow travelers held all the necessary power in their hands with which to control the administrative apparatus of the country. Moreover, as a consequence of the nationalization of industrial plants, the Communist Party extended its domination increasingly over the economic processes. B-lists (the Hungarian equivalent of reductions in force) and the arbitrary firing of so-called "reactionary" civil servants proved a convenient means for placing the entire executive apparatus under Communist Party direction. The final process of personnel control was greatly accelerated beginning in 1948.

Judicial power became a fiction with the liquidation of an independent judiciary. In the chaos immediately following the end of war, the institution of People's Courts was introduced under Soviet and communist pressure. When decree 81/1945, emanating from the Prime Minister's office, and Public Law 7/1945, had been enacted so as to weaken judicial independence, the non-communist parties still could not see that the Communist Party would sooner or later smuggle its own people into this new court system, consisting of six lay judges and one professional judge. The Communist Party excelled in exploiting the passions felt against fascists after the war, and they succeeded in filling the courts with their own members, generally non-lawyer graduates of Party schools. By 1948, People's Courts had already adjudicated show trials without opposition.

The power of the head of state in the Hungarian Republic was severely circumscribed by Public Law 1/1946. In 1948, nonetheless, a need was felt by the communists to place this office with its emasculated role into entirely reliable hands. Therefore, the head of state, an office usually falling to the majority party, was removed. He was replaced by a frightened and compromised former leader of the liquidated Social Democratic Party.

Thus, a long evolutionary trend has been reversed. In the course of its history, Hungary through repeated effort had succeeded in carrying out the basic principle of the separation of powers. The country had fought a centuries old struggle against the system of absolute monarchy. But with this latest communist-dictated development the separated powers ceased to exist and lost their significance. They were replaced by the toughest kind of absolutism: all power was channeled to Communist Party headquarters, where it was exercised by the general staff of a small national minority.

After delivering the supreme power into the hands of a few men, some important political work still remained to be done:

Limitation of Church activities;

Destruction of autonomous municipal and county organizations, thus mutilating a system worked out in the course of

Hungary's millenium, coupled with the disruption and replacement of any still existing autonomous social organizations;

Putting an end to private peasant holdings, which had in part found its origin in the land reform carried out in 1945, and which had, in part, existed and had been operated by the peasantry for centuries. Communism does not feel its power secured, unless small private holdings are replaced by large estates, either state owned or led by communist officials.

The local scene had been well prepared for these changes. A supreme communist power quickly invented coercive economic means of bringing recalcitrant property owners and free institutions to heel. If the economic coercion turned out to be insufficient, the secret police was always ready in the background to crush the stronger individuals and group resistance.

In Hungary, the traditional majority of the population had been and remains Roman Catholic, looking back upon a history of a thousand years; the Church has had a considerable role not only in religious life, but also in other spheres, especially in education.

The Calvinist and Lutheran Churches played a similarly influential, but somewhat smaller, role in Hungarian life.

The smaller religious communities, such as the Jewish, Greek Catholic, and Unitarian, had exactly the same rights and responsibilities as the larger churches.

The spiritual power of the churches was one of the greatest obstacles in the way of communist political expansion. This is why the crushing of church authority and the curtailing of religious freedom was numbered among the most important and immediate communist aims. This could be done with success, however, only after all power was securely in their hands. Attacks started against the leaders of the three great churches. The concentrated communist attack was directed mainly against the Roman Catholic Church, and especially its Hungarian leader, since he was the most significant personality around whom almost the entire country could and might rally. Jozsef Cardinal Mindszenty was finally arrested on false charges at Christmas, 1948 and later convicted. With him gone the last bulwark of wholesale national resistance was removed.

Churchmen were taken over as state officials. Their life, as you read in an earlier chapter, depended on whether they bowed before communist power.

Town and municipal autonomy likewise was wiped out in part by enacting a new law and, in part, by forcing upon the provinces a measure of state financial support which in effect controlled communal activities.

Public Law 1/1950 introduced a "system of councils." In carrying out this law, the communists placed their own men on the boards of these councils. The law of councils deprived counties, towns and municipalities of their autonomy. The situation of Budapest was a case in point. One-sixth of the country's population lived in Budapest. Hungarian statutes granted Budapest autonomous rights. These rights automatically ceased in 1948 on directive of the communists. Control measures of this type led ultimately to my resignation as Mayor of Budapest.

A similar fate befell all autonomous institutions.

Of these, I want to mention briefly only the trade unions, which might have been the citadel of labor resistance. The communists seized the trade unions movement and defined its official role: "It is the task of trade unions to popularize the aims of the Communist Party."

The trade unions were thus even deprived of the right to speak up on behalf of the working man.

Concomitantly with the organization of state political power, and as a corollary, economic life in Hungary was overtaken by the communists. Just as the takeover of power based on the support of Soviet troops may be taken for a general principle of communist expansion everywhere, the control of economic life followed general communist tactics as well. I might say that the preparation of the "Red recipe" is exemplified by the phases of this proccess which include land reform, nationalization of major industries, calculated inflation and ruination of private enterprise and small business. These are factors which will be discussed in the next chapter at greater length.

Communist tactics consisted in raising new political and economic demands incessantly, demands supported by demonstrations and strikes. No time is given to discuss and thresh out the demands. They aim at bringing about an unstable condition of both the society and the economy. It is designed to cause the citizen to lose his head and turn giddy in the whirlpool of galloping events. The chief role in the communist struggle for power is played by disintegration. Victory is achieved when the country is thrust into a political condition of permanent revolution. Disintegration is carried out simultaneously in the political and economic spheres.

But even economic disintegration was difficult to achieve in Hungary. Many businessmen finally had to be removed as "reactionaries" or "politically unreliable elements" before the communists could achieve their ultimate aim. The constant existence of a variety of unstable conditions, previous to the complete takeover of power, resulted from an unremitting and relentless assault by the Communist Party. Should the battle slow in the political arena economic troubles were conjured up, and vice versa. If the battle stalled on both fronts, the secret police stood ready to intervene. The AVO dealt with unyielding characters only. It was not interested in pliable men of weak character for these could be bought. But everyone who placed obstacles in the way of powertaking landed in the cellars of the secret police to see if he could not be persuaded to change his opinion.

The classic timetable of the communists, applied in countries which resist them forcefully, is well illustrated by the conspiracy trials which took place in Hungary.

At the end of 1946, the trial of military men and politicians belonging to the majority party,

In 1947, Soviet proceedings against Bela Kovacs, secretary general of the majority Smallholder Party,

In 1948, proceedings against the remaining leading members of opposition parties. The same year, proceedings were instituted against the representatives of foreign owned business firms. In this way these firms could be nationalized and, at the same time, personnel of foreign legations could be reduced,

Still in 1948, proceedings were begun against church leaders. In this manner, the strongest pillar of resistance, Mindszenty, was eliminated,

In 1949, purge trials within the Communist Party itself started.

Later trials served no other purpose than to send to prison

or cemeteries anyone who, as a strong personality, might potentially have served at any time as the focal point for any anticommunist movement.

Disintegration was complete in Hungary by the end of 1948. The powers of government had become confused. Personal independence was largely lost. The new situation thus created had now to be formally sanctioned.

This was done by Public Law 20/1949. The first three paragraphs read as follows:

1. Hungary is a People's Republic.
2. The Hungarian People's Republic is the state of workers and toiling peasants. Every power in the Hungarian People's Republic belongs to the working people. The toilers of towns and villages exercise their power by elected representatives who are responsible to the people.
3. The Hungarian People's Republic protects the freedom and power of the Hungarian toiling people, the independence of the country, fights every form of the exploitation of man, and organizes society for the purpose of building socialism. In the Hungarian People's Republic the close alliance of labor and toiling peasantry is being realized under the leadership of the working class.

This was the text of the leading paragraphs of the new Public Law. It was promulgated on August 20, 1949 and thus this day became "Constitution Day," a day for communist sports. Previously, August 20 had been a great national holiday. In memory of King Stephen, it was commemorated as Saint Stephen's Day. On this day, the Hungarian nation celebrated its traditions of a thousand years.

Communism in Control

Public Law 20/1949 formally established the communist state. The peculiarity of this people's state is that the citizenry has no role within it. Nominally, the state is the state of the "working people and toiling peasants." But they are represented in voiceless fashion by the Communist Party.

The toilers of towns and villages exercise their power through representatives "responsible to the people." This means in practice that legislators were not elected for a certain term, but could be removed at any point during their regular term, whenever deemed expedient by the Communist Party.

The Public Law proclaims the "leading role of the working class." In practice, this means the Communist Party, since the working class can act in an organized way only through this Party.

After enacting this law, the communists had only to see to it that their power was solidified and that Hungarian society accepted the new order of things. To achieve this, they adopted the method of rendering personal and social existence entirely insecure. Everyone had to feel that his presence, future, and livelihood were in the hands of the Communist Party every minute of every day. This could be brought about by economic and moral pressure. Economically, independent existence vanished. Nationalization was gradually extended to cover everything.

By nationalization law and decree, all citizens were forced to turn to the state employment agencies which classified people not only according to vocational qualifications, but, more basically, according to origin. Those descended from middle class families could obtain only the poorest jobs. At the same time, the schooling of "reliable" dependents of working people was accelerated. Middle class youth was first removed from the educational system, as you have seen. The future of a man was determined by his cadre file. This card contained all the data concerning the secrets of family and private life. Political inferences drawn from the general characteristics of an individual decided the course of his life. Whoever happened to be typed as a class enemy by the cadre card was scarcely able to keep body and soul tremblingly together.

Communism sentenced the middle class to a slow and cruel death. The only exceptions were physicians, engineers, scientists, and artists, provided they accepted the omnipotent role of the Communist Party. I personally know of a girl in her late twenties, who, a surviving member of one of Hungary's old banking families, was prevented from accepting employment of any kind, despite fluency in four languages, in the regime's hope that she would be reduced to prostitution in order to exist, thus affording the communists an opportunity to hold her up as an example of the decadent and corrupt middle class.

To this economic pressure, a moral pressure was added. The secret police dealt with outstanding men through charges of spying, sabotage, conspiracy or currency offenses. Resistance and opposition leaders were sentenced to death or life imprisonment. An awful fear held society in its grip, a kind of horror stemming not only from the insecurity of economic existence, but from the insecurity of physical existence itself. No one could be certain of his rights. Communism is the only current form of government on earth which does not provide for principles within the framework of which the natural rights of a citizen are inviolable.

The Hungarian communist government was inspired by the principle of utility. A citizen was free so long as he was useful to the Communist Party. As soon as his existence was no longer considered useful to the Party, he became subject to disappearance. The secret police acquired more and more skill in carrying out such acts. The number of non-communist families, one or another member of which has disappeared without leaving a trace, is ever-growing.

Thus society is beset by permanent fear. Weaklings tried to escape from this fear by applying in ever-growing numbers for admittance into the Communist Party.

The most interesting part of communist tactics was the question of Party membership. At the start, 1945 in Hungary, the Communist Party enticed with flattery the members of the middle class to enter the Party. They were welcomed as members and were immediately offered prestige positions. As the Party gradually took over the power of government, the practical advantages deriving from being a member became ever clearer. However, by the time the takeover was complete, admittance to the Party was made more difficult. Early in 1948, the communists launched one last oversized campaign to induce people to enter. However, when the number of memberships reached a total of 800,000, recruitment stopped. Henceforth, the Party emphasized it was a distinction to be admitted to membership.

Meanwhile, purges within the Party started. The purpose of these purges was to enforce the loyalty of every Party member to the ruling clique, and also to shake the feeling of security in Party members themselves. The principle of utility demanded that even a Party member should not feel equal to his leaders, but profess his loyalty daily by idolizing the leaders and their methods.

The effort made by the Communist Party to obtain a great number of members hides a second intention directed at securing the future. The majority of the citizens must be made responsible for the crimes committed by the leading cadre of the Communist Party itself. In 1949, Matyas Rakosi, the omnipotent first secretary of the Hungarian Communist Party, coined the slogan: "For everything that happens in this country, we communists are responsible."

This shifting of responsibility upon all members of the Communist Party served the purpose of decreasing the number of those who still had confidence in the ultimate liberation of the country with the attendant establishment of a government based on moral principles. Communists more and more emphasized that in the case of the country's liberation dire retaliation would be in store for members of the Communist Party. The high number of Party members, totalling 800,000, with many new candidates and many expellees on the periphery, revealed the communist intention to break the country's power of resistance by involvement. The convenient way of stabilizing communist state power was to compromise the moral integrity of more and more people by involving them directly or indirectly in communist malpractices.

In the western world the question is often debated whether economic troubles in one or another communist country will sooner or later entail a change in the political line, and might even result in a rupture of the system. I am sorry to say this view seems to me quite erroneous. The communist order is not at all interested in the living standards of the masses. Only the long term stability of the Communist Party matters. The general standard of living is quite incidental so far as communist dictators are concerned. The question of political power is always decisive. If living standards can be conveniently raised in the interest of communist stability, then it may possibly be done. In comparison, the question of economic policy is of secondary importance. And this is quite natural. Communist dictators are in a position to exploit the masses to their hearts' content. There is no social agency in existence which could raise its voice in successful protest. Whoever wanted to exercise healthy criticism had to reckon with being instantly spirited away. In the communist order the masses generally live on the same level. This low level of living is not overly offensive, since it is shared by all. At worse, this low level could descend right down to universal destitution, a condition which would make the power of the communist rulers even more complete.

The complete consolidation of communist state control began in 1949. This new order gradually replaced the previous social and economic order, duly atomized and disintegrated. In the course of this process of consolidation, a trend opposite to dis-integration could be observed.

For the communists now aimed at forming large dominated units. In agriculture, for example, the many independent farm-ers could cause trouble to the Party. Accordingly, the number of independent farmers had to be reduced to a minimum. The peasantry was forced into collective farms. Two kinds of farms were developed: state farms and cooperatives. The state farm was but a new form of the old system of large landed estates, with the difference, however, that the big landowners were directly eliminated and replaced by the state, in effect, the Com-munist Party. In cooperative farms, reliable men of the Com-munist Party held the key positions of control and supervision.

The method of coercion into joining was simple. Unbearable taxes and deliveries were levied on peasants not belonging to cooperatives. If they did not break down under this treatment, the secret police, the AVO, took over.

Economic life entirely lacked the healthy regulatory effect of supply and demand. All price-building factors were in the hands of government. The state was able to set prices useful to political ends. Thus, the fortunes of the peasantry no longer depended on crop results, but were determined in a very real way by the communist leaders themselves.

In industry, similarly, the communists aimed at building larger units more easily controllable. After nationalizing small industry, an opportunity presented itself to establish smaller factories using the equipment of several small tradesmen. Within middle-size industry, significant regroupings were carried through as well. Enterprises were "profiled," an expression by which the regime meant consolidating those factories equipped with the same machines into a single, large common factory organized to manufacture a single article.

Stabilization of the communist state order required the formation of large units in other fields as well. In education, in youth organizations, even in the field of scientific research, big collectives mushroomed.

The power of communist bureaucracy soon became more and more evident. This vast bureaucracy was but a natural concomitant of the system. Power in the communist state was and still is exercised in two ways: First, by administrative action in the form of departmental and governmental decrees and decisions; and second, through the agencies of the Communist Party.

Departments of government in the communist state lost the significance they had had under non-communist administration. They deteriorated into subordinate agencies of execution, even though the number of their personnel was higher than ever.

In order to control fully the state apparatus without opposition so as to govern completely, the Communist Party had to build an apparatus almost equal in number to the government staffs. Thus, even apart from the numerous superfluous administrative agencies and offices designed to replace the liquidated private sector of the economy, the state administrative staff was just about duplicated by the Party apparatus. This vast number of people, all occupied with some function of leadership, amounted to the vanguard of the Communist Party. Instead of doing hard physical work, as many of them formerly had done, they now occupied high positions of communist bestowed dignity, coupled with authority and personal privilege, such as the exclusive use of official cars. The Communist Party secured extraordinary advantages for all of its faithful. They enjoyed wealth, select vacation resorts, even special shops, where this "new class" could obtain imported luxury goods at low prices. In this way, a new aristocracy was imposed on the country within two years of the takeover, exceeding both in numbers and in power the role of the old aristocracy. This artificial social class might perhaps be fittingly labelled the "proletarian aristocracy." Having forsaken their class goals, which their own Marxian creed dictated that they honor, Party members usurped power crudely and undeservedly.

The formation of such a new aristocracy is an indispensable process in any communist country. Only such a class, abruptly developed, may serve as the reliable support for a ruling clique. It also serves, for a time, as a façade hiding the truth from public view that a dictatorship has been established, not by the proletariat but by a small fanatic band receiving its orders from Moscow.

The dualism of the communist exercise of power often plays a trick on western opinion and thus secures an advantage for the communists. The western world is apt to believe that discussions with communist heads of state, ministers, and other leading officials, may have significance and that their declarations are something to build upon. Yet the dualism of government and Party always renders such an expectation doubtful. In general, negotiations by communist ministers aim merely at sounding out the other side with regard to intention. They obtain data for Communist Party functionaries who hold the power of decision in their hands and whose names are often unknown. Decisions are always made within Communist Party councils, not in government departments.

In communist countries, all the lines converge on one focal point, the first secretary of the Party. Only a man able to maintain, under the pretense of communist slogans and ideology, a personal dictatorship is fit to hold this position.

The first secretary of the Communist Party and the prime

minister of a country may be the same person. But such exceptional coincidence used to occur in extraordinary cases only,
such as war, or political crises of particular gravity.

In Hungary, the communists who built the new communist
order feared a world war and, accordingly, the first secretary
of the Communist Party was also the nation's Prime Minister.

This period under Matyas Rakosi saw the country's complete
subordination to the Soviet Union. What up to that time was
going on only in a disguised and rather clandestine manner
was now officially announced as policy by the Prime Minister
Rakosi himself. Every act of his Government was prescribed by
Moscow. By this time the *Cominform,* an agency of coordination
existing among the various Communist Parties, had lost its importance. Complete subservience to Moscow was guaranteed by
the person of the dictator.

Communist Political Science

I sense that in a communist state antagonisms fraught with
crises arise sooner than in a non-communist state. The exercise
of absolute power in the Soviet bloc has always required the
rule of a single Communist Party clique. This has naturally
developed the requirement that other cliques born of human,
personal, or ideological antagonism had to be exterminated.
And, as the inexorable logic of totalitarianism dictates, if such
rival cliques did not emerge, they must be artificially created.
The ruling class definitely needs such rivals. It must deliver a
blow on someone, or upon some group, in order to make someone responsible, even if within the Party organization, for the
troubles which have persisted and will continue to persist in
more and more obvious forms. This in turn has brought about
the various trials against communists, as the Rajk affair in
Hungary, and its counterparts in other communist countries.
It was the purpose of such trials that the real or supposed rivals
of the dictator were to be crushed. Developments in Hungary
showed that in the wake of these communist trials a fairly great
number of the accused managed to survive and some of them

along with their sympathizers within the very ranks of the Communist Party. There were many communists living in perpetual anguish, fearing that they would be taken to task for their friendship with one or another of the accused or executed communists. This mental torment created a perpetual latent antagonism within the Party.

Another natural source of danger within the communist state has been the continuing fear aroused in those of the new aristocracy, whose careers have been something less than successful, due to sprouting economic and organizational troubles, especially in the area of the bloody injustices committed under communist leadership. They feared then and now that they, too, would be taken to task if one day the western world should prove ultimately victorious against them despite all manner of communist ideological assurance. There emerged a wide mass of Party members who, bridging the chasm between slogans and truth, fought a momentous battle with their own consciences.

The realization that no one could quit the Party voluntarily, for whoever did so would instantly find himself in difficulty if not in prison, had a dual effect. On the one hand, while it forged a tight unity, it also generated centrifugal forces within that same tight Party unity. As a result, the opportunists who entered the Party because they were weaklings, or craved their daily bread, lived in perpetual torment lest by a possible change in political fortune they would find themselves responsible for all the crimes and inhumanities a dictator had committed in the name of Soviet socialism.

The period of greatest stability in the communist state order in Hungary was 1952. The omnipotent first secretary of the Communist Party held power literally over life and death. His limitless rule had been openly admitted by the controlled press. At this point Rakosi took a step, both necessary and fatal, which later proved to be one of the causes of the collapse of communist statism. He had the head of the secret police (AVO) arrested and convicted of crimes essentially attributable to Rakosi himself. This was necessary in order to make someone responsible for the bloodbaths. At the same time, data referring to the real causes of these bloodbaths had to be spirited away. The step was fatal because it shook the self-confidence and security of the secret police.

The dictator took this step because he considered himself now strong enough to oversee the activities of the secret police directly without an intermediate chain of command. But in his calculations he overlooked a basic danger which at once materialized. The secret police was overcome with fear.

It is appropriate that I say a few words here of the communist effort to replace the traditional morality by a new standard. A communist state order wants us to believe that communists are a kind of superman, better, wiser, and more mature than all other men. For instance, Soviet and Hungarian films depict the Communist Party secretary as an *Uebermensch* who is able to solve all the different and complicated problems of life. Communists try to create a new kind of hero worship which bestows a halo on their own heads. They preach an heroic view of life, which despises material success. This sophistry has naturally produced glaring contradictions in real life. For men have come to discover that Party secretaries and other Party officials, portrayed as austere heroes in films, rolled in riches and exhibited too many known human weaknesses. Meanwhile, the worker who toiled for low wages, and was asked to live a heroic life, could not attain even a minimum of material success.

All this generated an antagonism deep within the souls of men. The outward expression of this feeling could not in discretion go beyond the limits of a joke, a witticism, a passing comment. By the end of 1952 with criticism strictly contained the communist dictator and his ruling clique could well believe that power never had seen so safely in their hands.

But Stalin, the Soviet dictator died in 1953, and overnight this created an entirely new situation. In the Soviet Union, the groupings which had waited so silently for so long began to compete for power. As a first result, Rakosi, the first secretary of the Communist Party, had to resign as Prime Minister of Hungary.

On July 4, 1953, the new regime leader, Imre Nagy, who during the communist dictatorship felt the strong tension generated in the Party as well as in the country, presented a program which he himself described as being bounded by "socialist legality."

No sooner was this program announced than a battle broke out between the Government and the Party. The first secretary of the Party saw clearly from the initial reactions to the announced program that popular wrath would ultimately sweep away his personal dictatorship. Accordingly, he did everything in his power to frustrate the program and to replace Prime Minister Nagy who was a Party member, it must be remembered, by a man submissive to Rakosi's orders.

This period abounded in measures adopted, only to be withdrawn. Among the decrees adopted were the dissolution of internment camps, permission for internally deported people to return to their homes, revision of cases of political prisoners and regulation of the procedure for rehabilitation, easing the burdens levied on the peasantry, the raising of wages, and several other first steps toward liberalization. In the course of carrying out the Nagy program, the Communist Party sabotaged a portion of it and amended still other provisions of the plan. Although the first secretary of the Communist Party did his best to revive the old, stormy traditions of dictatorship, criticism was stirring everywhere throughout the country.

Some communists hoped that the dictatorship could be transformed, and the memory of the crimes committed might fade, while a form of state could still be maintained in which power was exercised by the Communist Party.

The first secretary, Rakosi, succeeded in removing Prime Minister Imre Nagy on April 19, 1955, but he no longer had the strength and power to have Nagy executed as in the days of old. Nor did he possess strength enough to answer the accusations of relatives and friends of those executed in the wake of earlier communist trials. Finally, on orders of Moscow, Rakosi once more vacated his position as director on July 18, 1956.

All this, of course, happened within the larger context of the weakening of the dictatorship in Moscow and the long struggle being fought out in the Soviet Union. In February 1955, Soviet Prime Minister Malenkov resigned and handed control over to First Secretary Nikita Khrushchev and Prime Minister Bulganin. The struggle continues with Khrushchev appearing victorious.

In Hungary, communist rule continued as before under the lordship of Soviet power through 1955 and part of 1956. Political and economic life dragged on, almost exclusively by way of its own inertial force.

The Warsaw Pact, which formally joined the Soviet occupied countries into a military alliance, came into being on May 14, 1955, prior to the Geneva Conference of Heads of Governments. The dating of the Warsaw Pact seems to indicate, at least to me, that the removal of Prime Minister Imre Nagy had been required by the Soviet Union. For the Soviet leaders could not know whether or not Nagy would have placed obstacles in the way of concluding such a Pact.

The Geneva "summit" Conference, July 18-23, 1955, had a decisive influence on the development of the Soviet occupied countries, Hungary among them. The Conference's results prompted the Soviet Union to issue directives requiring the stabilization of the communist order in Hungary. But it proved difficult to maintain that order. The liberalization process begun in 1953 made public an ever growing series of abuses. Through the gates of prisons men who had been convicted and sentenced on the basis of false charges walked out into life. The ranks of the communists split. Writers and other intellectuals were eager to cast off the shackles placed on free expression. The youth, endowed by nature with a good sense for discovering abuse, now delighted in making it public. Shame and bitterness accumulated in the public mind of a nation violently subdued and controlled. The inner struggle raging within the Communist Party relaxed the merciless grip of dictatorship.

People longed for reforms. By way of reaction, communist oppression produced a general longing for freedom.

When the new Party first secretary, Ernoe Geroe, answered the demands of youth assembled on October 23, 1956, he had nothing to offer but threats and further repressive measures. The accumulated bitterness of the years burst forth and the revolution started.

The cruel terror which has followed the Soviet armed crushing of the revolt in Hungary has furnished new evidence to verify the experience that communism can be maintained in only one way: foreign armed might, the gallows and prison.

Ironically, the post revolt dictator, Janos Kadar, who launched the wave of terror is the same man who, two years ago, had demanded that Rakosi be impeached for his crimes. These sad and tragic happenings furnish additional conclusions for the lesson of history: communism is man's worst dictatorship guided by a single principle, the principle of egoistic expedience.

The Hungarian Economy in the Communist Era

BY DR. BELA BALASSA

In an examination of the causes of the Hungarian Revolution, usually not much weight is assigned to economic reasons. Yet the economic situation of Hungary greatly contributed to the outbreak of the uprising. In stressing the importance of economic causes, however, I do not want to de-emphasize the impact of political and ideological factors. The limited Hungarian liberalization due to the policy of partial de-stalinization, the intellectual freedom movement and the collective psychical resistance against communism were also factors of primary importance.

In 1945, the Communist Party appeared on the scene with reform claims which played a role in the program of non-communist parties as well, and which enjoyed popularity with the great majority of Hungarians. In substance, these demands aimed at changing the structure of a still somewhat backward feudal type society.

Land reform was one of these demands. Nearly all parties agreed that land reform was a social need. But serious differences cropped up as to the manner and pace of its accomplish-

*Dr. Balassa is a Hungarian economist.

ment. The communists understood this problem only too well
and brought from Moscow ready-made land reform blueprints.
With the aid of their Soviet friends, the Hungarian communists
introduced the plan at once. The non-communist parties just
emerging from an underground existence had no time to study
the proposed legislation and suddenly, it seemed, land reform
was accomplished. In the course of its enforcement, abuses occurred which could not be corrected later. The non-communist
parties found themselves in a situation where to object would
appear to dispute major points of their own programs. This they
could not do and, consequently, the enactment of Public Law
6/1945 amounted in substance to placing a communist land
reform bill on the statute books.

The difference between the non-communist parties and the
Communist Party on land reform can be summarized. The non-
communist parties wanted desperately to solve this long post-
poned economic question by means of land redistribution: to
replace large estates with healthy small holdings. In the eyes
of the communists, however, land reform served merely the
purpose of dissolving the existing social order, and they were
completely indifferent to the question of whether the emerging
new conditions were to be healthy or not.

From the beginning, the Communist Party also demanded
nationalization of major industries and mining. The democratic
parties themselves aimed at establishing modern social and economic conditions. As a result, they were unable to parry communist agitation because the non-communists could not undertake the defense of industrialists a part of whom collaborated
with the Nazis. The communists for their part dictated a legislative pace in transforming the economic order which Hungarian
society could not follow without jolts and jars and, in retrospect,
their innovations proved indigestible to a considerable extent.

Financial difficulties went hand in hand with the reckless
handling of important economic issues. Looking back with a
measure of historical perspective, one has the impression that
a runaway inflation was intentionally conjured up by the communists to accelerate reconstruction through a decrease in real
wages, at the same time blaming the industrialists for the infla-

tionary spiral. As a matter of fact, inflation reached its most hectic pace at a time, the summer of 1946, when the Government fought most doggedly against communist demands for further nationalization.

At a time when the non-communist parties eventually agreed to nationalize public utilities including coal mining and electrical combines, the communists had already demanded nationalization of banking and industry other than public utilities. The majority Smallholder Party, advocating as it did the idea of private property, could go no further down this road under any pressure beyond nationalization of banking. Even this measure proved an economic reform of very dubious value for serious troubles ensued in its wake In all fields of economic life. But the communists, in their resolve to dominate, aimed at disintegrating the entire economic structure and thus, through this tactic, achieving the annihilation of the ruling democratic party.

In 1948 and 1949, the communists accomplished their specialization plan. In place of the individual enterprises mammoth "industrial centers" were formed. Later, similar institutions emerged depending on political utility throughout the entire economic fabric.

The industrial centers were subordinated to corresponding departments of government, which were in turn controlled indirectly by Moscow through the Party.

Hungarian industrial plants were reorganized in 1950, and according to the new order, the meshing in with Soviet industrial needs was the next step. The Soviet Union instructed each of the satellite countries what industrial products they had to manufacture.

The Peace Treaty, signed by the Great Powers in 1947, could count on implementation in one category only. The Soviet Union mercilessly collected her reparation claims. In the period of the gradual downfall of non-communist political influence these reparation payments, because of the inordinately low prices set by the Soviet Union on all deliveries, weighed on the country as an intolerable burden.

Economic life under communism is characterized in general

by two phenomena: incessant reorganization and change of norms. It is widely known that communist economic life is directed through "Five Year Plans." The first Five Year Plan in Hungary began in 1950. This plan listed vast investment and production projects. The economic specialists at communist headquarters knew, as did anyone else with some knowledge of the Hungarian economy, that these plans were unattainable. The plans were made deliberately unrealistic because productivity and consideration of efficiency were subordinated to the Soviet orders and the requirements of rearmament.

The Essence of Planning

One cannot investigate economic phenomena such as described above without looking into psychological, political, and sociological matters, and here I shall deal with the impact of psychological and sociological phenomena and of political matters on the economy, rather than the other way round.

The Hungarian economic situation before the revolution was critical. The inherent deficiencies of collectivist economic planning and the catastrophic economic policy had caused the national standard of living to fall below the prewar level. And more depressing, the Hungarian people did not see any possibility of improvement within the framework of the communist system. The years of planning and communist policy had amply proved to the populace that the deficiencies of the system were inherent. Thus, given the opportunity, the Hungarian people had no recourse but to try to change the system itself.

One of the fundamental causes of failure of the communist economic system in Hungary, a consequence of collectivist economic planning itself, was the lack of initiative. In comparison with a free enterprise system, a collectivist system cannot exhibit individual incentives necessary for the best possible realization of economic possibilities. Collectivist planning neither is nor can be an equivalent substitute for private initiative.

Besides the lack of initiative, which might be termed the psychological factor, there is the political factor, the impact of the political attitude of the Hungarian people on the economy. Whatever the mechanical faults of the economy may have been the hostility of the Hungarian people towards communism contributed in considerable measure to the failure of the communist economic system. Nor should the importance of Soviet exploitation, which in its various forms impaired the economic situation in Hungary, be underestimated.

Another important factor which contributed to the failure of communist economic policy in Hungary, was the catastrophic agricultural policy of the regime. Instead of intensifying the development of agriculture, the Government embarked upon enforced collectivization. This policy led to the impairment of the peasant's initiative and meant, in reality, a step backward. Communist investment policy involving the neglect of economic balance in connection with the achievement of military and political goals also loomed large in the destruction of economic society.

Another aspect of the human equation in communist economics is the problem of premium payments which appeared as a Marxian substitute for profit, and which enveloped both the national wage policy and the matter of trade unions in its vicious snare.

Some consideration must also be given to the Hungarian national income and its distribution, as well as to the standard of living.

Marxist-Leninist theory does not admit the role of psychological factors in a collectivist economy. It rather asserts that after the abolition of the capitalist system "the rational behavior of rational man" will be dominant. It further argues that the aims of society will be substituted for the self-interest of mankind as the fundamental aim both of collective and individual behavior. Communist theory does not recognize the possibility, and the reality, of a clash between collectivism and individualism. This false belief is quite widespread not only among Marxists, but also among non-Marxists who favor some form of collectivism. Nevertheless, psychological factors do possess great importance within a collectivist economic system, and frankly it is simply not possible to assess the problems of a collectivist economy without giving due consideration to this phenomenon.

First and foremost among the psychological interrelationships linking human behavior and economic goals is the problem of initiative. Without going into a discussion concerning the role of proper private initiative in capitalism and the possibility of a divergence between selfish motives and the welfare of the community, it may be presumed that individual initiative in a free enterprise system greatly contributes to the development and employment of a nation's economic resources. The question naturally arises: what happens to personal motivation under a collectivist system? Does it disappear or does it contribute to the development of the economy? Communist authors and thinkers are inclined to assume, if not explicitly, then implicitly, that human nature tends to change in a collectivist system. These authors envisage a "happy" state of harmony between the interests of the community and those of the individual. However, neither logical reasoning nor the recorded experience of communist economies prove this premise. Personal or selfish motives of individuals constantly strive to find outlet in human activity. This is not simply a matter of theoretical interest, but treats rather of the real world around us and has direct applicability to the Hungarian and other Soviet-type economies.

The main material goal of the individual is still generally considered to be the achievement of his personal welfare. But in a communist society, with its limited legal possibilities in this area, the individual is induced to use semi-legal or illegal methods for the achievement of his objective.

This communist-created lack of outlets for private initiative and the consequent clash between individual interests and the interests of the Marxian community is reflected in two fundamental facts: there is no source of private initiative striving for the betterment of the economic system; and the course of selfish motivation frequently employs outlets of net disadvantage to the communist economic system as a whole.

State employees in the Hungarian collectivist system, for instance, rarely had desires to improve industrial techniques or reduce prime costs. In a free competitive economic system, every entrepreneur is forced to reduce costs to insure a competitive market position, and the reduction of costs eventually leads to the reduction of prices.

Is there any compelling force leading to reduction of costs in a collectivist economy? Is there any inducement which finally would lead to price decreases? The Hungarian experience has shown that there is no such drive. Managers of state enterprises were and are mainly administrators who must carry out the directions of their supervising ministries. There is no motive which would impel them to reduce costs. Communist authorities tried to induce managers of factories to decrease costs by paying premiums for plan fulfillment. Yet, this method led to an increase of prices rather than to a decrease of costs. Similar conclusions may be drawn regarding the quality of output. In a free enterprise system consumer independence is likely to shift from products of lower quality to those of better quality compelling producers to improve quality.

In a collectivist economy the situation is completely different. Due to extreme specialization of manufacturing there is a tendency to allot the production of one type of goods to one factory only. The consumer has no choice whatsoever and he is forced either to buy the product desired, regardless of quality, or refrain from purchasing altogether. On the other hand, Hungarian enterprises were inclined to produce poor quality goods because even those could be sold and the poorer the quality the greater the savings in cost, thereby increasing premium possibilities for the manager and his staff. In Hungary, an additional cause for the deterioration of quality was the incessant Party demands for quantitative results.

This deterioration of quality was felt most heavily in the fields of consumer investment goods. This fact was even acknowledged by the Government. *Szabad Nep* (Free People), the official Party paper, wrote on June 19, 1956, "the quality of a number of consumer goods has deteriorated owing to our exaggerated drive for quantitative results. Because of this situation new purchases became necessary more frequently due to the poor quality of the commodities and as a result real wages were correspondingly reduced."

Modernization of plant and industrial techniques are still other aspects of initiative. In a free enterprise system the entrepreneur is compelled to modernize in order to keep up with the forces of competition. In a collectivist system such compulsion does not exist. Application of new techniques becomes an administrative question. It is not at all certain that the best technique would be applied at the proper time and place. Modernization is also subject to political considerations. Take the case of Hungarian light industry. Political and military considerations favoring heavy industry led to neglect of even the proper maintenance of machines in the light industrial area. The drive for quantitative results, the general lack of personal interest in the proper maintenance of machines in all areas of industry on the theory that the state will supply another one if necessary, led to the deterioration of productive equipment and machinery throughout the nation.

The individual is not at all interested in the welfare of the state, he is interested in his own welfare. In the communist system he does not connect his individual welfare with that of the state. He takes into consideration his general situation and dismisses the possibility that his personal gain might eventually harm the state's welfare. He is willing to see the communist state suffer a loss at the instance of his personal advantage. There are countless examples of this reaction in communist Hungary. Negligence in connection with material, machinery and tools annually inflicted immense losses on the economy. Considerable material stock was stolen each year, generally without assigning responsibility for it. No one, absolutely no one, cared about state owned property. This phenomenon found its origin not only in the needs and motives of the individual but also in the popular attitude toward the entire communist system.

What was the attitude of the Hungarian people towards the communist system and what were the repercussions of this attitude upon the functioning of the Hungarian economy? Communist propaganda asserts that Soviet style governments lack any contradiction between state and people. In contrast to this assertion one could refer to the divergence in material interest, as outlined above, or to the divergence of political interest and its effect upon the economy. "The factory no longer belongs to the capitalists, it now belongs to you, fellow-workers," has been a frequently used slogan of communist propaganda since Lenin's time. But workers in general are sufficiently mundane to prefer higher wages here and now to an alleged proprietorship which falls short in its most important respect, pecuniary gain. It is not saleable and the alleged "proprietors" have no influence whatsoever on the management of the enterprises. Workers' logic is very simple: Hungarian factories were socialized between 1948 and 1950. Has the standard of living risen since then? The answer is no. In the meantime, despite communist efforts to the contrary, the workers became acquainted with some of the facts regarding the standard of living in free enterprise countries. They heard about the favorable results of a free enterprise system in West Germany and the corresponding failure of the East German communist economy. At the same time, they heard the ceaseless propaganda about the superiority of the communist system over capitalism. Yet the facts seemed to prove the opposite.

Workers in communist Hungary felt that they were not in fact the owners of the factories. But who did own the factories? Who was the real owner? There must be somebody, some group controlling industry and not only the factories but virtually the whole country. This line of thought reasoned: the owners of the factory, the owners of the whole country are those who reign and rule in the country, who enjoy special privileges and a considerably higher standard of living. This is the new ruling class—people who hold the highest positions in the Party and state apparatus, the privileged minority. The workers felt that a small group held both political and economic power and the worker was literally compelled to labor for this class. The worker did not share a common interest with this group, but rather felt that the interests of the new class were, in fact, opposite those of labor. Political suppression made him feel that the state represented the hated communist ruling class. As a result, if he damaged factory property, the worker felt he had damaged property belonging to his enemy.

These political and psychological factors frequently led workers in Hungary from acts of simple negligence to conscious sabotage. Hostility against the communist state often resulted in deliberate impediments being placed in the path of economic objectives. One additional point should be mentioned here, the consequence of compulsion. If a man acts freely, he normally feels he is acting in the best possible way. Yet if he is forced to do or not to do something, he feels himself denied, though in reality this might be only a subjective feeling. Compulsion and limitation of alternatives, however, lead ultimately to a decrease in the individual's subjective welfare. The collectivist state exercises compulsion over the entire area of economic life, limits individual opportunity and thereby creates a climate for adverse psychological consequences. As examples, there were the limited alternatives in available goods, the compulsory delivery system in agriculture and the restricted possibilities in the choice of occupation. All these conditions had similar effects on the subjective welfare of the individual ending in communist control of his activity.

Agriculture Under Communism

Before the Second World War, agriculture held a dominant position in Hungary. In addition to satisfying domestic agricultural needs, agricultural products comprised the main Hungarian exports. But Hungarian agriculture also had its shadowy side. The distribution of land holdings was exceedingly unequal, a semblance of feudalism was still evident. As a result, cultivation was extensive. Before the war there had been a strong movement towards individual farming and intensification of cultivation. The land reform of 1945 at first gave some hope for further development. Yet instead of development, the last decade has displayed the steady deterioration of Hungarian agriculture. Hungary is no longer able to export products of the land in considerable quantity. In fact, Hungary has been compelled to import food. This deterioration of agriculture was due directly to communist policy. To examine communist agricultural policy in Hungary, I must go back briefly to the teachings of Lenin who urged the fight against the kulak (an independent farmer who owns more than twenty five acres of land) and who declared the necessity of agricultural collectivization as a support for socialist industry. The Hungarian communist leaders did their best to fulfill these goals. However, was it reasonable to apply the methods of Soviet agriculture to Hungary?

In the Soviet Union the kulak held important political and economic power before his decline. Soviet leaders endeavored to destroy the leading elements of the peasantry, therein strengthening communist rule in the villages. In Hungary, kulaks held neither strong economic nor political power. After the land reform of 1945 there were no differences in wealth in Hungary as was the case in Russian villages. Yet the enterprising, individualistic Hungarian kulak was the most industrious element of the Hungarian peasantry, which had reached a somewhat better economic position in life largely through its own personal efforts. Hungarian communists caused a serious setback in agriculture by separating the kulaks from their property. Marketable production had come primarily from the kulak surpluses. Furthermore, crops were usually of better quality on kulak lands. And to make matters worse, the lower middle class of farmers never felt quite safe through fear of eventual classification as kulaks with the pressures that brought from the regime. Personal initiative in terms of production was considerably reduced by this fear of persecution as kulaks. The adverse consequences of the liquidation of the kulak were felt throughout the entire economy. Lenin's dictum prescribed the collectivization of agriculture. Without assessing the success or failure of collective farms in the Soviet Union, I should merely like to suggest some of the major existing differences existing between Soviet and Hungarian agricultural realities and experience. Firstly, the density of population is approximately indexed at four per square mile in the USSR and thirty-nine in Hungary. These figures alone indicate that the problems of Hungarian agriculture differ considerably from those of Soviet agriculture. To translate this into a more familiar setting, it is inconceivable that the extensive methods of cultivation generally applied in the United States would be practical in Denmark.

The methods of extensive cultivation of land operate with relatively low unit costs and yield per acre based on mechanization and low labor costs. In the Soviet Union extensive cultivation in large units is feasible. But as one would not compel the Danish farmer to imitate American production methods, it was as wrong to apply a production organization and methods employed in the Soviet Union to Hungarian agriculture. A dense population coupled with a low land laborer ratio required intensive cultivation which is better obtainable in small units. Adoption of this system had also led traditionally to export possibilities for Hungarian agriculture. Yet political considerations induced the Hungarian communist government to imitate the Soviet example: to enforce collectivization, thereby creating large units under inefficient cultivation. Thus the trend of earlier Hungarian agricultural policy dating to the twenties was reversed, bringing about a general decline in Hungarian agriculture.

Communist collectivization had its beginnings in 1949. Yet despite the considerable regime effort, only twenty percent of arable land was collectivized by 1956. The attainment of the goal of collectivization in different regions of the country varied in direct ratio to the pressure employed. The failure of this policy is reflected in the fact that during the revolution about ninety percent of the kolkhozes (collective farms) were disbanded. After the Soviet army had crushed the uprising, not even the pressure of the new communist regime could prevent the complete dissolution of fifty percent of the former collective farms.

The extent of the failure of collectivization in agriculture can best be shown by an examination of relevant production figures. According to data the Hungarian Ministry of Agriculture published during the revolution, the productivity (crop/acre) of communist-run state farms was some twenty percent and that of individual privately owned farms some fifty percent above the productivity of the kolkhozes.

The inefficiency of kolkhozes can be traced mainly to psychological factors. An outstanding characteristic of the Hungarian peasant is his individuality. The Russian peasant had long been accustomed to collective style farm work in his *mir* which existed before the First World War. The Hungarian peasant has always preferred to work individually. He did not feel any direct connection between his work in the kolkhoz and the benefits he derived. For example, the fact that peasants were inclined to work a shorter day in the collective farms than they formerly worked on their own farms accounts for about a ten to fifteen percent decrease in productivity. A small piece of land (up to one acre) for personal use was left to those peasants who entered the kolkhozes. Usually the peasants tried to concentrate their effort on the plots of land left to them, rather than to participate actively in the work of the kolkhoz. There was no incentive to cultivate the collective farms. Thus common land under intensive cultivation yielded less than it had under property ownership. The effects of such activities on communist agricultural policy can be guessed.

For example, production of coarse grains declined five percent in the years 1950 to 1954 from the level achieved in the period 1936 to 1940. Such decreases were common and ranged from a seventeen percent drop in tobacco productivity over the 1936 to 1940 period, to a drop in the production of bread grain from a yearly average of 2.79 million tons during the period 1911 to 1915 to 2.63 million tons in the span 1950 to 1954. Thus in communist Hungary production at times dipped even below the level of the 1911 to 1915 period. This depressing fact is made even more startling if we examine comparative population figures. The population in Hungary in the 1911-1915 period reached some eight million. By 1954, Hungary's population was close to ten million. Hence, if one adds this consideration to the formula, per capita production in bread grains, to cite one example, decreased by about twenty-five percent in comparison with the pre-World War I period. A decrease in per capita production naturally resulted in the reduction of real consumption and export figures.

In considering per capita production of basic coarse grains, the decrease amounted to fifteen percent relative to the level of 1911 to 1915. Since coarse grain serves as fodder in Hungary, a decrease in per capita figures indicates an ultimate reduction in national meat consumption.

The figures outlined above serve not only as indicators regarding the present situation in agriculture but also serve to reflect the impact of communist agricultural production on the standard of living.

Completely aside from the various unfavorable production results affecting standard crops, considerable additional damage was incurred by forcing upon a reluctant countryside production of crops such as cotton and rice, whose cultivation was in no real way economical or practical in Hungary. However, the headlong drive for autarky within the Soviet bloc led almost inevitably to such absurd cultivation projects. For several years certain farmers were compelled to produce cotton on parts of their land. The fact that production costs of cotton were about ten times as high as the world market price was not sufficient reason to militate against attempts at cotton production. Only after a series of disastrous harvests, when the yield was less than the grain sown, did the regime finally decide to end this fruitless and costly experiment. The results of rice production were not significantly better. Production costs in an essentially temperate climate were many times higher than in warmer climates. Yet for want of free trade, rice production is still continued. This decline in Hungarian agriculture was also detrimental for foreign trade. In 1955, as a result of the loss of an exportable surplus, the value of agricultural imports amounted to a significant seventy-five percent of the total value of agricultural exports. This decrease in exports was especially marked in the quality products of agriculture such as wine, fruit, and horticulture since collectivization of agriculture generally discourages cultivation of labor and time-consuming products. Furthermore, not only were quality farm products curtailed, but there was an accompanying decrease in the export of staples, such as corn and rye. To be sure, the decrease in the export of quality products and staples was partially counterbalanced by the export of poultry and dairy products which resulted in a permanent domestic scarcity of meat, poultry, and butter. This chaotic situation brought forth such strange happenings as the export and import of the same products. It was not uncommon for wheat to be exported in the fall of the year, when the Government needed foreign exchange, and imported in spring, when wheat stocks were no longer sufficient to cover the minimum needs of the population. The regime strove to export products of higher quality and to import items of lower quality for the consumption of the people. For example, the best Hungarian wheat was always exported and French wheat of a lower quality was imported. In the fall of 1954, wheat valued at some 4.6 million forints was exported, while the following spring wheat was imported at a cost of 17.4 million forints. The same year butter exports yielded 2.9 million forints in revenue while imports costing 2.8 million forints were required.

These figures involving productivity, per capita production and foreign trade amply reflect the failure of the regime's policy and its effects on the whole of agriculture, the national standard of living and Hungarian foreign trade. The picture painted is certainly no tribute to the efficacy of communist planning.

Economic Exploitation

Soviet rule in Hungary had its impact on politics and ideology as well as on economic matters. Moscow dictation of economic life consisted not only in servile imitation of Soviet methods and policy, but also in the deliberate and planned exploitation of Hungarian resources for the overall advantage of the USSR. Exploitation of the Hungarian economy and more generally the economies of the satellite countries assumed various forms. Exploitation through reparation payments was used against the former allies of Nazi Germany: Rumania and Hungary. Fiscal malpractices, overvaluation of the ruble and a dual standard of quality for goods imported into the USSR as compared with good exported from the Soviet Union were constantly employed. Exploitation was also carried on through the use of Soviet and mixed (Soviet-satellite) enterprises established in the captive countries. A very profitable technique involved compulsory satellite support of Soviet troops garrisoned on their territories.

Economic exploitation of Hungary dates back to 1945 when it was decided that Hungary was to pay reparations to the Soviet Union for damages caused during the Second World War. Reparation payments were fixed in the amount of two hundred million dollars based upon the value of the dollar in 1938. Reparations were to be supplied in the form of commodities. In practice, the value of the commodities to be delivered was much higher than the amount originally stipulated. This result was achieved through various manipulations of the Soviet authorities. The value of the U.S. dollar had decreased by about fifty percent from 1938 to 1946. The Soviets made up reparation lists in such a manner that they favored commodities whose prices had increased more than one hundred percent. The reparation lists contained many commodities whose prices had actually increased by two to three hundred percent. Hence, the Soviet Union got more for their "reparation dollars" than just the average value difference between the 1938 and 1946 dollar. A considerable proportion of the goods sought as reparations by the Soviet Union was not available in Hungary. In certain cases, the Soviets pressed the Hungarian authorities to obtain these goods from abroad. These demands naturally laid an additional burden on the Hungarian economy. By reason of her unfavorable export position, Hungary had to export goods below their production costs in order to fulfill her obligations to the Soviet Union. In certain other cases, the Soviet Union cleverly accepted the delivery of alternate types of goods, but only at the expense of still more favorable terms.

Undervaluation of goods supplied as reparation to the Soviet Union was quite customary. The Soviets set very high quality control requirements on delivered goods and frequently they applied quality discounts on inconsequential or non-existent quality defects.

According to the best estimates, the real value of the goods supplied by Hungary to the USSR was some sixty to eighty percent higher than the value of the reparation payments originally stipulated.

A most important form of Soviet exploitation was manipulation of foreign trade. After the Second World War a complete change occurred in the traditional pattern of Hungarian foreign trade. It was Soviet intent to cut the trade ties of Hungary with western capitalist countries and alternatively to develop multiple trade relations inside the Soviet bloc. The compulsory nature of these trade relations was obvious from the most cursory glance at Soviet methods. The USSR required the Hungarians to deliver products whose production was completely uneconomical. Hungary, on the other hand, had to import commodities such as industrial machinery from the Soviet Union which were easily obtainable on better terms elsewhere. In the first year, Soviet orders were not discernible in any pattern. The fulfillment of these orders caused considerable harm to the fragile Hungarian economy since the production of these required goods demanded frequent switch-overs in the production plans of the affected Hungarian factories.

Price manipulations were also frequently used in trade between Hungary and the Soviet Union. The Soviets often fixed prices below the world market for goods imported into the USSR. On the other hand, iron ore exported from the Soviet Union to Hungary was priced above the world market level. Furthermore, iron ore destined for the Hungarian steel plant at Sztalinvaros was not only priced above the world market level but its contents were lower in quality than the contents of the standard ore available on the world market. The aim of Soviet trade exploitation, bilateral as well as multilateral, was to create a world-wide trading relationship by which the USSR could acquire precious western currencies through satellite exports to the West.

For example, Egypt asked for bids on the construction of an electrical power plant at El Tabin. The Hungarian offer was the lowest bid although it was evident that Hungary could not build the plant for anything near the stipulated amount. By bidding the lowest figure, Hungary's offer was accepted. The contract price amounted to 1.6 million Egyptian pounds (about 6.4 million dollars). The real cost of construction had by October 1956 amounted to some 600 million forints and still the plant had not yet been finished. Thus the costs incurred in construction were about ten times the price paid by Egypt. Yet Hungary had to bid low for the award since Egyptian pounds were among the scarce currencies desired by the Soviet bloc. These Egyptian pounds were sorely needed by Hungary, obviously, but the amount received from Egypt was not poured into the Hungarian economy. Hungary had to buy cotton with the pounds and then resell the cotton to the Soviet Union. Thus the construction deficit was borne by the Hungarian people and the beneficiary was the USSR.

Then there is the example of Soviet exploitation of several satellites in series. For many years the USSR bought coal from Poland at a specific price and resold it at a higher price to Czechoslovakia and Hungary. The coal was transported directly from Poland to the ultimate buyers without ever touching Soviet soil. The Soviet Union here employed the simple technique of middleman's commission.

The misuse of Hungarian uranium mines has become well-known as a typical example of Soviet exploitation. Prior to leaving Hungary, I worked with a Hungarian construction trust which was responsible for building roads and underground sites in the uranium mining area. My experiences are first hand and indeed revealing. After months of exploration, a considerable strain of uranium ore was found in the neighborhood of Pecs, a middle-sized town in southwest Hungary. Immediately, a Soviet enterprise was established to control the mining of the ore. Only the workers were Hungarians in the new enterprise; the managers, engineers, technicians, geologists were all Russian. No Hungarian could ever expect to obtain any information whatsoever regarding work in the mines, uranium content of the ore, quantities of ore mined and tonnage transported to the Soviet Union. The enterprise was directly responsible to the Soviet ministry in Moscow which deals with problems of atomic energy.

The Soviet uranium complex resembled the colonial enterprises of the by-gone days of colonization. Hungarian soil was being drained of its strength by this project, but the Soviet company was not subject to Hungarian laws, through communist insistence that the Hungarian state had absolutely no jurisdiction over such USSR projects. Buildings and mines were guarded by Soviet soldiers, and Soviet authorities held sole authority on who was or was not to enter the mines and official buildings.

Soviet engineers and technicians were relatively well paid in comparison to normal Hungarian salaries. While the average Hungarian engineer earned about the equivalent of $128 to $153 a month, Soviet engineers working in the uranium complex received, in addition to their full salary in rubles, a "colonial" forint allowance averaging some $427 monthly. Soviet technicians were paid a ruble salary plus a monthly allowance of $215. There was no civil or social intercourse between the Russian colony and the Hungarian population, a policy of "splendid isolation was rigidly preferred." The contribution of the Hungarian economy to the massive Soviet uranium effort consisted not only in giving up national ore deposits but the economy was forced to supply construction workers and the required material. It goes without saying that the construction of industrial buildings, dwellings, roads, and underground sites was supervised by Soviet authorities. Soviet management did employ some few Hungarians to assist in the supervision of the construction work, but all major decisions regarding problems of construction and price arrangements were made by the Soviets. Overnight the uranium mines became the most important Soviet investment in Hungary. As is generally typical in a totally planned economy, construction work in the mines initially developed a great shortage of materials. Yet this work had the highest priority under urgent Soviet insistence. The necessary material was to be provided, even if it required requisitioning from other Hungarian projects already underway. The completion of many critically needed workers' housing developments in Budapest and other Hungarian cities was interrupted for the sake of the uranium mines. Priority shifting of materials from various places of construction not only caused unnecessary transport expense, but, in terms more harmful to the

Hungarian people, resulted in the discontinuance of many practical construction projects.

Hungarian communist officials came in droves to the uranium mines, listened attentively to the orders of the Soviet representatives, and hurried back to Budapest to carry them out. The uranium mines assumed a privileged position in the distribution of such scarce materials as bricks, iron, and cement. Abuses were compounded at the direction of Soviet authority. Highway construction in the mountainous Pecs area was needed—quickly and without regard for cost. Thus work began in winter contrary to all professional advice. Construction proved impossible, as originally suggested by Hungarian engineers, and ultimately the road work was finished the following spring and summer. This needless waste was estimated to have cost the Hungarians eight times the normal cost per mile of highway construction. But there were no regrets, no apologies.

There is no reliable data in existence regarding the quantity of uranium extracted. The uranium was usually transported in the form of ore and the various extraction processes were carried out in the USSR. As a result, Hungary had no accurate data on the uranium content of the ore. According to a consensus of Hungarian escapee information, the total quantity of uranium ore transported to the USSR up to the date of the revolution was not great since work in the mines had not actually begun until the winter of 1955, but the ore was said to be very rich in uranium content. The strict non-interference of Hungarian authorities in matters concerning the uranium mines is well illustrated by the statement made during the revolution by Professor Janossy, a leading Hungarian scientist and member of Hungary's atomic energy commission, according to which he had not even been officially informed that uranium mining was going on in Hungary.

One of the first revolutionary demands was the nationalization of the Soviet uranium enterprise, the first instance in history, incidentally, when a communist "socialist" enterprise was to be nationalized. Free Hungary wished to mine her own uranium ore and should she desire to sell her uranium to do so on the world market. Following suppression of the revolt, the

Soviet "owners" resumed their work in the mines, then damaged by the insurgents, and uranium ore is still controlled by the Soviet Union as before.

Investment Policy in Hungary

To examine the communist investment policy in Hungary, one first should take a look at the broad objectives of overall economic policy. The main economic goal in communist Hungary was the achievement of a collectivist system based upon the model of Soviet planning. There was nothing new or original in this economic approach either in Hungary or in the other satellite states, since it was nothing more than servile imitation of the Soviet example. Therefore, similar to the Soviet Union, Hungarian authorities, upon the socialization of private enterprise, endeavored to emphasize the development of heavy industry coupled with the collectivization of agriculture.

A review of the Soviet example reveals that after some years of indecision the USSR authorities decided to devote their energies first to the development of heavy industry. Their reasoning seems to have been founded in the desire for autarky and the priority accorded military considerations. Soviet leaders in their fear psychosis aimed at self-sufficiency. They wanted to ensure their political and economic independence from western capitalism. The Soviet Union wanted to close her territory to the economic, political and ideological influences of capitalism. The development of heavy industry was to spark the growth of the entire Soviet economy. The USSR had another major reason for building up her heavy industry. It was to serve as a base for armament growth. In the light of the events of the Second World War this policy appears to have been reasonable. All of this was made possible by bountiful supplies of natural resources.

Following the takeover in East Europe, the Soviet satellite countries were compelled to pursue the same policy down to the last decimal point. The theory of a "single road to socialism" had led to the axiom that any deviation from the Soviet line was non-permissible. Thus, the investment policy of every satellite country aimed at the development of heavy industry to the neglect of light industry and agriculture.

In the formation of satellite investment policy valid economic considerations were almost entirely neglected. Policy objectives and methods were primarily based on political and military considerations. For example, the question of the ready availability of natural resources was not at all raised. No reasonable thought was apparently given to the fact that lack of convenient locations of natural resources would inevitably cause a considerable increase in the unit cost if the development of heavy industry was to be insisted upon.

It did not matter that Hungary lacked the very materials most important to the development of heavy industry. Hungary must, to cite a specific case, import eighty-five percent of her iron ore. Likewise, the labor productivity of the Hungarian coal-mining industry is but thirty-five percent of the neighboring Polish industry. Although Hungary could have enjoyed comparative advantage in some sectors of light industry and in agriculture, these fields were neglected in deference to Soviet directed objectives.

In a freely functioning system, ultimate profitability is the leading principle generally governing new investments. Every entrepreneur tries to improve his position by employment of new techniques and improvement of production methods. The market serves as a mechanism of checks and balances. The market reflects the profitableness of investments and reacts if investments prove unproductive. Under collectivism, investment decisions are made by the state. There is no natural market mechanism operating through the price system. And basically there is always present in communist countries the priority of politics and military considerations which ultimately govern economic decisions.

During the period of the first Five Year Plan ninety-four percent of investment funds serving industrial purposes was directed to heavy industry while six percent, an absolute minimum, was given over to light industry. This differential becomes even more marked if we take into consideration the fact that investment funds contain estimates for new investments as well as replacement of worn out equipment. Light industry's share of the fiscal pie was barely sufficient to replace obsolete and worn machinery. Since the regime's public posture required the construction of at least some new factories in the area of light industry, the supply of available investment monies to be allotted for older factories was not even sufficient to practice a sensible program of depreciation. Before World War II Hungarian light industry, especially the textile industry, held a favorable competitive world position. However, as a direct consequence of communist economic policy, Hungary by and large lost her markets. Even more frustrating was the fact of technological stagnation, at a time when western consumer research and technology were making major advances. The priority of political considerations over economic considerations is reflected in the frequent shifts in investment goals which usually followed rapid turns in the Soviet political line. As an illustration, the three main phases of Hungarian investment policy which followed the basic socialization of industry were:

1. From 1949 to 1953 about twenty to twenty-five percent of total national income was invested. The proportion of this investment allocated to heavy industry amounted to a high ninety-four percent.

2. In 1953 with the rise to power of Imre Nagy, the regime tried to achieve a better investment balance. The total amount spent for investments was cut. Heavy industrial investments in 1954, for example, amounted to only fifty-five percent of the previous year's rate. Some unproductive investments were discontinued and there was a marked tendency to expand investments in the agricultural field.

3. With the removal of Nagy from the premiership in 1955, the old obsession with heavy industry returned and the investment rate in this area once again shot up.

It is small wonder that these relatively frequent changes in the basic objectives to be sought caused grave difficulties in the Hungarian economy. In many cases adjustments to a new policy had not even been completed, when still another policy would be decided upon.

The equally decisive influence of military considerations was also easily discernible in Hungarian investment policy. Behind heavy industry obviously rested a communist military buildup. For on what other major premise can one justify such heavy expenditures of the Hungarian communist regime. It was certainly not necessary to sustain forced industrialization for peaceful purposes alone. Examined from the viewpoint of a peacetime economy, heavy industrialization of a small, poorly-endowed nation represents not only a waste of excess capacity but an unnatural balance of dangerous proportions. The history of Hungary's steel plant reveals some fundamental characteristics of this problem. After the Communist Party seized power in Hungary, construction of a new steel plant was decided upon. Work began at a site near the Yugoslav border in 1947. The plant was to be operated with iron ore imported from Yugoslavia and coking coal mined at a location convenient to the plant. However, with the Yugoslav-Soviet break in relations the plant was moved some 160 miles to the north, because the Hungarian communist leaders feared an eventual war with Yugoslavia, not to mention that they no longer received iron ore from Yugoslavia. An alternative supply was found in the Krivoy Rog region of the Soviet Union. The necessary increase in transportation expenses greatly increased production costs of the new plant. This increase in prime costs was in fact even more marked since the Soviet Union supplied low-grade ore which caused difficulties in the production process. Furthermore, the coal from the new mine fields which had previously been judged suitable for coking proved unusable. Coking coal had to be obtained from Poland. To make matters worse the equipment supplied by the Soviet Union was antiquated and unless the USSR could not supply it Hungary was refused permission to import needed machinery from western countries.

This economic excess and high handedness resulted in plant unit costs some sixty to eighty percent higher than unit costs of the old Hungarian plants. The ultimate cost of the steel plant, to cap the climax, amounted to ten percent of the entire gross investment covering the Five Year Plan period involved.

Plants serving military purposes were often disguised and registered as "hardware" or "chocolate" factories; two such plants were located in Sajobabony and Albertfalva. Further-more, it was customary practice to assign production of various military parts to different factories.

Aside from crash program priorities, neglect of investment development in the national economic life was basically at-tributable to a quirk in Marxist-Leninist theory. Marxism does not acknowledge the productivity of capital. Thus, in practice, communists, at least the Hungarian variety, tend to the ridicu-lous conclusion that any economist who might attempt to meas-ure investment yield and suggest recommendations on the basis of an examination of productivity was a reactionary. It is no wonder then that there was no development in the theory and practice of the measurement of productivity which naturally resulted in a completely non-scientific approach to proper economic growth.

Besides the unsatisfactory planning of investments in a wider sense, there were considerable deficiencies in planning of invest-ments in a narrow sense, that is, actual planning and organiza-tional work for individual enterprises. Deficiencies were gen-erally related to mistakes flowing from policy errors. Frequent changes in priority schedules and lack of scientific planning caused considerable extra and unnecessary expense due to the consequent need of duplicate transport systems, duplicate tech-nical planning and duplicate construction. At times, technical plans and designs were not even completed come the scheduled date for construction, thereby tying up work crews, losing many man hours of labor and setting back dates for future work and projects. This proved to be the sad history of both the electricity plant at Pecs and the uranium mine at Kovagoszollos.

Politico-military priorities frequently demanded relatively short time-spans for the completion of construction. It was often impossible to proceed in a normal economic fashion which, in general, would be first to build dwellings for the workers, roads for their use and sites for the job at hand. Almost always, prior-ities dictated that work on all fronts should be carried forward simultaneously with construction of the plant or factory itself. This parallelism put undue strain on transportation facilities and created great difficulties with water and electricity, not to mention damage to roads still under construction. Situations of this sort were characteristic in the construction of the steel complex at Sztalinvaros and the chemical plant at Kazincbarcika. Soviet technical intransigence added to the misery. Some priority projects, close to Russian hearts, were inappropriate in Hungarian surroundings. Yet the Soviet experts working with Hungarian authorities forced through these projects on the theory that what proved suitable in the USSR was suitable for a satellite. The fantastic cost of such economic delusion is perhaps best exemplified in the creation of the Sztalinvaros steel plant.

Frequently coordination and cooperation between different projects was completely lacking. An electricity plant was to be constructed at Tiszapalkonya using as an energy base coal which was to arrive by lighter over a canal system. But it turned out that there was an insufficient "investment credit" (the expression used to designate expendable amounts) for the construction of the canal. In the meantime, the power plant was finished, but since there was no canal for the transport of the coal, the formal opening of the plant had to be delayed. Finally, coal, transported by train at a much higher cost, was used to prevent both projects from becoming economic scandals. These examples are far from being the definitive list. Yet these cases may be sufficient to illustrate the fundamental causes of high industrial costs and weak industrial investment productivity existing in the Hungarian economy. The tragedy is clearer when it is realized that this waste of nearly one quarter of the national income came at the expense of an already overexploited people.

How to Get the Premium?

This question was frequently raised in private discussions of managers and directors of Hungarian industry. The "premium motive" in the communist system might be called a substitute for the profit motive which operates in a free enterprise system. There is no fundamental difference between the collectivist and capitalist systems regarding their principal economic objective: material reward. There may well be other important interests such as prestige and power but these are usually of secondary importance. While we all know that there is no profit as such in a collectivist system, there is in present day communist systems this sublimation known as the premium. Premium is defined as a bonus to be paid to managers, engineers, technicians and leading white-collar workers for the fulfillment of special obligations.

It was the practice of Hungarian industry to pay premiums for the fulfillment of production and/or cost plans. The income of the employees of state enterprises—as with salaries and wages generally—were extremely low in Hungary. Salaries barely covered expenses necessary for subsistence. Premiums might reach seventy-five percent of the basic salary, and great efforts were expended to partake of premium payments for this was really the only other legal possibility to better somewhat individual living standards. Theoretically, premiums could have served as a means to attain economic goals but in practice this objective was never achieved. For in reality managers strove to discover the easiest manner by which to obtain the highest possible amount of premium and the easiest way was generally to evade the regulations.

During most of the decade of communist control in Hungary, the only existing condition for receiving premiums in the construction industry for instance was the fulfillment of production plans. Supervisors showed no concern for a decrease in the cost of production. Increase in costs, waste of material, payment of excessive wages did not work to reduce the premium if the production plan was fulfilled. Consequently, the entire construction industry labored under a considerable deficit. To avoid further losses premium conditions were changed in 1956 and it was no longer sufficient simply to fulfill the production plan. If a particular construction enterprise labored under a deficit, the premium was not paid. One might think that these new conditions would have resulted in an almost immediate reduction of costs. This was not the case at all. Construction overseers had two choices: reduce costs or increase prices. They chose the latter, easier alternative and began to manipulate prices. In the building industry every product (buildings, roads, bridges, etc.) had its individual cost and price. Thus every new project could bring a new set of inflated prices. In the course of the year profit and loss statements of construction enterprises showed considerable change due to this boosting of prices. During this period I worked for a time with the largest Hungarian construction trust where I had responsibility for cost and price problems. The trust employed about ten percent of the entire labor force assigned to the Hungarian construction industry. In the year 1955 our deficit amounted to more than ten percent of the trust's cost. In the first half of 1956 the trust made a ten percent profit. What was the cause of this change? Easy—the increase in prices. People in western countries might wonder how this change was brought about. It was quite simple actually. In a free enterprise system there are two parties holding opposite interests in every transaction, the seller who wishes to obtain a reasonable profit and the buyer who is interested in expending the lowest amount of money possible for his purchase. In collectivist economies, as in communist Hungary, material reward took the form of a premium, a bonus, which in the example of the construction trade was not opposed by any equal and opposite investor's interest. The state employees of economic investment trusts were not at all interested in the reduction of prices levied by construction firms. According to the system of investment financing in Hungary, those charged with investment were interested only in the physical accomplishment of the expansion project and in allocating the investment-credit assigned for a given period. As a matter of communist consistency, the employees of investor trusts were themselves awarded premiums if expansion plans were fulfilled, that is to say, if the budgeted amount of money was spent. Plan fulfillment of investments was measured in forints; therefore, these officials were most interested in spending the entire investment credit as soon as possible and increasing prices was one excellent method. There certainly was no objection then on the part of this "purchaser," the investment firm. Furthermore, the initial cost of expansion was not chargeable to the newly built plant. Marxian economic theory does not accept the concept of an interest rate. Officials of new plants were sublimely indifferent to plant construction costs. This strange phenomenon wherein no one had a material interest in decreasing costs or price increases was one of the regime's seemingly insoluble problems.

Some of the devious methods of boosting prices included the use of more expensive materials, the employment of special mark-ups on the basis of allegedly existing special building conditions and billings for construction work not accomplished. Prices were supervised by the Ministry for Construction, but the ministry had no interest in containing price increases, since improvement in the balance sheets of individual enterprises also meant an improvement in the overall balance sheet of the ministry. According to estimates I made along with one of the leading officials of the ministry's price department, the increase in prices in the construction industry was about thirty-one to thirty-two percent between the years 1952 and 1956. During the same period the construction industry was said to have operated on constant prices. Official investment figures must, therefore, be deflated by more than thirty percent.

In contrast to the construction industry, premium payments and dodges in other sectors of the economy were subject to a more rigid control. Here the methods of evasion were somewhat different but the ingenuity of Hungarian managers and engineers could always find ways to get around the regulations. As in the construction industry, the fulfillment of production and cost plans were also the main premium granting conditions for other industries.

The weight of rubber wares in the toy industry was the criterion of plan fulfillment. Since rubber had to be imported, overfulfillment of the plan was not permitted. On the last day of each month the month's production output was weighed. If it proved to be deficient, the engineers got some air pumped in the rubber toys. If it was excessive, the opposite method was applied. In the case where fulfillment of the cost plan was also a premium condition, the accounting department assumed responsibility for securing the premium. In every Hungarian accounting course it was taught that the main difference between accounting under capitalism and under socialism was the falsification of the balance sheet in the former so as to serve

the interests of the capitalists, while the balance sheet of the
socialist enterprise always reflected the truth. So far as Hungary
and other communist countries are concerned, this statement is
ridiculous. The balance sheet of the various state enterprises
were permanently modified so as to take into account premium
requirements. If the possibilities of achieving a premium were
good, the balance sheet showed a profit, if possibilities were
not good, it showed a deficit. In many Hungarian enterprises
the profit-loss statement varied directly with production figures.
The leading employees of these state companies were among
those most interested in manipulating the balance sheets and
no one expressed a contrary interest. Balance sheet analysts and
inspectors did not notice the falsifications, or if they did, they
were not sufficiently interested to do anything about it.

Unions and Wages

In western countries unions represent the workers before
management. Trade unions are theoretically the representatives
of the workers in the communist system too. In practice, however, unions must accept the decisions made by the state. These
decisions deal with a wide range of important problems connected with wages, social security, insurance, retirement. But
the activity of communist trade unions is merely formal.

In a free enterprise system contracts are really contracts, collective bargaining is really bargaining. Agreements between
employers and unions are the outcome of mutual discussion.
These agreements determine wages, length of the work week,
holidays, working conditions, etc. If labor does not agree with
management on certain points, they may strike for the achievement of their demands. The contents of these contracts are the
same in communist countries. Yet this is purely façade. In the
communist system the substance of "contract" and of "bargaining" is missing. The trade union is merely another organization
of the state acting as national employer. It is led by the Communist Party, which also controls the state. Every single item
regarding collective contracts is determined by state regulation.
The workers have absolutely no right to strike. If somebody

does not agree with state regulations he is branded a reactionary. Communist authorities emphasize that unions are not
independent, they must comply with the directives of the Communist Party and the communist state. Union leaders are Party
functionaries assigned to this task. Each year the formality is
faithfully carried out when the union signs a contract in which
no one has any belief.

In seeking the underlying principles of wage policy in Hungary, one must once again return to the fundamentals of Soviet
policy. Lenin attributed great importance to modern methods
of scientific management and valued highly the work of Freder-
ick Taylor, the first American managerial scientist. The principal aim of Soviet wage policy was to increase the efficiency of
labor. Yet once more the inflexibility of the communist system
comes into focus. In the West piece work was employed only
if the circumstances permitted its application; the Soviet Union
desired to apply it universally. Over the last few decades there
has been a tendency in capitalist countries to adopt the qualified
hourly wage system which ensures better quality as well as
equity, but in communist countries the introduction of the piece
work system is still a central objective. As with almost every
economic issue, this problem also became a political question.
The slogan was "everybody has to be paid by the piece work
system." And directors, supervisors, trade union leaders tried
to introduce it, even if it was not really economical, even if it
did not increase labor efficiency. The economic question had
become a political question and nobody was permitted to criticize it. If one did not agree there was still no criticism since
opposition might bring with it the dangerous charge of reactionary. The situation was not unlike that of any army: com-
manders decide and subordinates comply.

What was the economic result of this enforced application
of the piece work system? Laborers doing work which required
great precision, for example, and who were paid per completed
piece, neglected precision so as to increase their wages. In some
cases even charwomen were paid by this system. They easily fulfilled their norms by reducing the quality of their work, literally
by sweeping the dirt under the rug. The experience of piece

work showed that the system resulted in work of a lower quality
and the establishment of arbitrary differences between working
groups. However, in many industries, construction being one
example, the piece work system was often a mere formality if
the wages paid to the workers in many cases did not jibe with
the amount earned according to calculations based on norms.
There are two methods of classification: either the wage, originally computed according to norms, was then "helped" by the
foreman in acknowledging receipts for unperformed work, and
the worker got his "normal" monthly wage, or monthly earnings
would be stated beforehand and norm cards submitted later.
This rigged difference in salary ran in some cases as high as
twenty to thirty percent. Another characteristic of the Hungarian piece work system was the constant tightening of norms.
Tightening of norms meant simply less pay for the same work.
In communist countries revision of norms occurred periodically
every three or four years. The norms were generally upped because of technical advancement, but not always. The workers
naturally tried to cheat or counteract any reduction in their
earnings. They could not fight the tightening of norms openly,
not only since they had no influence on collective contracts,
but a change in norms was a political question and thus dangerous to criticize. The fight was waged clandestinely by cheating
with the norms or doing poor work. The entire communist
period in Hungary is characterized by a form of permanent
struggle of workers against a state control under which they
were exploited.

As a counter measure to this attitude, the Soviet Government
some twenty-five years ago in its own experience launched a
movement named after Stakhanov, a deathless worker, commemorated in order to build labor productivity. The Stakhanovites were said to be workers of superior ability who overful-
filled their norms and thus "set an example" for their fellows.

As with all satellite countries in all these things, Hungary also
followed this Soviet example. The introduction of Stakhanov-
ism had a connection with tightening of the norms. Official
determination of norms was not to be simply based upon the
average work load. Rather, the progressive average was applied

with greater weight being given to the production achievements of Stakhanovites. The movement, therefore, became a method for the exploitation of labor through increasing the requirements assigned every worker based upon the Stakhanovite production curve. How then were Stakhanovites to be developed? In some factories Stakhanovites were workers of ability or skill, who innovated and improved upon the labor process thereby increasing their productivity. In other cases Stakhanovites were chosen by representatives of the Communist Party and the management on the basis of political reliability, Party membership, or amount of time spent in the factory. Workers of kulak origin could not become Stakhanovites because they were politically unreliable. Political reliability was not sufficient, however, to raise productivity. But the ever helpful Party assigned their would-be Stakhanovite comrades better machines, skilled helpers, permanent work, and so-called "well-paying" jobs where it would be easier to achieve better production results. This procedure might appear to be self-deceit in the eyes of a western observer, but actually it is only part of the self-contradictions upon which the communist system has been built. Since managers had to "produce" Stakhanovites and the Stakhanovites were people who supported the communist regime, the movement became a political, psychological, and economic offensive. Communist authorities wanted to have a group of workers who, being privy to higher incomes, would as a form of payoff support the communist system. For the regime's part the Stakhanovite movement was to serve as the leading force of "socialist competition" which is an euphemism for forcing workers to raise constantly the level of production.

National Income and Standard of Living

It is a difficult task to examine accurately Hungarian national income data. You have seen the example of the construction field where the data had to be deflated thirty-one or thirty-two percent, although constant prices were allegedly used. This situation generally pervaded the entire economy. The reasons for the unreliability of official communist data may be classified under two headings. First, some of the deficiencies were the direct consequence of a permanent economy-wide effort to boost production figures. The falseness of the published data was an everyday phenomenon in communist Hungary so as to show the "favorable" results of planning and quite as significantly to "prove" an increase in the standard of living. One form of deliberate falsification was the neglect of inflation in evaluating data in order to disguise actual deterioration in the standard of living. Other major types of falsification took the forms of the incorrect use of index numbers and the boosting of national income figures through the increase in turnover taxes.

There are only crude approximations available regarding the distribution of national income. Although these estimates might have an error of significant size, they are susceptible to comparison. It is very difficult, for example, to estimate the cost of armament in Hungary. These costs direct and indirect were hidden under the most varied of budgetary headings such as investment to public welfare. A comparison between the base year 1938 and 1955, the last year before the revolution, indicates that some four percent of the national income went to armament in 1938 and some fifteen percent in 1955. In contrast, prewar Hungary used eighty percent of its national income on consumption while communist Hungary devoted only fifty percent of its income to consumption type expenditures. The tremendous decrease in the share of consumption indicates a real reduction in the quantity of goods available for consumption, for national income did not increase sufficiently to counterbalance the decrease in consumption.

The percentage increase in economic expansion expenditures did not represent a similar increase in the real value of investments. As has been seen, a substantial number of investments during the communist period was unproductive.

The increase in public expenses reveals the immense growth of communist state bureaucracy and an accompanying increase in productive costs. It seems hardly necessary to remark that armament costs likewise did not serve the purposes of the Hungarian people; it was designed to strengthen the power of the Soviet Union at the expense of still further decreases in the national standard of living. In connection with consumption and standard of living figures, one can usually usefully check the number of dwellings constructed as an indicator of living standard. According to official Hungarian data, in 1955, some 32,000 apartments were built, in 1956, about 12,000 and plans involved approximately an additional 40,000 for 1957. In 1955, the number of apartments constructed was only 0.32 percent of the population, in 1956, 0.1 percent and the planned figure for 1957 approached 0.4 percent. Considering the housing shortage and the yearly 0.7-0.8 percent increase of the population, the number of the new dwellings constructed is not nearly sufficient. This analysis does not even take into account the discouraging fact that many of these apartments were built without bathrooms and, in general, were substandard and inadequate for family needs. To strike just one western comparison take France. France in 1956 constructed 240,000 apartments, 0.6 percent of her population, and France was below the western general average.

There are, however, no reliable Hungarian figures comparing standards of living under communism with the standard of the prewar period. According to different estimates, agreement on the decrease in the standard of living generally amounts to ten or fifteen percent.

Perhaps even more illustrative of communist inadequacies in providing for its captive peoples, even on a minimum scale, is the evidence reflected in a food, clothing, and rent survey. The United Nations Economic Commission for Europe drew up a list of different kinds of food containing 2500-3300 calories and 100 grams of proteins and fats per day. The quantities represented a food basket which the average adult required per month. The representative cost of the food basket in Hungary (the data was originally applied to Poland) in 1956 was roughly fifteen dollars. According to *Szabad Nep* of June 19, 1956, the monthly net wage in Hungarian industry at this time was the equivalent of fifty dollars for the worker. Thus, a month's work bought 3.2 food baskets. If one takes into account the expenditures necessary for clothing, rent, and other expenses, assessing forty percent of the cost of food for clothing, ten percent for rent and fifteen percent for miscellaneous expenditures, it totals the sum of twenty-four dollars. Thus, out of the average monthly wage of fifty dollars, some twenty-four were automatically committed, a situation barely adequate for the needs of two adult persons, let alone children. These circumstances forced women to seek work in order to fill out the earnings of their husbands. The earnings of one person were clearly not sufficient for the needs of a family.

The reader has now examined at least some of the principal characteristics of the Hungarian communist economic system. What conclusions can be reached regarding the failure of this system?

Some of the reasons are quite apparent: the inflexibility and unreality of collectivist planning, the absence of personal initiative, the lack of coordination in the areas of production and investment, the throttling of competition, and the maintenance of an expensive, excessive, and rigid bureaucratic apparatus. Other reasons emerge from the nature of communist economic policy: the priority of political and military considerations over economic sense, the counter-productive collectivization of agriculture, the frequent and rapid turns in the regime's economic exploitation of the country by the USSR.

Ten years of communist rule have resulted in the decline of Hungarian agriculture, in massive investment errors in the name of industrialization, in a ridiculous bureaucracy, in a substantial decline of the standard of living. The repercussions of these man-made failings were felt by the whole Hungarian people and contributed a major share to the spirit of the revolution. The Hungarian economy is not a special case; the lessons derived from it are applicable to the other Soviet dominated economies. For the thoughtful person, it reflects not only a failure of communist economics in Hungary, but in a very real sense the inherent inability of communism to provide its subjects with a reasonable measure of material advancement commensurate with the innate dignity and worth of the individual.

THE JUDGMENT

In Hungary today, and throughout Eastern Europe, the revolt is over but the revolution continues. In Poland, in Yugoslavia, and even within the USSR itself, the creeping questions of slow revolution make their mark. It is this persistence of unanswered questioning which arouses anxiety in the Kremlin. Hungary revealed a Pandora's box of trouble for orthodox communism. The slaves rebelled against the masters in the very form and for the ideals which Moscow has for so long piously propagated.

In the twenty months since the Soviet crushing of the uprising the symbol of protest, of independence, of national dignity, had come to repose largely in the personage of Imre Nagy, communist and Hungarian patriot. He was the man, who, for whatever reason, haltingly and even reluctantly, led Hungary to its brief freedom.

The spirit and even the legend of Nagy were made secure by the abject Soviet betrayal of Janos Kadar's sworn word to fellow communist Tito of Yugoslavia that Nagy's safety would be assured upon departure from Yugoslav diplomatic sanctuary. The betrayal of Nagy and his colleagues reached its logical climax at 11:00 P.M., June 16, 1958, when the Hungarian communist Ministry of Justice announced that former Prime Minister Imre Nagy, his defense minister General Pal Maleter, police official Jozsef Szilagyi, and journalist Miklos Gimes had been executed.

What had transpired in those twenty months from November 1956 to June 1958? Why had betrayal been compounded? Why did a Soviet Government so sensitive and alert to world propaganda advantage permit an action which sickened the entire civilized world, and revealed once more the unchanging face of communist inhumanity?

A perceptive student of Hungary has referred to the 1956 uprising as a "Poets' Revolution—the kind that changes the world." He was right and the proof resides in Soviet counteraction which, with the execution of Nagy and Maleter, reaffirms communist concern with the continuing spirit of revolution.

Following the suppression of the revolt, the immediate problem which faced the Soviet overlords of Hungary and their appointed communist representatives was the re-establishment of control. This concern which occupied the Kadar regime for all of 1957 was resolved in the most brutal fashion. The list of techniques would include deportations, illegal trials, executions, secret police terror, total censorship and complete disregard of United Nations attempts to establish some measure of justice and international order.

This communist perfidy can no where be more starkly summed up than in noting Kadar's public promise made November 4, 1956: "the Government will not tolerate workers being persecuted, under any pretext whatsoever, for having taken part in the most recent events . . ." Yet the highly respected International Commission of Jurists has reported that nearly 5,000 persons had been executed in Hungary in the first twelve months following the revolt.

The execution of Nagy is for communism both the closing of a chapter of history and the evidence of a gigantic failure. In his execution we have the admission that Nagy did not break, he did not retract, and true to this symbol his country has followed him into persecution. To a Soviet-oriented communist the highest crime is rebellion against orthodoxy. Nagy, therefore, was a traitor of the worst sort, and his crime was compounded by his refusal to recant even unto death.

While a single opponent is bad enough, the Soviets were faced with an entire nation in opposition. From a Party strength of just under one million members, the Hungarian Communist Party is able today to boast of a paper figure esimated at 300,000 persons, most of whom are devoid of ideological fervor and devoted to only one goal: physical survival. This is in itself a shock and Kadar seems well justified in his full-time concern with organizational matters. But it doesn't end there. The intellectuals of Hungary have been on "strike" since the revolt's suppression. Concerted and relentless pressure by the communists, alternating promise and threat, has so far failed to force the leading writers of Hungary to surrender. They adamantly refuse to create for their masters despite the arrest and imprisonment of several of the country's outstanding authors.

If you couple these facts with the sullen refusal of the population—adults and children alike—either to support Kadar or the increasingly powerful Stalinist minority, it is possible to sense the magnitude of the problem constantly facing Soviet officials.

A final and dramatic proof of Hungary's continuing national resistance is reflected in the abortive visit of Soviet leader Khrushchev to Hungary during the spring of 1958. The world leader of communism was snubbed, insulted and so badly treated by his captive audiences that many commentators openly speculate that the rebuff helped convince the Kremlin that any measure of moderateness must be rejected for Hungary.

But there is more. The execution of Nagy represents not only the final stages of repression in Hungary, which may bring the uneasy Kadar to a similar fate, as well as complete reversion to traditional Stalinist cultural, economic and political practices, but it stands as the failure of a policy —a policy generated by Khrushchev himself. As you have read earlier in this book, the February 1956 de-Stalinization speech of Khrushchev precipitated a general thaw and ferment throughout the satellite area. This liberalization led directly to the rise of Gomulka, to the Hungarian revolution, and to the sustenance of Titoism. Now the results are in; the Khrushchev experiment, if it can be labelled so, has failed and the fateful sign of retreat was signalled openly by the murder of Nagy.

Thus what is happening in Hungary today, and what happened to Nagy and Maleter, is intended by Moscow as a warning—a warning to Poland, to Yugoslavia, to the other captive nations, to us here in the Free World.

And what is this warning? It can be read in various ways. But principally it recalls the determination of Moscow ruthlessly to control the subject peoples; it cautions the West to be alert and on guard; and it signifies the fear with which the monolithic structure of communist tyranny looks upon freedom, nationalism and ideological revisionism.

The ways of freedom often move in strange directions, and are even more often lost to history's view. Two such examples perhaps typify the cause of Hungary—and, for that matter, of free men everywhere.

Geza Losonczy was a communist member of Nagy's last cabinet. When communism first came to power in Hungary, Losonczy, as a deputy minister of culture, supervised the burning of books blacklisted by the Party. Among the books was Hungarian-born Arthur Koestler's classic study of communist purges and death, *Darkness at Noon*. It is one of history's ironies that included in the official announcement of Nagy's execution was the revelation that Geza Losonczy, Hungarian patriot and anti-Soviet, had died in captivity before he could be brought to trial, the living embodiment of "darkness at noon."

Miklos Gimes, journalist, was executed with Nagy for having defied the Soviet Union. Gimes had for years been a communist until his questioning of the Hungarian regime's policies brought his Party expulsion. He joined Nagy. As Soviet forces crushed Hungary's freedom, Gimes led his wife and child to the border and safety. He returned to Budapest with full knowledge of the fate awaiting him. He was prepared to pay the price of freedom. And so with Hungary. She also was prepared to pay the price for her freedom.